WAYNE DOWLER is Associate Professor of History at Scarborough College, University of Toronto.

Native Soil was a mid-nineteenth-century Russian reaction against materialism and positivism. It emphasized the need for people to live their lives and develop themselves naturally, so that class differences might be reconciled, the achievements of the West fused with the communalism and Christian fraternity preserved by the Russian peasant, and the Russian nation united in the pursuit of common moral ideals. The metaphor 'Russia and the West' summarized much of the intellectual and political debate of the period: how Russia should use its indigenous and its 'borrowed' cultural elements to solve the political, economic, and social problems of a difficult period.

Professor Dowler presents a detailed study of Native Soil conservatism from about 1850 to 1880 – its various intellectual facets, its leading thinkers, and its growth and gradual disintegration. In this utopian movement, literary creativity, aesthetics, and education took on special significance for human spiritual and social development. Dowler therefore examines the writings of two of the most gifted exponents of Native Soil – F.M. Dostoevsky and A.A. Grigor'ev – and looks at their circle and the journals to which they contributed in an assessment of their responses to the challenges of the period of Emancipation.

WAYNE DOWLER

Dostoevsky, Grigor'ev, and Native Soil conservatism

UNIVERSITY OF TORONTO PRESS
Toronto   Buffalo   London

© University of Toronto Press 1982
Toronto   Buffalo   London
Printed in Canada

ISBN 0-8020-5604-0

TO MY PARENTS

Canadian Cataloguing in Publication Data

Dowler, Wayne, 1945–
   Dostoevsky, Grigor'ev, and native soil
   conservatism

   Bibliography: p.
   Includes index.

   ISBN 0-8020-5604-0

   1. Soviet Union – Intellectual life – 1801–1917.
   2. Conservatism – Soviet Union – History – 19th
   century. 3. Grigor'ev, Apollon Aleksandrovich,
   1822–1864 – Influence – Dostoevsky. 4. Dostoevsky,
   Fyodor, 1821–1881. I. Title

   DK189.2.D68   947.08'1   c82-094629-x

This book has been published with the help of a grant from the
Canadian Federation for the Humanities, using funds provided by
the Social Sciences and Humanities Research Council of Canada,
and a grant from the Publications Fund of University of Toronto Press.

Contents

Acknowledgments

An earlier version of this work was accepted as a doctoral dissertation at the London School of Economics and Political Science in the University of London. There I was fortunate to have as my thesis director Professor Leonard Schapiro. I am grateful to him for the knowledge and wisdom that he so generously shared with me and for his encouragement and kindness. I wish also to thank Sir Isaiah Berlin for a suggestion at a critical moment in my work which did much to clarify my thinking about the native soil movement. I am indebted as well to the several anonymous readers whose comments were helpful in the preparation of the final draft of the book.

To the patient and helpful staffs of the British Museum in London, the Bibliothèque nationale in Paris, and the University of Helsinki Library I owe a further debt. For the even greater forbearance of Naida Mawson-Sonstenes, who cheerfully typed the manuscript more than once, I am grateful. Finally, I thank my wife, who in spite of the pressures of her own historical research and teaching was never without time to assist and encourage me.

The transliteration system used is that of the Library of Congress in a slightly modified form. All dates before 1918 are given in old style. In the nineteenth century the Julian calendar used in Russia lagged twelve days behind the western Gregorian calendar.

WD

Introduction

Conservatives in nineteenth-century Russia have not been accorded the attention by historians that their number and influence would appear to warrant. The collapse of conservative values during 1917 and the apparent vindication of the radical tradition in the Russian Revolution are at least in part responsible for the relative neglect of the conservative tradition. A major hindrance to the study of conservatism in Russia has been the difficulty scholars have had in coming to grips with conservatism as a universal political and social phenomenon. The conservative mentality and its political expressions have yielded less readily to analysis than the more topical and cosmopolitan liberal and radical ideologies. The complex of values, institutions, and traditions that have gone into the making of the conservative frame of mind in particular societies remains a relatively uncharted territory.

Conservatives in Russia have not, of course, been entirely ignored. Some of the leading conservative personalities have been served by fine biographies, and a few useful studies have been made that encompass Russian conservatism in a wider embrace.[1] Recently, new sources have emerged from both Soviet and Western archives.[2] As a result, it is now possible to trace the evolution of conservative thought in the nineteenth century and to differentiate the various elements that made up the Russian right with greater precision. The recent and unexpected resurgence of Russian conservative thought, spearheaded by Aleksandr Solzhenitsyn, has made this task all the more relevant, urgent, and interesting.

Conservatism found expression in a variety of forms among a number of institutions and social groups in nineteenth-century Russia. The official Orthodox church and the bureaucracy remained bulwarks of the conservative temperament in spite of the presence of a few liberal individuals within both. The peasants, for the most part, persisted in their stubborn traditional loyalty to the myth of the just tsar as their paladin against the depredations of the landlords. Although the liberal constitutional movement spread impressively among the gentry in the post-Emancipation period, the majority trusted their conservative instincts and clung to their conservative opinions. Finally, a highly articulate philosophical conservatism, which brought the element of reflection to the other, more traditional conservative forms, appeared around the middle of the century among a significant segment of the Russian intelligentsia.

What united all of these disparate conservative voices was the belief in the appropriateness of authoritarian rule for Russia. Until October 1905 when, under duress, absolutism at last gave way, at least in theory, to limited monarchical government, the defining characteristic of conservatism was support for the autocratic principle, according to which all political and legal authority rested ultimately with the monarch. Not all Russian conservatives approved of the autocracy as it was actually constituted, but none would have welcomed the imposition of either formal legal or institutional restraints on the authority of the tsars.[3]

The existence of dominant conservative elements within the church and bureaucracy and among the peasantry and gentry is hardly surprising. All of them were in some way reacting to the threat of social, economic, or cultural change. The church had traditionally resisted, more often passively than actively, the encroaching secularization and westernization of Russian life, and the pace with which these forces advanced was especially brisk in the nineteenth century. The bureaucracy had long before become a virtually autonomus institution with its own raison d'être. It was dedicated above all to self-perpetuation and fiercely resisted any political or administrative adjustments that seriously threatened the position and livelihood of its members.

The situation of the peasantry was more complicated. Its conservatism was in part the product of ignorance, which the customary mode of village life only reinforced. The peasants had centuries earlier identified the enemy – the gentry and, increasingly in the nineteenth century, the bureaucracy – but in the absence of any other earthly prospect of attaining justice had doggedly adhered to the desperate hope that a just tsar would one day intervene to deliver them from their tormentors and the usurpers of their lands. It was a barren but not uncomforting illusion. Peasant conservatism was, therefore, habitual but perilously unstable, capable of unexpectedly metamorphosing into revolutionary anarchy.[4]

The object of peasant discontent, the gentry, had been uneasily aware of the peasant danger since at least the Pugachev rebellion in the early 1770s, and fear of the peasants' axes had traditionally been a mainstay of gentry conservatism. During the nineteenth century, particularly in the wake of the Emancipation in 1861, its conservative inclinations were reinforced as its economic position generally deteriorated in spite of government efforts to stop the rot. Along with diminishing economic power came the threat of displacement from social pre-eminence. As the economic position of the gentry declined, its members clung ever more tenaciously to the still considerable remnants of their status and power and to the memory of a more secure and comfortable past.

Conservatism among these groups was largely reactive; it rested on solid traditional, temperamental, or pragmatic grounds and fell well within the range of normal scholarly expectations about political behaviour. It is more difficult to account for the advent of a conservative outlook within the intelligentsia. It was a relatively new group; the state accorded it no juridical status and officially resented its intrusion, but had to rely more and more on its education and skills. The intelligentsia had no tradition and little past of its own to defend. Themselves the product of modernization, the *intelligenty* could, ostensibly at least, best advance their own interests by promoting further change rather than by seeking to preserve the status quo. What, then, could have induced a portion of the intelligentsia to adopt and defend a conservative position?

In the scholarly literature on Russian history, the term *intelligentsia* has been applied to a wide variety of groups in a number of socio-economic settings.[5] But however diverse have been the groups that *intelligentsia* has been asked to describe, they all shared a distinctive ethos. All held ideas that conflicted with 'official' or accepted values and all were dedicated to serving the people in some way. The social composition of the intelligentsia changed over time, and the ways in which its members proposed to serve the people varied and were often at odds. But its general stance of opposition to established values and to the existing state and social order as well as its orientation towards social service remained a constant.

The rise of the intelligentsia to prominence in the middle decades of the nineteenth century was a complex process that extended as far back as the reforms of Peter the Great in the first quarter of the eighteenth century. The technological and administrative innovations that Peter imported from the West were inevitably accompanied and supported by a large share of the intellectual apparatus of Western societies. Not least among the tools acquired by the Russians was the spirit of criticism that was emerging as the basis of intellectual inquiry in western Europe. Peter had himself encouraged the growth of a secularized critical élite as a counterweight to the religious culture of the Muscovite past that his childhood experiences had taught him to despise and fear. The subsequent development of Russia for the rest of the century was in some ways not unlike that which occurred in the monarchies of western Europe. During the eighteenth century a number of European rulers, for a time at least, successfully harnessed the critical spirit of the age to their own uses, as kings allied with philosophers against the traditionalist forces of feudal society. 'Enlightened despotism' had its limits, however, and the contradictions between enlightenment and absolutism in the end tore the alliance apart.

In Russia, too, the state showed itself to be a progressive force during much of the eighteenth century. Even the shock of the French Revolution was only a temporary setback. Emperor Alexander I, who came to the throne in 1801, led his country through an important series of far-reaching administrative, legal, and educational changes. It was only after the defeat of Napoleon and the ensuing conservative settlement at the Congress of Vienna in 1815 that Alexander, a victim of the wave of reactionary mysticism that swept Europe in the wake of victory over France, withdrew the Russian state from its leading role as a force for progress. The disillusionment generated among forward-looking Russians by Alexander's reactionary stance in time precipitated the Decembrist conspiracy of 1825, during which a group of army officers, noblemen all, attempted abortively to create by force a constitutional monarchy in Russia.

The treason of the Decembrists further undermined the already shaky confidence of the state in its ability to manage the changes it had itself put in motion. Under Nicholas I, the brother of Alexander, the Russian state was transformed into a powerful instrument of conservatism. Nicholas and his officials were not reactionaries; they did not oppose all change, but the reforms that they introduced were designed to tighten the bonds between government and society and served to undermine the autonomy of the latter. It was during the reign of Nicholas that the idea of society as a counterweight to the conservative tendencies of the state emerged. Society began to see itself and its concerns as distinct from the state and its interests and to cast itself in a new, progressive role.

Society had been in preparation for its new role since at least the 1820s. The educational reforms of Alexander I not only extended education but also raised the quality of Russian learning as well. The restrictive educational policies practised by Nicholas I could only retard but not halt the cultural development of his subjects. The lengthening subscription lists to an increasing number of journals, newspapers, and magazines during his reign reflected the growth in Russia of a small, élite reading public. Pockets of articulate public opinion and cultural sophistication, often directed by one or another of the large, monthly 'thick' journals, began to form. Among the main indicators of Russia's almost imperceptible advance towards modernization in the reign of Nicholas was the growth of a viable urban culture. The new sophistication of city life spelled, among other things, the growing differentiation of social classes and the disruption of the traditional noble, peasant, burgher designations of the estates. In the 1830s Nicholas was compelled to create a new estate of 'hereditary honorary citizens' in order to incorporate the rapidly growing professional and commercial groups into official society. The demand for services in the urban centres drew an increasing number of peasants from the countryside, although most of these new urban dwellers remained officially listed on the rolls of the peasantry.[6]

The growing intensity of urban life, along with the sharper social differentiation it entailed and the deepening interest of the public in cultural matters, had a number of important consequences for Russians. For the first time in its history, the country was able to support, albeit meagrely, a group of independent literati. In addition, the potential for dissatisfaction with Russian conditions as well as the pool from which the disaffected could be recruited were considerably enlarged.

The feeling that society was becoming more and more divided and the undefined sense that all was far from well in the empire of Nicholas I were heightened. Nicholas's secret police intuited the restlessness in Russian society. In 1840 the tsar came across this troubling passage in one of his gendarme reports:

There is hidden everywhere a certain general dissatisfaction, which can be expressed in a statement written to the Chief of Gendarmes from Moscow: '*I do not know exactly, but something is wrong*,' and this expression we now hear often from the most well-intentioned people. Of course, nothing bad has as yet happened, but unfortunately this kind of an expression is a reflection of a state of mind and feelings which is less propitious than at any time during the entire last fifteen years, and which proves that all the estates in general find themselves in some sort of awkward condition, for which no one can account, even to oneself.[7]

It was this restless atmosphere that provided the necessary pre-conditions for the formation of the Russian intelligentsia.

The intelligentsia was the creation of Russia's slow and uneven advance towards modernization.[8] The impact of cultural modernization on a few extruded a tiny minority of educated individuals out of the antiquated economic, political, and social order, enabling it to escape from the narrow confines of its class outlook and prospects. Its members were few in number, but the capacity of the rigidly structured Russia of Nicholas I for social readjustment was still too slight to reassimilate even these few displaced persons easily. They came from no class in particular. Some were the sons of the landed gentry, many more were children of the bureaucratic nobility whose families had earned noble status by advancement on the Table of Ranks, and a few came from the lesser bureaucracy, merchant families, and other non-noble groups. They had in common their education and the fact that they were, at least temporarily, separated from their class origins and the traditional occupations of their families.

It was, of course, the intelligentsia that formulated the 'accursed questions' of Russian life and consecrated themselves to answering them. Ideas are seldom merely responses to other ideas. More often they are programs of action designed to meet and overcome an unsatisfactory state of affairs. Both the personal situation and social condition of the members of the unattached intelligentsia in Russia were eminently unsatisfactory. They had refused to follow the occupations and life-styles of their parents and, even if their families encouraged them, were, at the very least, culturally estranged from their family environment. Personal alienation was accompanied by a profound social alienation. The high standard of educational achievement of the intelligentsia placed an insurmountable barrier between it and ordinary Russians. Wards of the new urban culture, its members lived and worked either on the fringes of or completely outside official society and could claim no legally recognized class affiliation. As one of the more extreme manifestations of the new social diversification of Russia, they were particularly sensitive to the many nuances of heightening social tensions. They were steeped in the latest intellectual trends of the West and acutely aware of the discrepancy between the vitality of western Europe and the apparent stagnation of Russia under Nicholas I. Their attempts to express themselves in prose and verse were often frustrated by the close scrutiny of a suspicious state.

Alienation was only one of the features common to the Russian intelligentsia. Another was its nearly unanimous distaste for the liberal-capitalist societies forming in western Europe. As intellectuals who were not entirely immune from an élitist disdain for 'trade,' its members were repelled by the commercial spirit and capitalist morality of the Western middle classes and the putative vulgarity of their thought and habits. They further rejected the legalism and impersonality of the liberal contractual state, which appeared to them to preclude the possibility of a true community. There were, of course, exceptions, but hostility to the bourgeois state and to a social order based on the rule of law was endemic among the intelligentsia and powerfully shaped its vision of Russia's future political and social order.

Both radicals and conservatives among the intelligentsia feared the growth of capitalism in Russia and adopted remarkably similar positions towards industrialization and the introduction of liberal constitutionalism. Both camps, until the advent of Marxism in the 1880s, envisaged a predominantly agrarian communal society in which industry, though not unimportant within the economy, remained on a small scale under community direction. Both preferred a self-governing federation of communes in which the powers of the central political authority were drastically few. Both profoundly distrusted positive or formal law, seeing the key to social regulation instead in the inner moral convictions of individuals and in a sense of common social purpose. Securing the freedom of the personality and the moral salvation of the individual was likewise a primary concern of both parties. Neither side was content with the status quo but envisaged a Russia morally and socially transfigured.

The members of the intelligentsia shared one additional characteristic. This was their common intellectual origins in the utopian spirit of the romantic period. Romanticism was rooted in the longing for a return to the imagined social harmony, simplicity, and spiritual unity of pre-industrial society. Utopian socialism, which in one or another form provided sustenance to the radical vision of Russia before Marxism, participated in this fundamentally conservative longing. The utopian socialists idealized the agrarian communalism of the past and several among them dreamed of a return to the self-regulating communities of the guilds. One historian recently concluded that 'much of what has been called Utopian socialism ought to be seen as essentially conservative in outlook.'[9] Small wonder, then, that the great literary critic V.G. Belinsky, who was educated and wrote in the atmosphere of romanticism and utopian socialism, should later have served as the inspiration for both Russian radicals and conservatives, or that significant elements of Slavophilism in the 1840s should have reappeared in populism in the 1870s. Nor is it surprising that some *intelligenty* began at one end of the ideological scale and ended at the other; the distance they had to travel was not very great.

The Russian intelligentsia was therefore bound together psychologically, ideologically, and intellectually. Its members were motivated by a
shared experience of personal and social alienation, they defined their
political and social objectives largely in terms of their opposition to the
middle-of-the-road, politically moderate, liberal-capitalist ideology of the
West, and they had a joint intellectual and spiritual centre in the visionary
utopianism of the romantic era.

In spite of having so much in common, the intelligentsia was,
nevertheless, sharply divided between proponents of the right and of the
left. This division owed less to differences concerning ends than it did to
divergent views about means, which were in turn dictated by opposing
conceptions of man and the world and of the nature of the socio-historical
process. Once having separated himself by means of his education from
the special interests of his class of origin, the *intelligent* was confronted
with a choice. Either he could elect to associate himself with the interests
of a particular class, usually the most downtrodden, on whose behalf he
tried to speak and act; or he could choose to work towards a syncretic
solution to class antagonisms through the discovery of a principle that
transcended and reconciled class interests.[10]

In conformity to this pattern, a radical wing formed within the
intelligentsia during the middle decades of the nineteenth century; for
the most part, it aligned itself with the interests of the peasant class. The
devotion of the Russian left to the peasantry continued almost unabated
until the 1890s, when the accelerated pace of industrialization revealed to
at least a section of the radicals the revolutionary potential of the
proletariat and split the left wing of the intelligentsia. At the other
extreme, a conservative camp grew up within the intelligentsia; it
attempted to reconcile class differences by appealing to the higher
principles contained in nationality (*narodnost'*), which, for all its divisive
ambiguities, the conservatives viewed as a common denominator stronger
than the sectional interests of the various social estates.

The class origins of individual members of the unattached intelligentsia
reveal little about the route they later chose to follow. Individuals with
similar family and educational experiences were to be found in both the
radical and conservative camps. Broadly speaking, the intellectual profile
of the Russian radical commonly included philosophical materialism, or
often positivism, and atheism. The conservatives usually were, in contrast,
philosophical idealists who acknowledged the existence of some kind of
transcendental power. The idealism of the conservatives was frequently
accompanied by aestheticism, or a highly developed artistic sensibility,

which prompted them to value art for itself and not as a mere tool for didactic purposes as was more often the case among the radicals. Early family training and educational exposure may have contributed to these differences, but no pattern of behaviour obviously emerges.[11]

Rather than reflecting a sociological determination, the selection of routes would appear to have been an individual affair, arising from life experience, personality, mature moral choice, and personal contact with one's peers. The importance of the latter factor should not be overlooked. Friendships were often conducted within a framework of formal or informal intellectual circles where the magnetic influence of a strong personality could prove decisive for the whole group. The dominance of A.S. Khomiakov among the Slavophiles and Belinsky or M.A. Bakunin among the westernizers exemplifies a process that must have been repeated often in less well-known circles.

The division between those who identified with one class and those who preferred social reconciliation did not always follow along strictly radical-conservative lines. The theme of reconciliation sometimes appeared persistently in the thought of thinkers usually associated with the radicals. A.I. Herzen, for example, incorporated the idea of reconciliation into his social philosophy, particularly during the early years of the Emancipation period. A similar notion re-emerged in the populist writings of N.K. Mikhailovsky. Such crossing over should not be surprising. Both the conservative intelligentsia and the radicals, as has been shown, were responding to a similar personal and social dilemma and both were inspired by a shared intellectual inheritance. Nevertheless, reconciliation tended to remain incidental to the thought of the radicals but central to that of the conservative *intelligenty*.

In *pochvennichestvo* (the native soil movement) the philosophy of reconciliation attained its fullest expression. Through their journal *Vremia* (later *Epokha*), which was owned and edited by the Dostoevsky brothers in the early 1860s, the *pochvenniki* (men of the soil) achieved a brief period of modest public recognition, though scarcely wide acceptance. The origins of the movement go back to the beginning of the 1850s when a group of young aesthetes – the so-called 'young editors' – took control of the literature and literary criticism sections of the Moscow journal *Moskvitianin*. The native soil movement retained its early, close ties with literature and criticism, and it was from its literary concerns and convictions that the social philosophy of the *pochvenniki* developed. *Pochvennichestvo* was central to the evolution of F.M. Dostoevsky's moral, social, and political views after his return from Siberian exile at the end of

1859, and he remained loyal to many of its most important tenets until his death in 1881.

Contemporaries most often thought of the native soil movement as an attempt to reconcile Slavophilism and westernism. But both the 'young editors' and later the *pochvenniki* believed that they, like the times, had moved beyond the debates of westernizers and Slavophiles. During the early 1860s, the 'men of the soil' not only undertook a sophisticated critique of nihilism but also tried to provide young Russians with a positive alternative to the radicalism of Chernyshevsky or Pisarev. Critical as they were of the Russian radicals, the *pochvenniki* were also at pains to distance themselves from other conservatives. Although they admired and in some respects emulated the early Slavophiles, they differed from them in a number of crucial ways. They also engaged in heated debates during the 1860s with such publicists of the right as M.N. Katkov and I.S. Aksakov. Few of the major concerns of the day escaped their scrutiny.

The native soil movement is sufficiently rich in ideas and personalities to merit a study of its own. Dostoevsky's contribution to the group and the relationship of his thought to that of its other members has been too little appreciated in the literature. To date, no major attempt has been made to place Grigor'ev's 'organic criticism' within the wider, both Russian and European, intellectual currents of his day. But a study of the *pochvenniki* has wider implications. The comparison of the philosophy and ideology of their movement to those of other conservative tendencies as well as to the ideology of nihilism sheds new light not only on the conservative tradition in nineteenth-century Russia but also on the psychology and behaviour of the whole Russian intelligentsia.

1

Conservatism and the search
for national originality

Russian conservatism emerged in the nineteenth century within the traditions of the larger European conservative experience. From the time of the Enlightenment, the challenge of the parties of progress had elicited a joint counter-offensive on the part of conservatives throughout Europe and armed them with a shared ideology. Though latecomers to the family of modern European conservatism, Russian conservatives were also compelled to face the threat posed to traditional values by the advent of economic, social, and cultural modernization. In spite of their basic kinship, the separate branches of European conservatism were as noteworthy for their dissimilarities as for their family resemblance. The conservatives, who made it one of their cardinal principles to preserve the heritage peculiar to each distinct nation, were directed by their own logic to emphasize the differences rather than the similarities among the institutions, culture, and behaviour of separate national groups. In the case of the Russian conservatives, Russia's long history of religious exclusiveness probably served to strengthen this particularist trait among them. The conservatives' insistence on national particularism meant that while what was considered worth conserving varied widely from country to country, the general framework of the conservative philosophy remained more or less the same. Conservatism was, therefore, characterized less by a commitment to a specific form of government or social order than by a certain attitude towards the world, man, and history.

The first stirrings of modern conservatism in Europe were as old as the origins of the modern state.[1] As kings and princes took measures in the seventeenth century to enhance the power of the central authority at the expense of regions, estates, and corporations, a defensive conservative mentality was rudely awakened. In the eighteenth century determined rulers found new allies in the *philosophes*. The 'party of humanity' indecorously assailed the traditional institutions, beliefs, and privileges which, sanctified by centuries of usage, sustained the old order and, in its view, stifled the individual and deprived him of his natural rights. The aggressive assertions of the *philosophes*, which were rooted in an elaborate social philosophy, compelled conservatives to formulate a philosophical defence of the life they had formerly taken for granted. Since modern ideological conservatism was originally a protective reaction to the philosophy and practices of the Enlightenment, its character was conditioned by the very principles it opposed.

At the heart of Enlightenment thought was an optimism, that had been building since the Renaissance, about the intelligibility of the universe and the essential goodness of human nature.[2] By the outbreak of the French Revolution, the more radical individuals among the *philosophes* had removed the source of evil from man himself and relocated it in corrupt and corrupting social institutions and traditions. The principal bequest of the Enlightenment to both radicals and liberals of the modern era was the belief in the perfectibility of man and the sufficiency of human will and reason for the regeneration of human nature by the creation of a rational social order. Freed from the restraints that traditional society imposed on his thoughts and actions, the new rational man in the renovated social and political order would be subject only to those limits that derived from his own reason and that he willed on himself.

In order to examine human nature more clearly in the pure light of reason, the *philosophes* abstracted man from his existing historical associations and from the traditions that they believed debased him and placed him in a metaphorical state of nature. In this imaginary condition, they argued, the true nature of men became apparent: they were autonomous beings, possessed of reason and equally endowed with a number of inalienable natural rights. The universalism of the *philosophes* was balanced by a realistic eighteenth-century assessment of the strength and persistence of local and national differences. Later radicals were less inhibited, and the notion grew that societies ought to be constructed less on the particular historical experience of individual nations than on a body of abstract and universal assumptions about humanity.

With rationalism came utilitarianism. Most of the *philosophes* agreed that man's primary motivation was concern for his own security and comfort. It was this concern that, in their minds, lay behind the creation of a political society on the basis of a social contract. Through the social contract, the contracting parties sought to secure their personal wellbeing by the political regulation of relations among competing individuals within a framework of civil and universal human rights. The state was no longer seen either as an independent creation of Providence or as a unique product of a particular historical experience but principally as an instrument created by humans to promote the conditions under which the citizen was freest to advance his own economic and social interests. In such a state, regional particularism and traditional social distinctions were expected to give way to a more homogeneous and open society of equal citizens or, in later radical thought, to almost total social levelling.

Conservative thinkers were quick to grasp the implications of the Enlightenment's views of man and the world and to attribute to them the worst excesses of the French Revolution. In order to counter the radicals and liberals effectively, the conservatives had to demonstrate that the workings of the universe were not as accessible to human reason as the *philosophes* had supposed and that the reason and will of man were alone inadequate to reorder society successfully and regenerate human nature.[3] The conservatives had none of the optimism of the *philosophes* about the innate goodness of man. They contended that evil was not an ephemeral product of an irrational environment but a permanent and even necessary aspect of the human condition. Nor, given their philosophy of imperfection, would conservatives entertain fantasies about human perfectibility. Edmund Burke, who with the publication of his *Reflections on the Revolution in France* in 1790 emerged as the acknowledged leader of the conservative forces, remarked with heavy irony that conservatives were 'afraid to put men to live and trade each on his own private stock of reason, because we suspect that this stock in each man is small.'[4]

Since the conservatives believed that unassisted human reason could avail so little, they were not unnaturally sceptical about the possibility of a society in which men obeyed only the dictates of their own reason. Internal or self-imposed restraints were seen as inadequate to contain the destructive sides of human nature which the optimists overlooked. External restraints were also necessary, and history had been a long and painful struggle to uncover ideals and institutions suitable for subduing the beast in men. Rather than trust to abstract human reason, Burke recommended that men should rely on concrete, historical experience, 'the general bank and capital of nations and of ages.'[5] Rationalistic social engineering could result only in chaos or tyranny. Customs and traditions bound societies together, gave them order, stability, and continuity, and provided the surest guarantee of individual liberty against the encroachments of the state. To attack and destroy them was to invite the shambles of the French Revolution.

Along with the abstraction of Enlightenment thought the conservatives also dismissed its universalism. They scoffed at the notion that men in all times and places were the same. Even among the tradionalists, who had a more static view of the world than did the next generation of the romantics, historical relativism crept in: every age and every nation produced institutions, ideas, and social arrangements uniquely appropriate to them. Conservatives gloried in variety. Everywhere men were different because everywhere they were steeped in particular national and local traditions and customs. Joseph de Maistre, who after Burke was the most influential spokesman for the conservatives in the period of the French Revolution, insisted that 'every age and every nation has a special distinctive nature which must be carefully considered.'[6]

The main failing of the *philosophes*, according to their conservative critics, was their inability to see men and society as they really were: their entire methodology was suspect. It was contrary to common sense to strip the human being of the attributes bequeathed to him by the milieu into which he was born and to place this abstract, residual man in a mythical state of nature where he was inexplicably but conveniently endowed with natural rights.[7] The idea 'man' was to the conservatives an abstraction that had no real existence. There were only men, real individuals, who lived, worked, and died under particular historical circumstances in concrete social settings. Their rights were not innate but derived from the position in society into which they were born. The social estates and the distinctions and privileges they conferred were not the products of chance or human malevolence but the work of Providence, sanctified by history. It was social rank that gave men definition and moral purpose. The various classes together, each with its own innate principle, constituted a sacred corporate organism that harmoniously performed all the necessary functions of society.

The intent of conservative political thinking was to secure the individual from interference, in the name of reason or the public good, by the state. Conservatives advocated a politics of limits.[8] The regulation of social relations rested on ingrained habits and practices and on the traditional rights and privileges of the duly constituted social estates. It did not depend on state control. The conservatives did not see it as the purpose of the state to manage the anarchical clash of individual wills but to symbolize a nation's unity and oversee the smooth workings of a social organism ordained by God or history.

The French Revolution seemed to confirm the worst fears of the conservatives. Under the banner of liberty and equality, chaos and destruction spread through France and seeped into neighbouring countries. Napoleon imposed order of a sort, but the liberal ideas on which the Revolution had originally been launched gained even wider currency in the constitutional settlements that followed hard on the conquests of the imperial army. With the defeat of Napoleon and the convening of the Congress of Vienna in 1815, the conservative reaction got under way. Throughout Europe, whatever of the old régime that could be restored was restored. The patience of the traditionalist conservatives on the Continent, who during the Revolutionary and Napoleonic periods had confidently looked forward to a restoration, was rewarded as monarchs turned to them to furnish ideological sustenance for the reactionary policies to which they were committed. The Holy Alliance of Russia, Prussia, and Austria, with its dedication to the eradication of liberalism wherever it was to be found, aptly symbolized the siege mentality of conservatives in the restoration period.

The restoration should have sated the forces of European conservatism after 1815 but did not. Conservatism itself turned out to be no proof against the romantic longing that infected almost a whole generation in the post-Napoleonic period. During the romantic age, a new generation of conservatives arose that was dissatisfied with the solution imposed on Europe by the traditionalists. The reasons for their discontent are not hard to find. Since 1789, Europe had experienced an unprecedented series of changes. After the stolid decades of the old régime, almost anything now seemed possible. The return to the pre-revolutionary status quo had been partial at best. A great deal had changed and was still changing. The restoration, therefore, brought order but not stability. The uncertainties of the age heightened the sense of loss among conservatives and nurtured a longing for a total transformation of society. Few conservative romantics were simple defenders of the status quo but were utopian visionaries intent on rebuilding the world.[9]

The conservative romantics took as their own most of the theories of the traditionalists but placed new emphasis on old ideas and added some original thoughts of their own. Like the traditionalists, the romantics had little faith in the powers of human reason. They did not disparage the rational faculty but believed with Coleridge that 'man is something besides reason.'[10] They stressed instead the importance for man of the 'integrated personality' in which intellect and feeling were held in an equilibrium. For the romantic conservatives, the human personality consisted of a complex of faculties which incorporated reason but included also emotion, intuition, and faith. The elevation of one faculty over the others occasioned an imbalance in the human soul, destroyed its wholeness, and separated the individual from the inner meaning of the universe. Harmony with the external world rested on perfect harmony within the internal world of the individual.

The core concept of romanticism was that reality was fundamentally thought or idea. The romantics conceived of history as a dynamic process in which the idea of the universe gradually revealed itself and attained consciousness in the minds of men. Most conservative romantics, therefore, rejected the static conception of a world governed by the God-given, absolute standards characteristic of the traditionalists and adopted a thoroughly relativistic and historical position. Each age or nation was held to make a unique and valuable contribution to the creation of the whole fabric of the universe.

The place of individual nations in some universal scheme was an especially intriguing question to conservatives in the romantic age. They were not the first; J.G. von Herder had anticipated their concern in the last quarter of the eighteenth century. He contented himself with the notion of the fullness of the universe in which every age and every nation contributed some small part to an unknown and unknowable universal plan. The German idealists, most notably Hegel, spoke of world nations that were specifically designated by the 'World Spirit' to dominate the intellectual and cultural life of an age and provide a temporary vehicle for the furthering of a universal design. Near the end of his life, Hegel's countryman the poet Schiller contrived to have the best of all worlds. He graciously conceded the invaluable service rendered to history by all nations while reserving the crowning achievement for Germany. 'Each people has its day in history,' he wrote, 'but the day of the German is the harvest of time as a whole.'[11] The confusion of philosophy with history and the fascination with cosmic second guessing were traits shared with the Germans by many Slavs, and Schiller's optimism could be and was easily adapted to Russian needs by the simple expedient of substituting Russia for Germany.

In the relativistic scheme of the conservative romantics, change was seen as inevitable and even salutary. The theory of change that they most often settled on rested on an analogy with biology, the most vital of the sciences in the early nineteenth century. Unlike the *philosophes* who had viewed societies and nations as mechanisms, conservatives saw them as organisms that were born, matured, and died according to some unseen, inner necessity. Not all of the conservatives intended that the organic analogy be taken literally. Burke, for example, used the term but only as a metaphor in order to convey the fundamental importance of gradualism in historical development. In his view, change in history was essentially an empirical process achieved through cautious trial and error. The idealist philosopher Hegel, in contrast, saw in history a teleology or hidden purpose that was gradually working itself out in the affairs of men and nations. It was only the German romantics, led by Novalis and Adam Müller, who most consistently urged a literal application of biological organicism to society, state, and nation, but they were less influential, particularly in Russia, than might be supposed.[12]

It needs to be pointed out that it was not quite the same thing to argue that the separate parts of a society were organically joined in a single purpose as it was to insist that society was a living organism. The jurist Friedrich von Savigny best expressed the organic idea as it was most commonly understood when he wrote in 1814 that what bound a nation into one whole was 'the common conviction of the people, the kindred consciousness of an inner necessity.'[13] For the conservatives, it was this inner necessity, and not the disruptive rationalism of the social reformers, that dictated true change. Legitimate change was internal and spontaneous, not external and conscious.

The store of common conviction to which Savigny referred was, for conservatives, the minimal requirement for the survival of a nation. It was an unwritten bond, more durable than the external unity imposed by written constitutions and positive laws. Men were dependent creatures whose moral convictions arose from a shared social experience. The conservatives feared that the utilitarian pursuit of pure self-interest could end only in social disintegration since, in their view, social harmony rested on the subordination of individual interests to long-established communal values. Liberal individualism was tantamount to atomization and an estrangement of man from man that no society could for long endure.

The conservative romantics were not in complete agreement on the issue of individualism. Some of the Germans, such as Novalis and Müller, went so far as to subordinate the individual completely to the higher unity of the community. They interpreted freedom to be the total identification of the individual with the aspirations of the group. This view culminated in Fichte's conception of the state in which individuals were entirely subsumed in the whole. Other romantic thinkers were more sensitive to the dangers posed to the individual by the glorification of the community. They envisaged a society in which each individual, through the full development of his own personality, furthered the growth of the whole. Hegel's fellow idealist F.W.J. von Schelling was particularly aware of the tension between the individual and society and maintained that cohesion was greatest in that society in which the individual was freest to cultivate his unique personality.

The organic conception of the nation, which carried with it the notion of the moral solidarity of the individual and the community, was accompanied by a further idea that was to be of great significance for intelligentsia conservatives in Russia. This was expressionism, an idea that originated with Herder. In his criticism of the universalism of the Enlightenment, Herder had stressed the value to the individual of membership in a specific cultural group. He went on to argue that since individuals were products of a particular time, place, and culture, all their acts, especially their artistic endeavours, constituted an expression of the personality of the whole nation. The conclusion that the Russians, among others, drew was that nationality was most fully expressed in art.[14]

The European inheritance of the intelligentsia conservatives in Russia was exceedingly complex, and it is virtually impossible to trace specific influences with any confidence. The Russians were most profoundly affected by the Germans, with their dynamic, idealist, and relativist view of history and their organic, expressionist approach to the nation. Even within the German tradition, however, differences were evident that were later to provoke passionate arguments among the Russians. The ambiguities of the German bequest raise complications enough, but the Russian conservatives were never loath to borrow from any source, even from their ideological opponents, to make their case. The product of their eclecticism was a unique Russian variation on the general theme of European conservatism.

The continuous background of Russian conservatism was the highly durable Russian autocracy. Until the turbulent reign of Peter the Great, the Orthodox church had supplied the substance of Russian conservative ideology. The alliance of church and state was sealed in the opening years of the sixteenth century, and for nearly two hundred years the absolutist claims of the princes and tsars of Muscovy rested on the sanction of the church. The powerful monopoly of the church in Russian cultural life and its almost pathological hostility towards the religion and culture of western Europe early accustomed Russians to think in terms of the contrasts between Russia and the West, a habit that was later to become a fixed characteristic of the conservatives. Towards the end of the seventeenth century the church began to lose its independence in relations with the state and, even before the reign of Peter, had ceased to be a partner and become the adjunct of the secular authority.

Peter vastly accelerated the process of the secularization of Russian life
that had been going on since the Time of Troubles at the start of the
seventeenth century. In his efforts to combat the dead weight of the past,
he created a westernized élite within the upper groups of the society.
Peter may have intended to promote little more than a technological
revolution in Russia, but in the long run the cultural revolution that
resulted from his reforms proved to be of more lasting significance for his
subjects. It symbolized a clear break in Russian history between the
religious culture of the past and the westernizing, secular culture of the
future and created a cultural gulf between the upper and lower classes of
the society. To be sure, the gap between the educated and uneducated in
most societies is large, but in Russia the problem was exacerbated. Peter
demanded that the upper classes reject traditionalist assumptions, but
these still underlay peasant life. There was resistance to Peter's reforms,
much of it centred around the church. The old boyar aristocracy also
protested the loss of its status and privilege that accompanied the
introduction of the Table of Ranks. The last great spokesman for the old
aristocracy was Prince Mikhail Shcherbatov who in his *Corruption of Morals
in Russia* bitterly denounced the life-style of the westernized gentry and
the frivolity of the court.[15]

Shcherbatov's strictures made little impression on the Russian gentry.
Unlike the boyar aristocracy from which Shcherbatov was descended, the
gentry had been the beneficiaries of Peter's reforms. It is true that they
deeply resented the compulsory service to the state which Peter imposed
on them for life, but after the great reformer's death they succeeded in
having the term of service shortened until in 1762 it was abolished
altogether. The first and most important step towards the emancipation
of the gentry took place in 1730. During the succession crisis of that year,
which was precipitated by the unexpected death of the new emperor,
Peter II, the boyars made a final, desperate attempt to impose their
authority on the autocracy. They proposed a constitutional settlement
that would have subjected the decisions of the monarch to the approval of
an aristocratic council. The gentry, which preferred the rule of one to the
rule of the aristocratic few, came to the support of the new empress,
Anna. In return for a few concessions, it formed a partnership with the
autocracy against the old aristocracy. The dyarchy of autocracy and
gentry formed the new foundation of Russian conservatism until the
middle of the nineteenth century. The Decembrist revolt of 1825, in
which many prominent gentry families were implicated, shook the
alliance, but it endured with few modifications until the Emancipation
reforms of 1861.

The gentry ideal of correct relations between the autocrat and the nobility was patriarchalism. The Russian nobleman had traditionally preferred the resolution of social conflicts through the personal intercession of the tsar to the regulation of society by the impersonal authority of the law. Since the operation of the patriarchal ideal rested on direct access to the monarch, the gentry deeply resented the growth of a bureaucracy that increasingly interposed itself between the ruler and society. Bureaucratization was not, however, a process that either the monarchy or the gentry could readily control.

The expansion of the bureaucratic machinery of imperial Russia was partly the consequence of the impressive growth from ca 1750 of the population and the increasing social and administrative complexity that the greater numbers entailed. The first half of the nineteenth century saw the beginnings of the urban transformation of Russia. As old administrative or religious centres acquired new economic functions and new commercial and industrial centres arose, the urban population of the empire increased by roughly three million people between 1812 and 1857. From approximately 5 per cent of the population at the turn of the century, the proportion of city dwellers rose to nearly 10 per cent of the total by 1863.[16] The greatest increase occurred among the commercial and industrial middle classes and the factory workers.

The first steps towards urbanization, one indicator of modernization, were accompanied by another: the slow but none the less significant advance of education. Alexander I had undertaken a thorough restructuring of the education system from top to bottom. His successor, who was reluctant to extend more than bare literacy to the lower social orders, restructured the system to his own tastes and took care to control and manipulate the curricula of schools and universities. But the government could no longer dispense with a pool of educated citizens to effect the nation's business, and under Nicholas the number of Russians in schools steadily increased. Whereas in 1804 the Ministry of National Enlightenment had only some 33,000 students in attendance at schools within its jurisdiction, it had more than 125,000 in 1856.[17]

The second stimulus to modernization as well as bureaucratization was the pressing need for Russia to compete successfully in the international arena with the economically and technologically more advanced nations of western Europe. Since the beginning of the seventeenth century, the autocracy had been caught on the horns of a persistent dilemma. On the one side was the urge to preserve the special shape and characteristic social relations of Muscovite society on which the authority of the tsars had traditionally rested. On the other side was the need to innovate at the very least in the areas of technology and administration in order to keep up with modernizing neighbours in the West, but at the risk of disrupting the peculiar social order that favoured the preservation of autocratic government. In the nineteenth century international competition was intensified by the spread of nationalism and the need for continuous modernization became more urgent.

The dilemma presented by the demands of modernization was never resolved in Russia. During the nineteenth century successive generations of government officials grappled with the problem of adapting existing institutions to the needs of a modernizing society, but a satisfactory balance between stability and change was not struck.[18] If the efforts of Russian statesmen to preserve the social order awoke the spirit of radicalism among some elements of society, their attempts to 'systematize' Russian government through controlled change intensified feelings among conservatives − and others.

In spite of its abiding suspicion of most change, the Russian nobility had not been standing still. Following Peter's reforms, the successive generations of the Russian gentry came more and more to resemble their noble counterparts in the West both by outward appearance and inward conviction. To the best of their ability, most members of the gentry who could afford it emulated the cosmopolitan style of life that was rooted in the West.

The gradual Europeanization of the gentry was paralleled by a second important development. During the second half of the eighteenth century, a handful of Russian intellectuals painstakingly pieced together the foundations of a Russian national consciousness.[19] They were proud of their Muscovite heritage and even prouder of Russia's accomplishments since Peter. The dualism of the Russian inheritance not unnaturally generated tensions in the minds of the patriots. As early as the latter part of the eighteenth century such tensions began to be expressed in the metaphor 'Russia and the West.' It stood for the break between Muscovite and Petrine Russia, the cultural separation of the educated and uneducated, and increasingly, as will be seen, the rift between the proponents of a more traditionalist policy and the advocates of further westernization.

One of the more innovative and influential resolutions of the tension between traditionalism and Europeanism was first proposed in the nineteenth century by the novelist and historian, and most eloquent apologist of gentry conservatism, N.M. Karamzin. In 1802 he observed that 'Peter the Great, who *united* us with Europe and showed us the benefits of enlightenment, did not long humiliate the national pride of the Russians. We looked at Europe, so to speak, and at one glance we assimilated the fruits of her long labours.'[20] The implication was that it was part of the nature of Russians to be able to assimilate the achievements and accumulated knowledge of other nationalities and make use of them within a purely national context.

The War of 1812 and the victory over Napoleon heightened Russian feelings of national pride. In the 1820s and early 1830s Russian romantics turned to German philosophy for an account of the meaning of history, especially Russian history. It was during the two decades following the Congress of Vienna that most of the philosophical underpinnings of the more thoughtful varieties of later conservatism first entered the Russian consciousness. Guided by the German idealists, Russian romantics believed implicitly in the creative powers of the human mind. Convinced that history was intelligible, they saw the historical process as an organic unfolding of universal consciousness. The agents of the advance of consciousness were individuals and nations. Each nation, they contended, contained a particular spiritual essence that progressively attained conscious expression in its history, art, and literature.

The Russian romantics demanded more of philosophy than the solution of theoretical problems. They insisted on unity and wholeness, on the fullness of life, the integral relationship of knowledge and personality, and the synthesis of ideal and real, thought and life. In the belief that all knowledge was concrete, they rejected rationalism and empiricism as abstract and one-sided and sought instead to poeticize the individual, the nation, and the universe. From the beginning Russian romantics freely mingled questions of philosophy with questions of nationality and found in the mysteries of the Russian nation the wholeness and universality that philosophy ultimately could not provide.[21]

Karamzin's type of faith in the universality of Russians persisted, therefore, throughout the romantic period in Russia. P.A. Viazemsky, for example, believed that Russians were able to make their own everything of beauty and value that came from the outside world.[22] Viazemsky, a writer and critic, was referring to the creations of Russian literature. But the idea soon re-emerged in philosophy. P. Ia. Chaadaev put the same notion to use in order to inject a new element into contemporary interpretations of Peter the Great. In his 'Apology of a Madman' Chaadaev argued that Peter's reforms were not alien to Russia but profoundly national and represented the logical outcome of Russia's cultural advance towards humanity.[23] V.F. Odoevsky also noted, in his *Russian Nights*, that Russians had for a long time been conscious of their universality. Peter, he maintained, had linked the elements of west European nationality with the love and unity that was inherent in the Russian soul and so had prepared the way for Russia's universal mission.[24]

In 1819, Viazemsky provided the Russian language with a new word, *narodnost'*. Within it he hoped to encompass all the supposed characteristics of Russian national originality. *Narodnost'* was a crucial element in nearly all social and political thought in nineteenth-century Russia, but it was the very heart of conservatism. It was not, however, a precise term. Conservatives not only disagreed about the proper content of *narodnost'* but differed also as to how it could be reinjected into and diffused throughout the life of the nation.

Originally *narodnost'* was intended to describe those elements that distinguished Russian literature from the literature of other nationalities, and it never entirely relinquished its early close associations with literature. Herder's expressionism prevailed in Russia in the idea that the native originality of any people was expressed in its literary creations. The great poet Aleksandr Pushkin suggested in 1825 that the religion, government, and climate of a country combined to 'give each people a peculiar physiognomy which is to a greater or lesser degree reflected in the mirror of poetry.'[25] Pushkin's view was to have a lasting influence in Russian literature and literary criticism. The artist, as the product of his time and place, was believed to be organically linked to the life of his nation. Literature revealed to man the hidden meaning of the objective world and gave conscious expression to the unconscious, hidden springs of nationality.

By the 1840s the tension between the Western and Russian ideals had become personified in two small groups of intellectuals, the westernizers and the Slavophiles. Both groups have been discussed amply and often elsewhere in the literature. It is sufficient to remark here that the debate between the two camps turned on the metaphor Russia and the West. In the Russia of Nicholas I there was no opportunity to address concrete social and political issues, and this metaphor served as a kind of substitute for the great ideological matters dividing progressives and conservatives in the more open intellectual atmosphere of western Europe. Both Russia and the West, as they were understood by the two sides, were abstractions that bore little resemblance to the reality of either. The West conveyed the progressive virtues and implied a rationalist solution for

Russia; Russia embodied the conservative virtues and foreshadowed a traditionalist future. The West stood for something that Russia did not have but should acquire; Russia stood for something Russians had once had but were imminently in danger of losing.

By the end of the decade, the controversy between the Slavophiles and westernizers had more or less reached an impasse. But the possibility of synthesizing the major ideas of the two camps and the two sides of the metaphor that they represented had always been present. Karamzin and the Russian romantics had already provided a means of bridging the gap between Russian particularism on the one hand and the greater world of Europeanism on the other. All that was needed in order to complete the synthesis was a number of individuals who were equipped by their social experience and intellectual interests for this complex task.

2

The young editors of *Moskvitianin*

The appearance of intelligentsia conservatism in Russia is usually associated with the rise of intelligentsia radicalism. Conservative thought among the *intelligenty* is said to have been provoked by the materialism, scientism, and utilitarianism of the radical nihilists in the early 1860s. This view is by no means entirely inaccurate. Conservative formulations in the post-Emancipation period bore the impress of just such a reaction. Nevertheless, major changes in ideology rarely occur overnight but generally require a lengthy period of intellectual gestation. The philosophical, historical, and national principles on which the new conservatism in Russia was based did not spring up full-blown from the clash with the nihilists. Instead, its fundamental tenets were worked out in a relatively complete form in the years before and during the Crimean War (1853–5) and simply applied by conservative *intelligenty* as a counterweight to nihilism in the changed intellectual and social atmosphere of the Emancipation era. The new conservatism first manifested itself as a theory of literature and literary criticism, but, as was often the case in Russia, literature and criticism opened broad avenues into philosophy and social thought.

In 1850 a group of young Moscow writers and poets, literary critics, and dilettante philosophers gathered in the editorial office of the patriotic journal *Moskvitianin*. Contemporaries dubbed the little band of literary bohemians the 'young editors' of *Moskvitianin*. While the founding, or 'old,' editor, M.P. Pogodin, retained control of the political or historical sections of the journal, his junior associates, from 1850 to 1856, assumed responsibility for its *belles-lettres* and literary criticism. For a short while at the beginning of the decade, the impact of this brilliant, if erratic, youthful coterie made *Moskvitianin* one of the most vital and widely read journals in Russia. The group, which had come together by chance and never formed more than a loose association, gradually disintegrated as disagreements among them multiplied. In 1856 it dispersed completely when *Moskvitianin* ceased publication. Before they went their separate ways, however, the young editors established sufficient agreement on fundamentals to create the ideological basis of intelligentsia conservatism in the Emancipation period.

Moskvitianin, which had been established in 1841, had assiduously cultivated a reputation for heavy-handed pedantry, punctuated only occasionally by flashes of determination and insight. Its editor, Pogodin, and his colleague S.P. Shevyrev, respectively professors of history and literature at the University of Moscow, had chosen the motto 'Orthodoxy, Autocracy, and Nationality' as the basis of their program. S.S. Uvarov, Nicholas 1's minister of enlightenment, had, of course, originally authored the slogan as an antidote to the formula 'Liberty, Equality, and Fraternity' of revolutionary Europe, and such blatant association with government-sanctioned ideology had done little to improve the reputation of the professors or their journal. *Moskvitianin* had become equated in the public mind (not entirely fairly) with the obscurantist proponents of 'official nationality' in bureaucratic and journalistic circles. The prospects of *Moskvitianin* were further jeopardized by the tortured prose of the two academics, which thoroughly disenchanted both new readers and old subscribers. The result was that by 1850 *Moskvitianin* was insolvent, and Pogodin was in desperate need of fresh talent.[1]

Opportunity presented itself late in 1849. Impressed by the manuscript of *Bankrot* (The Bankrupt), a play about merchant life in Moscow by the still novice writer A.N. Ostrovsky, Pogodin hastened to meet the author. Early in December he arranged a literary evening at which Ostrovsky read his play to a large company. Among the distinguished guests were N.V. Gogol' and A.S. Khomiakov. The performance was repeated a few days later at the home of the Countess E.P. Rostopchina, who was soon to become the young editors' patroness.[2]

Ostrovsky had already established friendly relations with a junior associate of *Moskvitianin*. In 1847 he had by chance met T.I. Filippov, an aspiring philosopher and a protégé of Pogodin, in one of Moscow's student taverns. Filippov introduced Ostrovsky to the budding critic E.N. Edel'son. Shortly afterwards two poets, B.N. Almazov and L.A. Mei, were drawn into the circle. The nucleus of the young editors' set was completed in 1850 when A.A. Grigor'ev begged, on his knees the story went, to be admitted to the group. The novelist A.F. Pisemsky was also involved with the circle until 1852. It was these young men who were directly concerned with the day-by-day editing of the literary section of *Moskvitianin*. Many others hovered on the fringes. The ready access the young editors enjoyed to the pages of a journal at a time of severe censorship restrictions inevitably attracted many ambitious authors to them at one time or another.[3]

Of the inner circle in 1850, Almazov, at twenty-three, was the youngest, and Grigor'ev, at twenty-eight, the oldest. The young editors were, therefore, roughly a generation younger than the early Slavophiles with whom they have most often been associated by historians. Almazov, who was the product of high Moscow society, boasted by far the best pedigree. The others, for the most part, were the sons of bureaucratic officials on the lower and middle levels of the Table of Ranks.[4] The offspring of lesser bureaucrats, they had not followed in their fathers' footsteps but had instead chosen literary careers. At least two of the young editors, Ostrovsky and Grigor'ev, were intimately acquainted with the life-style of the Russian merchants among whom they had spent their childhoods. Their understanding of merchant life was no doubt enhanced by the friendship of I.I. Shanin, a young merchant who was an intimate of the young editors' circle.

The collaboration of the old and young editors of *Moskvitianin* was not as unlikely as it at first appeared. Certainly, it was not as incongruous as some 'progressive' historians at the turn of the last century supposed.[5] It is true that Pogodin's preoccupation with his distinctive version of 'Ortho-doxy, Autocracy, and Nationality' seemed remote from the primarily aesthetic interests of the young editors. Money was rarely far from Pogodin's thoughts, and he was undoubtedly, at least in part, motivated by nothing more than purely financial considerations in his efforts to attract youthful contributors to his journal. His pecuniary expectations were not disappointed. In 1851, on the strength of Ostrovsky's plays and Pisemsky's stories, subscriptions to *Moskvitianin* more than doubled, to 1,100.[6]

In fairness, however, it should be said that the sources reflect a genuine sense of gratitude towards Pogodin on the part of a number of young intellectuals, a gratitude that was based on a natural affinity. Pogodin, who had risen from humble origins, had already developed some of the ideas associated with the conservative wing of the intelligentsia. He was not only a teacher, but in his modest way also a patron, and one more influential in Russian intellectual life of the mid-century than has commonly been granted. Almazov and Grigor'ev repeatedly proclaimed

Pogodin as their spiritual and intellectual mentor; Ostrovsky lived amicably in the irascible professor's home for some time in the early 1850s and continuously demonstrated his loyalty by publishing most of his new plays in *Moskvitianin* until 1855, in spite of receiving only fifteen rubles per folio page from Pogodin at a time when *Sovremennik* and *Otechestvennye zapiski* were offering fifty rubles.[7] Not all the young editors were so idealistically motivated. Pisemsky, for one, abandoned *Moskvitianin* as soon as he got a better offer. But for most there were more cogent reasons for allying with Pogodin than blatant careerism.

Pogodin was one of the pioneers in the exploration of Russian nationality. In company with Viazemsky, Chaadaev, and Odoevsky, he expanded on the idea of Russian universality earlier raised by Karamzin. In his patriotic writings, Pogodin offered a formula that combined the Slavophiles' preference for Russia before Peter with the westernizers' admiration for the changes Peter had brought about in the life and orientation of Muscovy. Pogodin's conclusions were grounded in his studies of Russian history. He began with the popular, and remarkably durable, theory that the Russian state had not been founded on foreign conquest as had the states of western Europe. Consequently, Russia had been spared the feudal tyranny and class strife that had ravaged and divided the nations of the West. Instead, Pogodin asserted, during the Russian middle ages, forms of self-administration, communal tenure, and patriarchal freedom had evolved that guaranteed social harmony. Pogodin accepted that such an idyll was not destined to last in a world of competitive nation states. Geopolitics had required Peter the Great to interrupt Russia's national (*narodnoe*) development. In order to safeguard their independence Russians had been compelled to crush their northern enemies and arm themselves with the weapons and tools of western Europe. Pogodin believed that in the century following Peter's reign the goal of external security had been attained. With the establishment of an autonomous Russian presence among the nations of Europe, the Petrine age had completed its mission, and the stage was set for a new era in Russian historical development. Pogodin was an admirer of Schelling and was deeply influenced by his vision of a universal culture in which the cultural and moral principles governing East and West were commingled in a new and higher civilization. He was convinced that Peter's reforms, by bringing the West to the East, had made such a synthesis possible in Russia.[8]

The essential elements of Pogodin's vision were his sensitivity to the organicism or continuity of Russian history and his relativist conviction that each separate phase of Russia's historical development was valuable in and for itself. Every part of the nation's history, including the Petrine era, was held to be an independent and unique expression of a greater, still unconscious whole. Pogodin recognized the necessity of the past – all of it – in the preparation of Russia's great future. If the Slavophiles denounced the entire Petrine period as a hideous error (though one with which Russians now had to cope), Pogodin welcomed it as a necessary and natural step towards the fulfilment of Russia's purpose. The prosaic and stifling reality of Nicholas I's Russia might not have been adequate in Pogodin's eyes, but he was supremely confident that something entirely satisfactory was destined to emerge from it. The relativism and immanentism that were intrinsic to his interpretation of Russian history were Pogodin's most important bequest to the young editors and to the subsequent development of Russian conservatism.

There were other affinities between the old and young editors of *Moskvitianin*. The young editors had originally been attracted to one another by their passion for the Russian folk-song.[9] Like their older Slavophile contemporary P.V. Kireevsky, they collected the traditional songs of the people and sang them with all the enthusiasm of the newly converted. The young editors revered Russia's national songs as spontaneous expressions of the national soul and offered them as evidence of the artistic and historical sensibilities of Russians in past ages. The folk-song, they were fond of repeating, put to the lie the facile assertion of some westernizers that Russia had produced nothing of cultural value before the time of Peter the Great. With their enthusiasm for the nation's traditional songs, the young editors were more amenable to collaboration with a journal that had for several years proclaimed the glories of the Russian middle ages than with those which denounced or altogether ignored them.

Finally, there was the crucial question of literary criticism, which was and remained the primary concern of the young editors. Almost all historians of the period agree that the quality of criticism in the progressive St Petersburg journals declined sharply after the death of Belinsky in 1848. It was, however, more the tendency of St Petersburg literary criticism than its quality that offended the young editors.

The period 1848 to 1855 saw the predominance in Russian literature and literary criticism of the natural school. On the dubious authority of Gogol's *Dead Souls*, natural school writers assumed a critical and negative attitude towards almost all aspects of Russian reality. Natural school literary critics, such as *Sovremennik's* I.I. Panaev, valued literature merely as a weapon for the realization of proscribed social aims. Panaev and even his less abrasive counterparts on the more conservative *Otechestvennye zapiski* denied the very existence of a native Russian literature and scoffed at Russian folk poetry as inartistic. The natural school of literary criticism represented the antithesis of everything the young editors stood for in art. Since Shevyrev, with some assistance from M.A. Dmitriev, had for several years been combating the natural school tendency in Russian literature on the pages of *Moskvitianin*, the young editors understandably deemed it to be an appropriate organ for their own ideas about literature.

Unfortunately for those who wish to study them, the young editors were more remarkable for the enthusiasm than for the symmetry of their thought. They were representative of a youthfully exuberant creativity, uninhibited by tiresome thoughts of consistency or polish. They lived intensely and wrote feverishly. Much of their thought was still vague and a great deal was left altogether unsaid. In later years Grigor'ev liked wistfully to refer to this chaotic period as the 'antediluvian' stage of the movement that was to possess him until his death. It was only after 1856, when the young editors had gone their separate ways, that he was able to impose a semblance of order on the thoughts that germinated among his youthful associates.

Looking back in 1857 to the heyday of the young editors, Grigor'ev identified the three principal components of their movement: art (*Iskusstvo*), democratism (*Demokratizm*), and immediacy (*Neposredstvennost'*).[10] In these three elements were contained the ingredients of a profoundly conservative outlook that was to have far-reaching consequences for the later history of Russian conservatism. In a slightly altered order they still provide the most satisfactory basis for an examination of the young editors' movement.

The young editors were cultural nationalists in the tradition of Herder and the German romantics. Like Herder and his romantic followers they regarded the nation as a cultural entity and vigorously defended the value of belonging to a particular national culture against the universalizing claims of humanity. Again like Herder and a number of the German romantic conservatives, they believed that each nation was the possessor of an ideal which it developed during the course of its history and which, in time, contributed to the fullness of the universe.[11]

In their view of 'art,' the young editors were the Russian heirs of Herder's expressionism. By art Grigor'ev not only meant the primacy of artistic creativity over all the other activities of mind, but also intended to convey the notion that art, and especially literature, were a complete and independent expression of the national ideal. At the root of the young editors' aesthetic theory, therefore, was the assumption that art and nationality were inseparable. In an article in *Moskvitianin* in 1850, Ostrovsky argued that the literature of all advanced peoples grew in parallel with their social progress.[12] Or, as Grigor'ev put it in 1853, a given work of art was linked organically to the 'state, moral and social concepts' of a particular people at a particular time.[13] The life of a society, Ostrovsky continued, casts up certain character types for artistic depiction. The artist tested these national types against the universal moral ideal, which in Carlyle's phrase – and Carlyle was known to the young editors – 'lay in the hearts of all men' but to which the artist was particularly sensitive. If a type lived up to the ideal the artist legitimized it; but if it fell short it became the object of satire. Literature was not simply a mirror of national life but a prism by which the national experience was reflected through universal moral and aesthetic laws. Since every artist was organically bound to his own time and place, there could be no literature without nationality.

Ostrovsky's theory of types was not unique to the young editors but proved to be of great significance to them and later to the *pochvenniki*. Its importance lay in the fact that it established a reciprocal relationship between the development of *narodnost'* in life and in literature. Through the artistic depiction of types, nationality, which resided only unconsciously in the life of society, achieved conscious expression in literature and so returned consciously to life. The artist, by virtue of the superior force of his intuition, his gift, mediated between the real life of the people and its ideal essence. Consequently, the history of a nation's literature was the history of the organic progress of nationality towards self-consciousness.

If a work of literature was an intuitive and imaginative re-creation of the internal life of the nation, then, the young editors believed, it was the function of literary criticism to relate any given literary production to the whole body of national literature. They were particularly anxious that the criteria by which the place of a literary work in the whole canon of the nation's literature was determined not be too narrowly or mechanically conceived. Works of literature should be related not merely to other works of literature but to the life of the nation itself. The task of criticism, Grigor'ev insisted, was 'to show the relative significance of all works of literature in a mass, [and] to assign to each its appropriate place as an organic, living product of life.'[14] Good literary criticism, for the young editors, was relativist. They held that an old work of art was not superseded by its successor. Instead, it represented an independent and uniquely valuable artistic expression to be judged on its individual merits in terms of its own time and place and not solely on its position in a literary hierarchy.

From the great critic Belinsky the young editors had learned that every literary era was dominated by a personality who most fully expressed the contemporary level of national development in his art. For Belinsky, Gogol' had been the leading figure; for the young editors, the age of Gogol' had been succeeded by the age of Ostrovsky. Ostrovsky's plays about the life of the merchant class provided the focus of the young editor's thoughts about Russian nationality. The instincts of a great writer, they were sure, invariably prompted him to depict in literary types the fullest and most contemporary representatives of the national ideal. Ostrovsky had said a 'new word' (*novoye slovo*), and that word was nationality (*narodnost'*).

With the use of the term *neposredstvennost'* ('immediacy' or 'spontaneity'), Grigor'ev was consciously aligning the young editors with the so-called reversal of values in European thought that marked the transition from the Enlightenment to the romantic age.[15] This reversal involved a shift of intellectual focus from the abstract and general to the concrete and particular and from the universal truths of reason to the relative truths of historical experience. Grigor'ev reaffirmed the romantic conviction that immediately felt experience was superior to abstract reasoning as the basis of thought and action. The idea of immediacy, like almost every facet of the young editors' thought, grew out of their aesthetic theory. Immediacy, in fact, was the source of their quarrel with the natural school of literary criticism.

Legitimate knowledge of the nation, the young editors argued, arose entirely from the immediate perception of the historical experience of a people. Only in art was such immediacy attained. According to the young editors, therefore, art did not serve the narrow, abstract, and transitory social aims of ideologists as their rivals, the natural school writers, claimed. Instead, art was the agent of the concrete and living moral and spiritual forces that were immanent in a society and that constituted its nationality. In an interesting anticipation of Dostoevsky's aesthetic theories in his famous reply to Dobroliubov in 1861, Edel'son expanded in 1854 on the function of art: while it transcended utilitarian social aims, art, nevertheless, was useful to the human soul because moral, intellectual, and aesthetic enjoyment was necessary to 'every man and every society.'[16]

'Immediacy' had, however, implications wider than aesthetics. It also linked the young editors to the antirationalist tendencies of European conservatism. Like conservative nationalists in other parts of Europe, the young editors maintained that the imposition of rationally conceived ideals on the life of a nation served only as obstacles to its organic and natural development. In a study of Nikolai Stankevich's story 'The Idealist' in 1851, Grigor'ev wrote: 'Idealism is one of the sicknesses of our age. To demand from reality not what it gives of itself but what we determine [for it] in advance; to approach any living phenomenon with an abstract and, consequently, lifeless preconception; to recoil from reality the moment it rebuffs the demands of our ego, and to shrink proudly into ourselves: such are the most common symptoms of this disease, its inevitable course.'[17] Since the young editors themselves were unquestionably idealists, Grigor'ev's outburst appears odd at first sight. It is significant, however, that the author of the story in question, Stanke- vich, had been one of Russia's leading Hegelians before his premature death in 1846. Grigor'ev's critique, therefore, may reasonably be taken in general as a foray against Hegelian idealism and in particular against Hegel's historicism. The whole question of Hegelianism and Russian conservatism can best be dealt with in the following chapter. It is enough to point out here that the young editors vehemently opposed all attempts – either idealist or positivist – to discover the 'laws' of history and to deduce from them a universal theory of historical development. They regarded such universal laws as abstractions, detached from the concrete reality of the unique historical experience of individual nations and useless as guides to action.

It is evident from what has been said that the young editors were philosophical nominalists. Universals or abstract concepts were, to them, merely names with no corresponding realities in the world of experience. They were theories, the products of ratiocination and apriorism. The young editors opposed to such abstractions the concreteness of living experience in all its variety. Life was too rich and complex, too arbitrary, to be embraced by an a priori ideal. Rather, life had to be apprehended immediately through the kaleidoscope of individual and national exper- ience.

In light of the remarkable degree of interpenetration that the young editors believed to exist between art and life and their hostility to Hegelian historicism, it is not surprising that the relativism contained in their literary criticism extended also to their view of history. Just as every work of art was valuable for itself and not as a mere harbinger of its successors, so, they asserted, each stage in the life of a nation was to be judged according to its intrinsic merit and not on the extent of its contribution to some rationally conceived future end.

In 'democratism,' the remaining element of Grigor'ev's triad, was contained the foundations of the later conservative doctrine of social and ideological reconciliation. Grigor'ev intended by the term to underscore the essentially classless or integral character of Russian nationality. In an article of 1855, he insisted that there was 'no essential separation in the living, fresh and organic body of the nation.'[18] All social strata, despite superficial appearances to the contrary, were fundamentally joined in the unity of the national ideal.

If for the Slavophiles Russian nationality had been 'preserved' in the peasantry, for the young editors it was 'evolving' in the merchant class. The middle position that the merchant class occupied in society and its traditional contacts with all social levels made it, in the eyes of the young editors, the repository of all the forms and customs present in Russian life. The merchants combined 'both the ancient Russian life which whole centuries experienced and which had not been destroyed by alien influences ... and the full passion [among Russians] for the European comforts of life.' It is understandable, Edel'son continued in an article of 1854, 'that with such variety all the fundamental national features, whether they are subjected to the influences of multi-faceted civilization or are preserved in their pristine simplicity, are ... revealed in [the merchant class].'[19]

The emphasis the young editors placed on the merchant class as the bearers of Russian nationality has, understandably, induced some Soviet commentators to represent them as apologists for the emerging bourgeoisie in Russia.[20] Such a view, superficially at least, appears to be well-founded. It is important to remember, however, that the young editors believed, with Pogodin, that Russian nationality was in a process of becoming. In their opinion an 'independent Russian ideal has not yet finally been worked out up to our own day.'[21] Their affinity for the merchants arose less because they identified their own interests with a rising middle class – they were equally capable of an impassioned defence of peasant culture – than because they saw in the merchant estate a convenient composite of all the significant elements of Russian nationality. As far as they were concerned the merchant class represented no more than the partial embodiment of a much greater, future national ideal that would ultimately embrace Russians of all classes.

The young editors were not deceived in their optimistic assessment of the nationalist potential of the Russian merchantry. The decades from

1840 to 1860 witnessed among the élite of the merchant-industrial class, especially in Moscow, a transition from a narrow group perspective to a wider, Great Russian national consciousness. The transition was at first less political or economic than it was cultural, and the new nationalism of the merchants was most powerfully expressed in their patronage of Russian culture. During these years, several of the great late-nineteenth-century merchant collections of Russian art and artefacts had their modest origins. Alfred J. Rieber has pointed out that 'the merchant wing of the Moscow entrepreneurs asserted their fundamental belief in the superiority of the spontaneous, popular, private and national against the bureaucratic, aristocratic and foreign elements in Russian life. They claimed to place industry at the service of culture and, where possible, culture at the service of industry.'[22] Some of the young editors, notably Ostrovsky and Grigor'ev, were finely tuned to these new stirrings and found in the merchants' preference for the spontaneous, popular, and national an almost exact parallel to their own philosophical and aesthetic preconceptions. Far from taking offence at Ostrovsky's often cutting dramas about their way of life, many merchants encouraged him. Pogodin maintained intimate ties with Moscow's merchant élite, and at least one of the young editors benefited directly from merchant largesse with assistance in the publication of his works. Given the passionate sponsorship of Russian culture by the merchants, on the one hand, and the merchants' links with western education and technology, on the other, the young editors were at least in part justified in viewing them as a bridge between the two Russian cultures, the old and the new. It was not a fashionable position to hold. Most of the intelligentsia despised the merchant class for its materialism, its backwardness, and the petty tyranny of its family life which Ostrovsky, himself, did much to expose. But in light of the enormous services that the merchants were soon to render to Russian culture, the young editors proved to be more discerning and sensitive to actual developments in Russian life than most of their fellow *intelligenty*.

'Democratism' signalled an important change in thinking about Russian nationality. It marked a turning away from the sharp dichotomy the Slavophiles had drawn between the gentry and the peasants and the rejection of the near monopoly on nationality the Slavophiles had accorded to the peasantry. The nationalist concerns of the Slavophiles, which centred almost exclusively on the cultural and moral relations between aristocrats and peasants, began to give way to a more open conception of nationality. The change represented not only the earliest signs of a shift in the social background of the leading theorists of intellectual conservatism but also a new urban awareness of the growing complexity of Russian social life. The Slavophiles were for the most part landowners, drawn from the middle ranks of the gentry and actively engaged in the management of their estates. Their ideas were coloured by their rural experience and the patriarchalism of agricultural life in Russia.[23] The young editors had, on the contrary, become detached from any stable class affiliations. They had no resources in the land but lived as best they might by their pens in, what was to them, a highly unpredictable and unstable urban environment. And they did not regularly occupy a position in the official structure of the society.

Whereas the Slavophiles with their roots in the gentry, on the one hand, and with their sophisticated philosophical and religious concerns, on the other, straddled between gentry and intelligentsia conservatism, the young editors were among the first full representatives of the socially unattached conservative intelligentsia. Since both their official status and their social identity were nebulous, the young editors experienced a profound sense of rootlessness that manifested itself in the recurrent theme of 'wandering' in their writings. They attempted to overcome their disorientation and social displacement by embracing a classless and organic conception of nationality in which they, as artists and intellectuals, had a leading role to play.

The young editors were scarcely aware of all the implications of 'democratism.' Further elaboration by Grigor'ev and the publicist's talents of Fedor Dostoevsky were required to disclose its full significance. Nevertheless, its potential was already apparent. If the nation was an organic whole proceeding toward the conscious realization of an as yet unknown national ideal, the whole metaphor of Russia and the West and all it entailed was subject to a thorough re-examination. For it meant that Peter's reforms had not irreparably divided the nation and interrupted the natural direction of national development; it further implied that the westernized gentry and the traditionalist peasantry were equal partners in the creation of a national ideal that was still in the process of becoming; and finally it meant that the two guiding principles, Russia and the West, which peasantry and gentry respectively represented, were far from being mutually exclusive.

The young editors were not destined as a group to draw these conclusions. The early popularity that the novelty of their youthful exuberance had afforded *Moskvitianin* was not sustained. Relations with Pogodin steadily deteriorated. Even Ostrovsky's forbearance gave out at last in 1856. By the beginning of that year the general level of the critical articles and literary offerings of the journal had reached an appalling low. In August, the novelist I.S. Turgenev wrote that 'no one reads [*Moskvitianin*] and no one publishes in it.'[24] After fifteen years of anxiety and relentless scrimping, Pogodin bowed to what by now was inevitable. *Moskvitianin* fulfilled its subscription pledges for 1856 and then ceased publication forever. The young editors had already dispersed, but their ideals were preserved and extended by their most ardent proponent, Apollon Grigor'ev.

3

Grigor'ev and organic criticism

Apollon Aleksandrovich Grigor'ev has recently recaptured the attention of literary historians. A volume of his selected poetry has appeared in the Soviet Union and several of the best examples of his literary criticism have been reprinted in both Russia and the West. A few writers in the West and the East have also begun to probe the relationship between Grigor'ev and Dostoevsky.[1] Although the inquiry is not yet complete, little doubt remains that the critic's influence on the novelist was far from inconsequential.

Not surprisingly, less interest has been shown in Grigor'ev as an ideologist of conservatism.[2] He was, after all, a literary critic whose untidy essays were difficult to read and harder to understand. He did not consider himself to be primarily a publicist or popularizer and evinced no overt interest in public affairs or social matters. On the contrary, he more than once disavowed any such interest, grandly declaring that there were greater and more pressing issues facing Russians than the fleeting 'exigencies' of public policy. Yet his very conception of literature deeply involved him in some of the most burning issues of the day and carried him well beyond the commonly accepted confines of literary criticism. Many of his ideas were readily adaptable, and were adapted, to meet the intellectual and ideological needs of conservatives in the period following the Crimean War. Grigor'ev was an *intelligent* who could not but respond to the concerns troubling his fellow *intelligenty*. He was far from indifferent to the impact his ideas were making on the intelligentsia and was not always able to remain aloof from the 'exigencies' he professed to despise.

Unlike the other leading *pochvenniki*, Fedor Dostoevsky and N.N. Strakhov, Grigor'ev has not yet been favoured with an adequate biography.[3] His life, which was ravaged by poverty and alcoholism, and alternating bouts of ennui and spiritual anguish, was an extreme but not untypical example of the chaotic existence of many *intelligenty* in the 'age of intensity.' He was born in 1822, the illegitimate son of Aleksandr Ivanovich Grigor'ev, secretary to a Moscow magistrate, and Tatiana Andreevna, daughter of the family coachman. Within a year his parents married, and Grigor'ev was taken from the foundling hospital in which he had been placed at his birth to his parents' home in the *Zamoskvorech'e* district of Moscow. His father was modestly but adequately educated; his mother was almost illiterate. Grigor'ev spent his early years in the care of his doting mother and the household and yard servants from whom, he later recalled, he acquired a lively familiarity with the customs, legends, and songs of the peasantry.[4] His formal education began at age four at the hands of a medical student who lived in as Apollon's tutor for the next six years. The boy was a brilliant student, quick to learn, and especially able at languages. He acquired French as a child and in adolescence mastered German in six months in order to read the work of Hegel in the original. Later as an adult he learned English and Italian well enough to undertake masterly translations from the classics of both languages. At age sixteen he entered the law faculty of Moscow University, having first been tutored for the qualifying examinations by the then well-known historian I.D. Beliaev. Among his teachers at the university was Pogodin.[5]

The 1830s and 1840s were the decades of the student circle in Russia. Not to be outdone, Grigor'ev and his closest classmates formed their own *kruzhok* with Grigor'ev as its undisputed leader. The group, which congregated in Grigor'ev's bedroom nearly every Sunday afternoon from 1838 to 1842, comprised a distinguished membership. Among them were A.A. Fet, whose poems rank among the best in nineteenth-century Russia, Ia. P. Polonsky, a lesser but distinguished poet, S.M. Solov'ev, the great historian of Russia, Prince A.V. Cherkassky, a Slavophile sympathizer and an influential voice during the emancipation reform period, and K.D. Kavelin, a founder of the juridical school of Russian history, a rare Russian liberal, and, not insignificantly from Grigor'ev's point of view, future husband of his first and greatest love. Almost the whole of educated youth in Russia was at this time the ardent partisan of Hegelian philosophy. In this, at least, Grigor'ev's circle was unexceptional.[6]

Grigor'ev graduated at the head of his class in 1842 and embarked, prophetically as it turned out, on the first of a series of unsuccessful careers. To retain a permanent position seemed to be temperamentally beyond him. Record-keeping, he once wrote, was a degrading occupation that in the future would be done by machines. Such tasks hindered the search for truth and freedom, the chief concerns of men. 'Anyone who feels God within him, that is, Man,' he complained, 'must be ashamed to squander half a day doing the work of a machine.'[7] He began as a librarian at the university but proved so generous with the loan of books to his friends and so unable to remember that he had lent them at all that the library officials were compelled to secure the collection by seeing him safely appointed secretary to the university council. The new post suited him no better than the old.

The taste of another, more alluring, career came to him in 1843 when he published his first poems in *Moskvitianin*. Appropriately enough, love accompanied poetry. In the same year he fell in love with Antonina Korsh for whom he retained an emotional attachment all his life, in spite of her marriage to Kavelin in 1845. Failure in love and the 'dogmatic structure' of Moscow life drove him to St Petersburg in 1844.[8]

For the next three years, Grigor'ev struggled to make his way in the world of St Petersburg journalism. He apprenticed for a career of writing with poems, autobiographical stories, critical articles, reviews, and theatre notices. His play, *Dva Egoizma*, an amusing satirical sketch of the utopian socialist Mikhail Petrashevsky and the Slavophile Konstantin Aksakov, foreshadowed his future independence from both westernizers and Slavophiles.[9] In 1846, he published a little book of poems and translations which Belinsky damned with faint praise in his 'View of Russian Literature in 1846.'[10]

Near the beginning of 1847, worn out by the 'mirage' of St Petersburg, he returned to the 'reality' of Moscow. Here he published his first important critical article, 'Gogol' and his "Correspondence with Friends."' In the face of almost universal hostility towards Gogol', Grigor'ev defended his 'Correspondence' as a continuation of and not a break with his previous work.[11]

Family responsibilities descended on the struggling critic late in 1847 when he married Lidiia Korsh, sister of Antonina who had spurned him in 1844. In order to underwrite his new life, he began a wretched period as compiler of the European review section of *Moskvitianin*. He also put his law degree to some use by teaching civil and land law at the Aleksandrinsky Orphans' Institute and then from 1850 at the Moscow Foundling Home. Here he formed what was probably a romantic relationship with E. Ia. Vizard, the daughter of the home's supervisor. Whatever the cause, his marriage showed the first signs of strain at this time.

Toward the end of 1850 he joined the young editors. In spite of his domestic troubles, these were the happiest years of his life, the period, he said, of the rebirth in his soul of his faith in the Russian soil. A thick, bearded figure, dressed for effect in peasant costume, he roamed from theatre to theatre, drawing room to drawing room, argument to argument, guitar in hand, always prepared to sing in his reedy voice the national songs he knew and loved so well. These were also productive years in which organic criticism began to take shape in the numerous articles and reviews he contributed to *Moskvitianin*. In spite of frequent quarrels with the parsimonious Pogodin, Grigor'ev remained faithful to *Moskvitianin* and its ideals long after it ceased publishing. Even as late as 1860 he was still seeking means to revive it.[12]

Once more cast adrift, Grigor'ev engaged in brief flirtations with several journals. Invited to take part in the Slavophile organ *Russkaia beseda*, he broke off the connection after contributing only one article because the editor, A.I. Koshelev, refused to grant him the absolute control over the journal's literary criticism section which he demanded. Koshelev's refusal provoked a reply from Grigor'ev in which he outlined some of his objections to Slavophilism.[13] In 1851 he had an opportunity to participate in *Sovremennik*, but here he was outmanoeuvred by N.G. Chernyshevsky who soon established himself as resident critic. The *Biblioteka dlia chteniia* also only briefly provided him with an outlet for his passionate urge to 'serve' with his writing.

Unable to eke out a living among the burgeoning journals and reviews of the Russian capitals, Grigor'ev set out for Italy in 1857 as the tutor of Prince Ivan Trubetskoi. Here he wrote little but renewed his study of Schelling's philosophy. The art and artefacts of Italy, France, Germany, and Austria moved him deeply. But to him they were all of the past. He found life in contemporary bourgeois Europe to be hollow, 'full of triviality and lacking in true breadth and poetry.'[14] He longed to return to Russia where on Christmas Eve a reverential silence prevailed, unbroken by the shouts of hawkers and the raucous singing of Verdi 'hits.' A heavy drinker before he left Russia, Grigor'ev slipped during his trip abroad over the fine line into the alcoholism that eventually killed him.

Salvation from his boredom and homesickness appeared in an unlikely shape. In Italy, he encountered Count G.A. Kushelev-Bezborodko, who had recently received permission to publish a new journal, the *Russkoe slovo*. The count invited Grigor'ev to become the chief literary critic of his new enterprise. By October 1858 he was in St Petersburg, where in the next few months he set out his 'course' of organic criticism in the pages of the new journal.

Grigor'ev was haunted by the contradictions of the time in which he lived. Though he referred to himself as the last of the romantics and embodied many of their traits, his critical insight and independence of thought secured him against bondage to any particular tendency. His ideas, which won him ridicule and sometimes scorn from his ideological enemies but also admiration and affection from the likes of Dostoevsky, Ostrovsky, Turgenev, and Tolstoy, ran counter to the predominant temper of his age. He felt his own superfluousness deeply. Once with tragic poignancy he signed an article 'One of the Many Unnecessary People.' His weakness was, as Turgenev pointed out to him on a visit in Florence, the incoherence of his thought.[15] But it was the incoherence of a man 'absorbed in the passionate quest for life,' as Berdiaev described him and not of a man unsure of his convictions.[16]

Grigor'ev was never a cabinet intellectual. He lived with great intensity, found routine unbearable, and always sought a new path. An enthusiast, he often adopted the most extreme positions. In 1856, for example, he told one of his friends that he 'kissed the knout,' yet by 1860 he was singing revolutionary songs and consorting with radical students. In spite of such violent swings of enthusiasm he remained inwardly consistent. His love for Russia's past did not prevent him from looking forward to the future. In many ways, he anticipated the vitalism of Bergson and would have been at home in the idealist revival at the beginning of the twentieth century when the concerns he had foreseen nearly fifty years before at last overtook the intellectual life of Russia and Europe.[17]

Grigor'ev was also the mirror of his own times. Few characters so perfectly exemplified the dilemma of the intelligentsia in nineteenth-century Russia. Rarely did an author's work so totally capture the central tendencies of the age or subject them to such penetrating scrutiny. In 1858 he had several productive years still ahead of him, during which he gained admirers and even followers. But he remained a lonely figure, a philosophical stirring (*veianie*) but not a philosopher or ideologist. His dearest convictions were largely ignored by an indifferent public; demoralized by his frequent stays in the debtors' prison and wracked by alcoholism, he died in September 1864.

Almost all of Grigor'ev's ideas were encompassed within his complex and sophisticated theory of organic criticism. His views about philosophy, history, and nationality were not simply appendages to his theory of literature, but were integral aspects of it. During the years following the collapse of *Moskvitianin*, Grigor'ev carried Herder's idea of expressionism to its limits. He saw in Russian literature the full and conscious image of the inner development of the Russian ideal within the life of the nation. His insistence on the organic unity of life and literature blurred the lines between literary criticism on the one hand and history and philosophy on the other, and from their amalgam an elaborate theory of Russian nationality was forged.

Long before Grigor'ev's earliest attempts at literary criticism, Russian critics had turned to the relationship between literature and nationality. The romantics of the 1820s had put their best efforts into distinguishing what was peculiarly Russian in the literature of their day, and the concern with nationality and art intensified in the 1830s and 1840s. The immediate ancestor of Grigor'ev's organic criticism was Belinsky's historical criticism. As a young critic, Grigor'ev had been unfavourably disposed towards Belinsky's work. But by the middle of the 1850s he had reread Belinsky, particularly his early output, while under the influence of the later writings of Schelling. From this new perspective he had revised his view of the great critic. For the rest of his life, he considered himself with pride to be Belinsky's successor and the continuator of his tendency in criticism. He insisted, with justification, that he had said almost nothing that Belinsky had not already said before him.[18]

Although the radicals were later to claim Belinsky as their own, the fact that he was the source of both the conservative and nationalistic organic criticism of Grigor'ev and the radical and utilitarian criticism of Dobroliubov or Pisarev came as no surprise to Grigor'ev's contemporaries. Shortly after Grigor'ev's death in 1864 A.N. Maikov observed: 'After Belinsky criticism became divided, just as was Belinsky, forming two tendencies 1) the natural Belinsky, as he was, and 2) Belinsky muddled by political tendencies. The last was perpetuated by Dobroliubov and now finally has attained its apogee in *Russkoe slovo*, but the first, that is, the good side of Belinsky, is in Grigor'ev.'[19] Maikov's view, though highly tendentious, was in essence correct. Throughout his life, Belinsky was deeply concerned with the question of literature and art and the relationship of nationality to literature; it was this side of his predecessor's work that Grigor'ev admired and emulated. But Belinsky also emphasized the ethical implications of art – its accusatory function and its civilizing role – and thus opened the door to a utilitarian interpretation of his work.

Unlike the utilitarians, Belinsky never lost his faith in the power of art to discover and reveal truth, and he never subordinated art to reality. For him, art was as independent as was life itself. Grigor'ev shared Belinsky's faith in the autonomy of art but carried it to an extreme. At no time did Belinsky raise art to a cult as did Grigor'ev. Grigor'ev was an aesthete for whom life was meaningless unless filtered through art; Belinsky was a great humanitarian with remarkable aesthetic sensibility.

Belinsky's views about art were substantially formed by the time he

BELINSKY :

wrote his 'Literary Reveries' in 1834, and they did not change significantly over the short span of his career. He wrote the 'Reveries' ostensibly under the influence of what little he knew of Schelling, but in reality the whole German idealist tradition stemming from Herder and his contemporaries lay behind the essay. Art, for Belinsky was the '*expression of the great idea of the universe and its ceaseless diversity of phenomena.*'[20] Since universal diversity was expressed primarily through nations, art was pre-eminently national. In Belinsky's opinion Russian literature was as yet by and large imitative, European in both its form and content. The reason was, he suggested, that true Russian nationality was almost completely foreign to the Europeanized classes from which most Russian writers were drawn. He concluded, therefore, that there could be little nationality in Russian literature until it freed itself from European tutelage. '*Absolute* nationality,' he wrote, 'is accessible only to a people which is free from alien, foreign influences.'[21] He defined the task of Russian literature in his day as the faithful portrayal of scenes from Russian life. Though some of his natural school admirers may have thought so, Belinsky was not suggesting that art was simply a copy of daily existence. In his 'View of Russian Literature in 1847,' he insisted that the artist must be able to pass the objects of reality through his imagination and 'give them new life.'[22]

nation

In criticism Belinsky maintained that a work of literature should be judged within its historical context. Russian literature, he observed, revealed throughout a 'living historical bond' in which the 'new takes its origin from the old, what follows is explained by what precedes, and nothing appears by chance.'[23] The artist was the son of his time and place and a work of art was joined organically to the environment in which it was produced. The artist proceeded by creating types that embodied the moral characteristics of the society in which he lived.[24]

historical
context

Grigor'ev found little to disagree with in Belinsky's aesthetic views. But Belinsky was dead, and the task of interpreting his life's work was open to all comers. Grigor'ev was, therefore, inescapably drawn into the debates about literature and literary criticism that raged in the 1850s.

At some risk of oversimplification, there were two rival tendencies in literary criticism during the period. The school of art-for-art's sake was premised on the belief that art should have no purpose beyond its own internal aesthetic requirements. The utilitarian school, on the contrary, demanded that art should serve the purposes and needs of society. Characteristically, Grigor'ev remained aloof from both tendencies and worked out his own independent position with Belinsky as guide and Schelling as companion.

47 Grigor'ev and organic criticism

As a young editor, Grigor'ev had already arrived at the position that art was organically joined to the moral, social, and political life of the nation. Now he found confirmation in Belinsky of the view that the artistic nature was shaped by the era and society in which the artist worked. 'Works of art,' he wrote in a review of Turgenev's *Dvorianskoe gnezdo* (A Nest of Gentlefolk), 'are linked organically to the life of their creators and through them to the life of the epoch.'[25] Again following Belinsky, and once more consistent with his views as a young editor, Grigor'ev maintained that the writer embodied all the ideals of a particular nation in character types. All the national types resided in every great writer simultaneously and in complete harmony. The artist was, consequently, the full representative of the entire breadth of national life and not of particular individuals or social groups. He was the voice of the ideals of the whole people. In this sense, art was profoundly democratic.[26]

[margin: Belinsky's Organic link]

Although art was the product of a particular time and place, it was not merely a copy of life. Rather, it was life's interpreter. In an essay of 1856, Grigor'ev argued that art should give meaning to life, should seek the causes behind life's phenomena and assign a place to each chance event or series of events. The artist performed this function by approaching reality with the highest moral yardstick, which was derived from the 'contemplation of the fundamental and most profound foundations and rational laws of life.'[27] Here, Grigor'ev resorted to the idealist notion that all men possessed in common certain simple, eternal truths, which were particularly accessible to the man of true genius. The artist approached these universal truths, not abstractly, but through the specifically national. 'From this, it also follows,' Grigor'ev concluded, 'that the world view of all true representatives of the literary epochs is one; only the colour is different.'[28]

[margin: ART + MORALITY]

Although art was by its very nature inseparable from morality, Grigor'ev did not conclude that it had to serve a conventional point of view. He distinguished sharply between social, or conditional, morality, which always attached to private interests, and absolute morality, which transcended immediate social interests and needs. 'Great artists,' he said, 'do not contend against ... the highest morality or against the ideal but against conventional moral yardsticks and ideals abstracted from the momentary, niggardly or false laws of reality.'[29] It was, of course, this point that drew Grigor'ev into conflict with the exponents of the utilitarian view of art against whom he defended the autonomy of artistic creativity.

[margin: MORALITY]

In spite of his implacable hostility towards the utilitarian school of literature, Grigor'ev was no closer to the school of art-for-art's sake, the adherents of which he dismissed as 'literary gastronomes.' In his mind, their theory of pure art was impossible because art could not be separated from life. 'Everything ideal,' he asserted, 'is nothing else than the aroma and colour of the real.'[30] No literary work was merely a contrived piece of decoration but was always born out of the real life of the age.

Although art was not based in narrow social utility, it nevertheless served men in a number of ways. 'Art,' Grigor'ev wrote, harking back to Edel'son and looking ahead to Dostoevsky, 'exists for the human soul'[31] and is necessary for its well-being. Moreover, truth or the ideal enter life, in his opinion, only through art. It has been suggested that one of the main reasons Grigor'ev was drawn to Schelling's philosophical system was Schelling's failure to reconcile the ideal and real except through the agency of artistic intuition and genius.[32] It was precisely on these grounds that Grigor'ev deified art. 'Everything new is brought into the world only by art;' he wrote, 'it alone embodies in its creations that which is invisibly present in the air of the epoch.' Here, Grigor'ev had worked out the full implications of the young editors' principle of immediacy. A work of art was an immediate expression of the life with which it was organically united. A theory, in contrast, was a logical construction deduced from the experience of the past. Thus only art was completely contemporary and it alone could bring the new into thought.[33]

Grigor'ev had not yet exhausted the 'utility' of art. Since it was a conscious expression of what had previously been only felt in an era, it was capable of explaining and clarifying the most complicated questions of life without, of course, setting for itself the prior task of doing so. In addition, art was prophetic. Grigor'ev believed that 'art often beforehand senses the approaching future as a bird beforehand senses fair or foul weather.'[34]

The barometric nature of art endowed it with enormous social significance. The work of any great writer, if properly understood, mapped the general contours of the future course of national development, and literature as a whole gradually unveiled the ideal towards which the nation was unconsciously striving. Pushkin was the essence of such a writer. In 1859 Grigor'ev sketched Pushkin's significance for Russia.

Pushkin is, for the present, the only complete sketch of our national personality, a man of natural gifts who assimilated, amidst all kinds of clashes with other particularities and organisms, everything that should have been assimilated and who discarded everything that should have been discarded; [he is] the full and

49 Grigor'ev and organic criticism

complete form of our national essence, not yet drawn with colours but only as an outline, a shape which we will still shade in with colours for a long time to come. The scope of Pushkin's spiritual sympathies excludes nothing that preceded him and nothing truly and organically [Russian] which has and will follow him.[35]

Life and literature met in the national ideal, acting reciprocally upon one another in a steady advance towards national self-consciousness.

Criticism was to art what art was to life: it explained and clarified the ideals contained in an artistic work.[36] The critic was not endowed with the artist's intuitive insight, but to him belonged the important function of determining whether the artist had lived up to his own ideal in his work. It was the task of criticism to discover the links that tied a work of art to the soil on which it was born and to examine the artist's relation to life. The critic's vision, being more akin to that of the theorist, was always narrower than the vision of the artist. For this reason it was not the business of the critic to lead the artist or to attempt to force life to conform in art to certain preconceived notions.[37]

Behind Grigor'ev's aesthetic theories lay a whole comlex of philosophical assumptions. He belonged, of course, to the idealist tendency in nineteenth-century Russian philosophy. Russian idealists of the 1850s and 1860s were not relic survivors of the 1820s and 1830s. They were, instead, part of a European-wide reaction to the rising tide of positivism at mid-century.[38] Like materialism, and unlike its other rival, positivism, idealism was a metaphysical philosophy that sought to get behind the world of appearance and to penetrate the mystery of ultimate reality. The idealist looked on reality as a unified whole and regarded the human soul as the highest manifestation of the whole. Whereas the positivist searched for truth in nature through the accumulation of scientific evidence, the idealist turned his inquiries inwards to the human soul where he sought to unlock the secret of the whole of reality. The idealist attached great significance to the autonomy of the soul and demanded freedom for the fullest development of the personality in all its many facets. For it was in the unfolding of individual and collective human experience that the ultimate truth about reality resided.

Idealists of the mid-nineteenth century were anxious to demonstrate the essential harmony of human experience. For this purpose they adopted the doctrine of divine immanence. God, in His several idealist guises, was gradually revealing His universal purpose within the growing consciousness of men through the strivings and accumulating experiences of individuals and nations.

European idealism was far from presenting a united front in the 1850s.

The disagreement that most concerns us here revolved around the question of the means employed by Universal Spirit in its quest for self-knowledge and the end towards which its efforts were directed. In Russia, as elsewhere in Europe, the whole issue had come to a head in the Hegelian philosophy of history.

Like many Russians of his generation, Grigor'ev objected to Hegel's teleology. Hegel's scheme of universal history did not apparently make provision for the autonomous development of independent entities. Rather, every particular was defined by Hegel, or so it seemed to his critics, not in its own terms, but according to its place in an all-embracing and progressive whole. In its dialectical march towards self-realization, the World Spirit relentlessly pursued a pattern of the employment of individuals or states for its own purposes, followed inevitably by their annihilation as a stage of development beyond them was reached and their usefulness exhausted. Instead of growing freely according to their own innate principles and towards their own unique ends, particular entities were reduced to mere instruments of a universal purpose that stood outside them at the end of history.

The impact of Hegelianism in Russia is well-known. In the previous chapter, we have already encountered Stankevich, whose story 'The Idealist' provoked one of Grigor'ev's earliest, though somewhat oblique, attacks on Hegelianism. But Stankevich was only one of many Russians to embrace the philosophy of Hegel. Bakunin and Belinsky shared an ardent and faintly comic Hegelian phase in the early 1840s and, for a time, revelled in their loss of ego to the greater purposes of the World Spirit. Hegel's teleology unquestionably retained a hold on Belinsky long after he had shaken off the other trappings of the Hegelian dialectic. During the period of 'Literary Reveries,' he had upheld the autonomous nation as the fundamental unit of human development. 'Every nation,' he had written, 'plays its own special role which Providence has assigned to it in the great family of the human race and put its own share, its own contribution, into the common depository of the progress of the race. In other words, every people of itself expresses one particular aspect of the life of humanity.' Belinsky believed that in order to make its contribution to the common life of mankind, it was imperative that each nation develop and live its own original life.[39] This was the voice of Herder and to a lesser extent of Schelling. Under Hegel's influence, however, Belinsky modified his earlier commitment to the unique potentiality of individual nations. By 1843, he was already arguing that separate development was only the first moment in the process of human unity. 'This unity,' he continued, 'is now understood in a different way and consists in the subordination of the great idea of national individuality to the still greater idea of humanity.'[40] This was little more than a restatement of one of Hegel's propositions in the *Philosophy of History*: 'The principles of the successive phases of Spirit that animate the Nations in a necessitated gradation are themselves only steps in the development of the one universal spirit, which through them elevates and completes itself to a self-comprehending totality.'[41]

Hegel's apparent destruction of the free personality pursuing its unique goals, and the general repercussions of his world-view in Russian thought, produced consternation not only among the younger generation of idealists, to whom Grigor'ev belonged, but also among older idealists such as Prince Vl. Odoevsky. And like Odoevsky, Grigor'ev sought the refutation of Hegel in Schelling, who had devoted his last years to that purpose.

Schelling's historicism was much less rigorous than Hegel's. Like Hegel, Schelling saw history as a sequential revelation of God. But for the latter, God's revelation was not accomplished through external compulsion as Hegel maintained. 'For only that is free,' said Schelling, 'which acts according to the laws of its own inner being and is not determined by anything else either within or outside it.'[42] In Hegel the personality of individual entities derived from and was subsumed in the life of the World Spirit; in Schelling, on the contrary, life resided only in the unique potentiality of particulars. Abstractions such as World Spirit could not of themselves confer life.[43] Whereas Hegel maintained that the historical process was rational and logical, Schelling emphasized the irrationality, illogicality, and complete unpredictability of historical life. 'Man has a history,' he commented, 'only because what he will do cannot be anticipated by any theory. Arbitrariness is, insofar, the Goddess of History.'[44]

Schelling's understanding of history, with its emphasis on the irrationality and universal relativism of the historical process, was more in keeping with the temper of conservatism and nationalism than were Hegel's rationalism and the dialectic. But Schelling had other attractions for conservatives as well. It is important to note that his general critique of historicism, and of its concomitant instrumentalism, could be and was effectively applied not only to Hegel but equally to positivists such as Saint-Simon or Comte who attempted to discover the scientific laws of history and from them to deduce a universal theory of human development through history. Conservatives, consequently, found in Schelling a useful ally in their later assault on nihilism.

Grigor'ev was deeply indebted to Schelling whom he hailed as the Plato of modern philosophy. He was particularly attracted by his relativism. 'The great significance of Schelling's formula,' he enthused, 'is that it restores both to nations and individuals the complete autonomy of their life and smashes the abstract spirit of humanity and its development.'[45] In the face of such resounding testimony it would be unreasonable to deny the importance of Schelling's philosophy for Grigor'ev's intellectual evolution. However, an examination of the substance of Grigor'ev's ideas about history, the nation, and the people suggests that while Schelling helped to reinforce his basic philosophical position, Grigor'ev drew on other, more immediately relevant sources. Wsewolod Setschkareff argued some years ago that the idea of national originality figured very little in Schelling's early writings and did not play a significantly larger role in his later works. Setschkareff concluded that the notion derived instead from Friedrich Schlegel who was himself reflecting the opinions of Fichte and especially Herder.[46] Indeed, most of what Schelling did have to say about the nation and its role in universal history was little more than a reworking of Herder. Grigor'ev had unquestionably read Herder. He was also conversant with the ideas of Friedrich von Savigny, one of the founders of the German historical school of law, and knew the work of Augustin Thierry, the French idealist historian. He once singled out both men as thinkers aware of the moral self-sufficiency of national organisms. Both Savigny and Thierry were themselves steeped in Herder's philosophy of history. Although it is obvious that the influences on Grigor'ev were many and varied, the original inspiration for much of his thought was Herder who, therefore, serves as a helpful point of reference against which to compare Grigor'ev.

HERDER

Herder's philosophy was rooted in his reaction against eighteenth-century rationalism.[47] He rejected not only the a priori reasoning by which the maxims of Enlightenment thought were reached, but also the abstractness of the universal assumptions which governed the outlook of the Enlightenment. 'Oh why,' he lamented, 'is man deluded by language into thinking that abstract shadow images represent solid bodies, existing realities?'[48] A priori, general ideals that governed the movement of history did not exist for Herder.

VS. APRIORI

Grigor'ev was equally critical of the rationalistic ideal of universal human progress that the *philosophes* had posited. The Enlightenment ideal had for him no basis in life or experience. A product of rational deduction from the narrow laws of Newtonian science, the Enlightenment had severed the living body of European tradition. Romanticism,

53 Grigor'ev and organic criticism

Grigor'ev continued, had been life's response to the theories of the Enlightenment. During the romantic period, thought had returned to its proper roots in experience. But romanticism, too, had failed. While worshipping the experience of the past, it had turned its back resolutely on the present, and finished by denying life's natural evolution. Grigor'ev believed, however, that in spite of its ultimate failure romanticism had produced one positive result, which he called 'historical feeling.' By historical feeling, Grigor'ev meant sensitivity to the organic unity of thought and life and recognition of the individuality and moral independence of every nation. In Hegelianism Grigor'ev saw a return to the rationalistic assumptions of the eighteenth century and the subordination once again of life to thought.[49]

The most flagrant error of the rationalists, according to their critics, was the notion of human perfectibility. The illusion of progress towards an ideal state of perfection reduced men to agents of a law or force outside them and beyond their control. Herder and, after him, Grigor'ev denied that there was a law of universal progress driving mankind towards perfection. Men simply were not perfectible. 'In reality,' Herder reflected, 'man always remains man and nothing but man.'[50] Grigor'ev complained in similar tones of the 'dreary faith' of his contemporaries among the positivists in the infiniteness of progress and solemnly declared that the 'human soul, with its multi-various strings, remains and will always remain the same ... Nor will the variegated colours of nationalities and individuals coalesce into a general, compact, healthy and monotonous mass of humanity.'[51] And life was not determined by external forces. Subject to their limitations as humans, men were otherwise completely free to develop their own innate potential. Every individual's happiness was relative to him alone.

The nominalism that was so apparent in Herder's and Grigor'ev's philosophy was accompanied by an experiential approach to knowledge. The basis of all valid thought and action, they believed, lay not in theory but in the concreteness of practical human experience. The conviction that human ideals and precepts arose from the specific conditions of human existence convinced Herder that there could be no single universal ideal of human culture. Contrary to the Enlightenment belief in the conformity of human nature, Herder argued that in different times and places men were not identical. Although all men had experienced a common origin, the very essence of human development was its diversity. Central to Herder's world-view was the theory of immanence. History was a process of becoming, propelled but not determined by an omnipresent,

ROMANTICISM

HISTORICAL FEELING

HUMAN PERFECTABILITY

NOMINALISM: (1) A THEORY THAT THERE ARE NO UNIVERSAL ESSENCES IN REALITY + THAT THE MIND CAN FRAME NO SINGLE CONCEPT OR IMAGE CORRESPONDING 2 ANY GENERAL TERM. (2) THE THEORY THAT ONLY INDIVIDUALS + NO ABSTRACT ENTITIES (ESSENCES. CLASSES OR PROPOSITIONS) EXIST — COMP. ESSENTIALISM. REALISM.

54 Dostoevsky, Grigor'ev, and Native Soil conservatism

yet unknowable force. This force manifested itself in a diversity of distinct national cultures, which together represented the greatest possible variety. Although national cultures evolved at different rates, no nation was without a culture. Moreover, each nation was the unique result of the particular influences of its own locale. 'Every cultural development,' Herder wrote, 'originated from particular individual needs and in turn fostered other such needs; the process was one of genuine experience, achievement and practical life in a circumscribed sphere.'[52]

Grigor'ev was fully in accord with Herder's understanding of history and the formation of nations. He was adamant that there was no such thing as humanity; there were only individuals, families, and nations.[53] He further agreed with Herder that each national organism had grown out of the primary unity of the human species by a process of geographical, climatic, and linguistic separation. In establishing its autonomy a nation gradually 'modified the primary tradition into its own traditions and beliefs.' These traditions and beliefs constituted an as yet unconscious organic ideal that the nation actualized during the course of its history. Eventually it contributed its now self-conscious ideal to the collective life of the world.[54] For Grigor'ev as for Herder, then, human ideals were distinguished not by their universality but by their localism (*mestnost'*).

In place of an instrumentalist approach to the historical process, Herder and Grigor'ev mutually subscribed to universal relativism. Every national culture was held to be as valid historically as any other; no historical age or event was viewed simply as a preparatory stage to something superior. Neither of them accepted that it had been the fate of previous generations and cultures to serve merely as stepping stones to the superior enlightenment of the present. 'Yet I cannot persuade myself,' Herder reasoned, 'that anything in the kingdom of God is only a means – everything is both a means and an end simultaneously, now no less than in the centuries of the past.'[55] Grigor'ev was only echoing Herder when he contended, against Hegel's dialectic of the Spirit, that no national organism was 'obliged to serve as a transitional form to another.' Nations, like individuals, were independent and organic wholes that grew according to their own internal laws, free from any external necessity.[56]

It was one of Herder's most important observations that real national identity arose not from a common government, but from participation in a common culture. He called this common culture the *Volk*. The meaning Herder attached to the concept of the *Volk* has more often than not been misunderstood. He did not view the *Volk* as a living body or person with a life of its own, but as a 'relational event' or a 'historical and cultural continuum.' The *Volk* was not a biological entity but a continuous process of the interaction of diverse organisms. The essence of the *Volk*, therefore, was its pluralism. Individuals and groups of individuals were necessary to the social whole and had to be permitted to develop their potential fully in order to make their contribution to the whole. Since the organisms of society were interrelated and interdependent, together making up the *Volk*, there could be no question of a single group monopolizing the national culture. Rather, it was by definition the joint creation of all the social strata.[57]

Herder's understanding of the *Volk* was reaffirmed by Grigor'ev, and, through him, it exercised a profound influence on the attitude towards *narodnost'* of a number of Russian conservatives in the second half of the nineteenth century. There was, of course, nothing new for Russians in the notion that it was a shared culture and not the state that united the people. It had long been one of the premises of Slavophilism. But the Slavophiles VOLK had been unwilling to grant that true Russian nationality was the common VS. possession of the whole of Russian society. Instead, they insisted, as is well SLAVOPHILES known, that since the time of Peter the Great, the upper classes had relinquished their *narodnost'* and become westernized aliens. Only the peasantry had remained faithful to Russian national principles and preserved them as best it could. It is true that at least one of the Slavophiles, Ivan Kireevsky, had been uneasy about the Slavophiles understanding of *narodnost'* and in a letter to his 'Moscow friends' in 1847 condemned the identification of nationality with the 'simple people' (*prostoi narod*) as one-sided, calling instead for a broader definition.[58] But neither he nor his Moscow friends were able to provide one.

Grigor'ev, building on the foundations laid earlier by Pogodin and Belinsky, dealt with the issue more squarely. He declined to accept as GRIGOREEV'S complete the narrow definitions of nation and nationality that the NARODNOST Slavophiles offered. Instead, he distinguished a dual meaning in these terms, both narrow and broad. By nation (*narod*) in the narrow sense, he meant that part of the whole nation which, in comparison with the other parts, was in the 'most natural (*neposredstvennyi*) and undeveloped condition' – the nation in potential. By *narod* in the broad sense, he meant a collective personality, embracing the 'features of all the strata of the nation, highest and lowest, rich and poor, educated and uneducated' – the nation actualized. By *narodnost'* in the narrow sense, he meant the unconscious ideals that governed the lives of the common people; in its broad sense, *narodnost'* (now redesignated by Grigor'ev as *natsional'nost'*) referred to a consciously held view of life peculiar to the whole nation.[59]

Grigor'ev persisted in seeing the truest expression of *natsional'nost'* in

Ostrovsky's plays about merchant life. He did not however view the merchants as an economic class. Rather, it was their cultural identity that interested him. His association of *natsional'nost'* with the merchants was akin to Herder's identification of the *Volk* with *Bürger*. He meant no more than did Herder a specific social group but rather a particular cultural outlook; his *narod*, in the broad sense, embraced all the traditional classes of Russia just as Herder's *Bürger* embraced all the traditional classes of Germany. In one way, Girgor'ev's view of *natsional'nost'* was more tolerant than was Herder's view of the *Volk*. For Grigor'ev included within his definition the westernized Russian gentry while Herder excluded the Frenchified German aristocracy from his.

The dual definition of *narodnost'* was by no means a new departure in Russian thought. Grigor'ev was well aware that as early as 1841 Belinsky had distinguished between *natsional'nost'* (*nationalité*) and *narodnost'* (*popularité*), and the inspiration for his own definitions doubtless derived from this source. In Belinsky's formulation, *narodnost'* referred to the life of the lower strata of the nation, whereas *natsional'nost'* meant the whole life of the 'conglomerate body of all social estates.' Like Grigor'ev, Belinsky had a dynamic conception of national development. For him, *narodnost'* was the initial manifestation of *natsional'nost'*, and *natsional'nost'* was the actualized potential of *narodnost'*.[60] Belinsky's interpretation made little impact, however, and it was left to Grigor'ev to reintroduce the notion that Russian nationality was the organic product of the collective strivings of the whole Russian people.

It was also left to Grigor'ev, though here as well he was anticipated by both Belinsky and his old mentor Pogodin, to insist that Russian nationality was the organic product of the entire Russian historical experience and not just of the period before Peter as the Slavophiles claimed. Here again Herder's views serve to clarify those of Grigor'ev. In Herder's dynamic universe, everything sought to develop and to attain its full potential. Perfection, in his view, was nothing more than the process by which a thing 'becomes what it can and should.' This was no less true of nations than it was of individuals. Moreover, the progress of a nation towards its 'perfection' was rooted in its tradition. Since a nation was constantly moving towards the realization of its potential – that is, progressing – tradition was not something fixed and immutable, but represented a continuous blending of old and new. Tradition and progress were 'interdependent variables' in the process of socio-political development.[61]

Grigor'ev agreed with Herder that the history of a nation was an organic whole; all of its episodes were linked in a chain of tradition, leading towards the full realization of the nation's potential. And again, agreement with Herder placed him at odds with the Slavophiles. They held that the chain had been broken in Russia by Peter the Great. Grigor'ev, on the contrary, maintained that the organicism of Russian development had not been ruptured. In 1859 he wrote: 'When we speak of the Russian essence, of the Russian soul, we mean neither the national essence of pre-Petrine nor of post-Petrine Russia, but an organic whole: we believe in *Rus'* as it is, as it has formed and *is forming* after clashes with other lives and other national organisms.'[62] In the simplest terms, Russia was what it was and was becoming what it could and should become; the 'oughts' of the Slavophiles or westernizers were irrelevant to the real process of national development.

Grigor'ev's contention that Russia was developing 'after clashes with other lives and other national organisms' cleared the way for him to take as his own the notion of Russian universality which, as will be recalled, had taken hold in the minds of Russian nationalists from the time of Karamzin. Although Herder had maintained that human culture was particularistic and pluralistic, he saw it also as accumulative. Each national culture, pursuing its own national course, developed and introduced into the world a unique principle or ideal. The maximum achievement of one nation could not be transmitted intact to another nation, but fragments of its total accomplishment as well as the lessons of its experience could be passed on. In this way, a continuous development from one nation to another took place, though no one knew, or could know, the end of that development. The manifestations of humanity were and would be infinitely diverse for Herder, but 'within the ever-changing husk, the same kernel of human substance and happiness can, and in all probability does, remain virtually the same.'[63]

Grigor'ev neatly wedded Herder's theory of cultural transmission from nation to nation to the idea of Russian universality. For him, as for Herder, the lives men led were everywhere different, but they were, nevertheless, united in the 'truth of the human soul' which was 'immutable' and 'not subject to development.'[64] In Grigor'ev's view, the Russians possessed certain characteristics that made them exceptionally receptive to the ideals and principles of others. He found evidence of this receptivity in Russian history, about which he had strong views, and especially in Russian literature.

Grigor'ev's strong anti-centralist views and the importance he attached to localism drew him into the contemporary debate about Russian history. He objected vehemently to the statist school of Russian history, which was, in his opinion, bedazzled by Hegelianism. He charged his old friend from university days, S.M. Solov'ev, with passing over the so-called prehistoric tribes in his influential history, except to portray them as raw material for a future body politic. Grigor'ev, on the contrary, saw the local, tribal phase as the quintessential national moment during which the nation's principles were formed. The outlines of Russian nationality had taken shape during the pagan period. The rapid conversion of Russians to Orthodoxy signified not the weakness of paganism but the status of pagan belief as an official, hence national, religion. The eastern church wisely took paganism over, thus avoiding religious conflict by fusing the national and Christian traditions.[65] Grigor'ev was highly critical of the official church and appealed instead to what he called 'humble Orthodoxy.' In his mind, Orthodoxy represented less a specifically religious ideal than it did a moral and particularly aesthetic principle. By Orthodoxy, he wrote in 1859, 'I mean simply a certain historical principle which is destined to live on and give new forms to life and to art in contrast to that other, already antiquated principle, Catholicism. This principle is in the soil of Slavdom, and in particular of Great Russian Slavdom which with the breadth of its moral embrace should renew the world.'[66]

Religion and aesthetics were inseparably bound up in Grigor'ev's mind. He identified Christ with Beauty and saw in them the only source of internal unity. Catholicism, official Orthodoxy, and Herzen and the St Petersburg progressives, he said in 1858, all subscribed to exactly the same error. They failed to believe in life, art, and the ideal. Consequently, only the external unity of outside constraint was within their grasp. By contrast, in 'humble Orthodoxy' was contained the inner force of Russian fraternity, potentially the redeeming principle of the world.[67]

When Peter the Great hurled Russia into the mainstream of European life, so Grigor'ev's argument continued, the old, exclusive national culture had undergone a violent process of expansion. During this process, Russians had found that they were sympathetic to and able to absorb all the national ideals that came to them in this turbulent period from abroad. Russian universality therefore opened the door to a synthesis of the achievements of European cultures with the very essence of Russian culture, the principle of fraternity.

And now Grigor'ev came full circle, from literature, through philosophy and history, and back to literature. The proof of Russian universality, according to Grigor'ev, was the nation's greatest poet, Pushkin. Pushkin had struggled with and finally mastered in his poetry all the foreign ideals that had entered Russia in the previous century. His personal struggle was a microcosm of the greater struggle that had taken place within the moral and intellectual life of the whole country as these ideals were assimilated to the native Russian cultural tradition. As a great artist, Pushkin sensed the trends (*veianiia*) of the times in the air he breathed. He translated these into consciousness through their embodiment in artistic types. There were, according to Grigor'ev, fundamentally two types contained in Pushkin's work: the rapacious or predatory (*khishchnyi*) type and the humble (*smirnyi*) type. They as yet furnished only outlines of the full-blooded types that would in time be worked out by Pushkin's literary heirs. Pushkin's Aleko, the hero of 'The Gypsies,' who best embodied the predatory type, was reared on western education and alienated from the soil; he was powerless to act in a national context. Lermontov's Pechorin and Turgenev's Rudin were also such types. The humble type, represented in Pushkin by Belkin, had to await Turgenev's *Dvorianskoe gnezdo* to achieve its fullest expression to date in the character of Lavretsky.[68]

Grigor'ev contended that in the superfluous man Turgenev had developed the predatory type to its logical conclusion. Lavretsky, in contrast, was Turgenev's protest against the predatory type in the name of the good, simple, and humble. 'Humility before the soil and before reality arose in Turgenev's soul as the soul of a great artist, from the soil itself, from the milieu, from Pushkin's Belkin.'[69] Grigor'ev was quick to point out that Lavretsky was not the Slavophile ideal personified. He was drawn from Russian reality 'as the Petrine reform made him.' And he was national, as imbued with Russian nationality as the most traditionalist and pious *peasant*.[70] Since Grigor'ev believed that the living tendencies of the age were reflected or even prophesied in art, Lavretsky symbolized for him the imminent return of eduated Russians to the native soil.

Grigor'ev's proposition that Russian nationality was still in the making and represented the joint enterprise of all classes and groups laid the foundations for a movement of social, intellectual, and moral reconciliation in the following decade. His dream was of a Russian nationality, transcending class, historical, and ideological barriers and embracing not only Russia's past and present but also the whole panoply of recently acquired western knowledge and experience. He did not wish to imply by his extravagant theory that Russia was charged specifically by fate with a unique mission to save the world. Later, he firmly repudiated such a notion.[71] Rather, he meant that Russians could benefit from western experiences and put to use the achievements of the West, in the manner Herder had suggested, without at the same time relinquishing their unique national heritage and distinct physiognomy. None the less, his ideas could not help but add fuel to the messianic fires that were already burning among conservative nationalists in Russia as the 1850s drew to a close.

For all the eccentricities of his thought, and obviously there were many, Grigor'ev's fundamental frame of reference was that of contemporary European conservatism. He drew on a number of foreign, mostly German, sources, adapting them to the demands of the peculiar Russian setting, which he fiercely loved, and to the theories of his Russian predecessors and contemporaries, in whose works he had steeped himself. At this stage of his career he had expressed few, if any, specifically political opinions. He was, in fact, never to take a strong stand on mattters of politics – they interested him scarcely at all – but during the Emancipation period, as will be seen, he was moved at least to declare himself publicly for autocracy and to set down a few, admittedly vague, political precepts. His significance for the development of Russian conservatism lies in his philosophical stance and his organic view of the nation and nationality. Grigor'ev was the perfect antirationalist, elevating concrete living experience and spontaneity above abstract, rationalistic theorizing and ratiocination as the sources of valid thought and practical activity. He eloquently cautioned the Russian intelligentsia about the dangers of abstraction (*ideinost'*) and about the need to take particular circumstances, time, and place into account. His defence of integral nationality, from which no social or intellectual group was excluded, and his firm belief in the immanence of Russian nationality were instrumental in transforming a backward-looking, static, and utopian conservative ideal into a forward-looking and dynamic form of evolutionary conservatism. If, with its antirationalism, nominalism, and relativism, Grigor'ev's theory provided a philosophical base from which to attack the rising forces of nihilism, it also furnished an ideological framework within which the conflicts troubling Russian thought and society could be resolved in an organic, living process of reconciliation, leading to national harmony and moral and spiritual unity.

4

Intelligentsia conservatism in the Emancipation period

The intellectual and political atmosphere in the wake of the Crimean War was especially hospitable to the philosophy of reconciliation that had taken shape in the previous decade. The government's decision to emancipate the serfs and to undertake a far-reaching program of related social and political reforms briefly fostered among the intelligentsia a sense of common cause and co-operation and reinforced the tendency of a segment of the *intelligenty* to seek a reconciliatory solution to social and intellectual conflicts. In the post-war period, the intelligentsia as a whole came into its own as a political force, and its conservatively minded component grew in proportion to the total. During the reform era, the avenues to history and social thought, which Grigor'ev's organic criticism had opened, were explored to their fullest extent, and the implications of his theory of nationality were worked out and forged into a comprehensive conservative ideology. Among the leaders of this transformation was the novelist and publicist F.M. Dostoevsky. Dostoevsky contributed little that was new to Grigor'ev's view of art and theory of nationality, but he was instrumental in removing the latter from the rarefied atmosphere of literary criticism onto the plane of social theory.

In exile in the remote vastness of central Asia even the genius of Dostoevsky would have been hard put to imagine a greater contrast than actually existed between the St Petersburg from which he had been escorted into exile late in 1849 and the city to which he eagerly returned ten years later. The death of Nicholas I, the humiliating defeat on Russian soil in the Crimean War, and the alarming increase in the frequency and violence of peasant disturbances had set Russia on a new course of social and political development. A half-century of prestige, won in the exploits of the Napoleonic wars, and the carefully fostered myth of the might of the Russian state were shattered in a single campaign. Nicholas's funeral in 1855 signalled the passing of an era. The new emperor, Alexander II, though by instinct nearly as conservative and by nature only half as resolute as his father, was compelled by circumstances to recognize both the external and internal dangers threatening Russia. He embarked on a series of reforms designed to strengthen the country and to secure the autocracy against growing revolutionary pressures from below. The immediate results were momentous.

Apart from the defeat itself, the most alarming feature of the Crimean War to bureaucratic officials had been the widespread indifference of the public to the outcome of what it regarded as the government's war. In the face of almost universal apathy towards its fate the autocracy realized that it had little choice but to attempt to restore its legitimacy and popularity by permitting some limited forms of public participation in the administration of the country. The unsettling task of such a major and rapid reform could not be carried out effectively without some measure of public consultation, and public opinion could no longer be completely muzzled. Pending the creation of formal institutions for public debate, however, a period of near chaos could be expected as censorship controls were loosened and pent-up public frustrations were released. It was to this heady climate that Dostoevsky returned at the end of 1859.

The half-hearted encouragement by the government of a public discussion of the concerns of the day inaugurated an exchange of ideas on a scale unprecedented in Russia. The trickle of Western political, social, and philosophical tracts which had animated the salons and circles of the 1830s and 1840s turned into a flood at the end of the 1850s. The trend away from aesthetics and philosophy to science and social thought, which had already begun in the 1840s, acquired new impetus among the intelligentsia after 1856. Debate was removed from the privacy of the salons to the publicity of the 'thick' journals. Approximately 150 new newspapers and journals were launched between 1856 and 1860.[1] For the first time in Russian history a broadly based body of public opinion came into being, not only in the cities but also in the countryside, where the establishment of the *guberniia* committees for the detailed working out of the emancipation reform forced a reluctant gentry to take an interest in public affairs.

The real or anticipated changes in the internal arrangements of Russia naturally had important consequences for the evolution of the Russian intelligentsia. In the new age of 'publicity' the function of the intelligentsia adjusted from that of private to public critic of government policy. A feeling of relief and excitement seized intelligentsia opinion. After years of cloistered and, what seemed to the new generation, barren debate the opportunity to act had finally presented itself. The emancipation of the peasants only reinforced the consciousness among the *intelligenty* of a new departure. For the first time millions of peasants were entering Russian public life. The peasantry remained an enigma, feared by many, viewed hopefully as a revolutionary force by some, idolized by others, and patronized by most.

Initially, the reforms awoke a feeling of common cause among the educated. N.G. Chernyshevsky's fraternal greeting towards the end of 1856 to the newly founded Slavophile journal, *Russkaia beseda*, symbolized the early sense of unanimity among rival factions in matters that counted: 'Agreement on aims is in essence so strong that it is possible to argue only about abstract and, therefore, obscure questions. As soon as the discourse turns to the firm soil of reality, and touches on something practical in science or life, there is no place for fundamental disagreements; only incidental errors on one or the other side are possible ... because here there is no disunity among educated Russians; everybody wants one and the same thing.'[2] From London, Herzen turned the as yet unsullied prestige of his *Kolokol* to encouraging the development of a broad reformist front and to accelerating the growth of a united public opinion in Russia.

Since the impetus for the reform had come from above, many educated Russians were at first hopeful that their most cherished aims would be realized by the autocracy itself. The state had traditionally performed a progressive role in Russia, and, in the early years of the reform period at least, few were willing to turn their backs on the emperor entirely. In spite of frequent disappointments as the limitations of the autocracy's reforming zeal became apparent, the mood of co-operation among the intelligentsia persisted until well into 1862. It reached its zenith early in the spring of that year with a literary and musical evening, ostensibly in celebration of the one thousandth anniversary of the founding of the Russian state. Most of the 'progressives,' Dostoevsky among them, were present.[3]

It is true that well before 1860 Chernyshevsky had privately concluded that the régime was incapable of reforming itself in any significant way and that the peasants stood to gain nothing tangible from the emancipation. He, therefore, broke with such 'liberal conservatives' as B.N. Chicherin and K.D. Kavelin whose cautious gradualism, Chernyshevsky believed, served only to strengthen the conservatism of the autocracy.

Herzen, too, openly disagreed with Chicherin's view of Russian history and institutions, especially the peasant commune, as early as 1858. He did not, however, formally sever his links with other Russian moderates until 1863. Neither he nor Chernyshevsky was averse to applying added pressure on the autocracy by creating an illusion of broad agreement among the educated on general principles if not on specific issues.

On the Slavophile side of the Russian intellectual scene, I.S. Aksakov began in 1859 to criticize the autocracy with as much verve and more radicalism than the nihilist journal *Sovremennik* had ever dared to exhibit. The censors responded predictably by suppressing Aksakov's new journal, *Parus*, after only two numbers.[4] Whatever their point of view, practically all members of the intelligentsia were agreed that a radical transformation of society was necessary. Moreover, most Russian publicists of the right and left, who shared an abhorrence of western bourgeois and capitalist social and economic organization, were convinced that the peasant commune should be the basis of the transformation and found common cause in their opposition to even such cautious liberals as Chicherin. In such a climate of apparent concord it was not hard for Dostoevsky and others to persuade themselves that the time of ideological disagreements among Russians was nearing an end.

It was, of course, an illusion. Neither the co-operative spirit of the moment nor a certain level of agreement concerning ends could paper over for long the great theoretical and practical differences that divided the intelligentsia. At the root of the discord were vast differences in philosophical outlook. The radical *intelligenty* of the 1860s were materialists or positivists who were inspired by Western scientism and utilitarianism. They rejected traditional Russian society and its mores outright and hoped ultimately to realize in Russia the most advanced social ideals emanating from the West. They had committed themselves wholeheartedly to the cause of the peasantry and were prepared to sweep the boards of society clean in order to liberate the peasants from their downtrodden condition.

The enthusiasm of the nihilists for the extremes of Western social philosophy was not, however, universally shared by the intelligentsia. Defeat at the hands of the Western alliance in the Crimean War had given birth among elements within the intelligentsia to a new patriotism which served not as an excuse for conservative retrenchment but as a goad to conservative innovation and reconstruction. The intelligentsia conservatives looked for the sources of reconstruction not outside but within the Russian tradition. There they found all the elements, including the benefits of Western knowledge, that they believed were required in order to renew Russian life. These elements had been created throughout the whole process of Russian history. The process would remain incomplete, however, until all the parts coalesced into a harmonious whole. The conservatives believed that Emancipation and its attendant reforms represented the culmination of the process and presented an historic opportunity to reconcile all the social, intellectual, and moral elements that would constitute the new Russia.

The opportunities presented by the Emancipation reforms and by the entrance of the peasantry into the public sphere, the changing role of the intelligentsia and the temporary concord (strained as it was) among them, and the reforming patriotism of a segment of the educated public facilitated to a remarkable degree the growth of the reconciliatory and evolutionary ideal of nationality that had originated among the young editors and was deepened and propagated by Grigor'ev. All the conditions necessary for a synthetic nationality embracing all classes and based on the living traditions of the country appeared to be falling into place. It is not surprising, therefore, to find Grigor'ev's theory making considerable headway among the conservative intelligentsia in the late 1850s and early 1860s.

While Grigor'ev was formulating the principles of organic criticism in St Petersburg, Fedor Mikhailovich Dostoevsky (1821–1881) was atoning for his role in the Petrashevsky affair by exile in Semipalatinsk, an isolated military settlement near the Chinese border. He had spent the first four years of his sentence, from January 1850 to February 1854, at hard labour in the fortress at Omsk. Here he was almost totally cut off from changes on the Russian cultural scene. A measure of relief came in 1854, when he was released from penal servitude and enlisted in the army. As a political exile, he was at least permitted to receive and write letters and to read books and journals. But the remoteness of his enforced place of residence frustrated any hopes he might have had of re-entering the mainstream of contemporary thought. Books that he requested from his brother, Mikhail, and from friends did not arrive, and in his letters he often chafed at his involuntary seclusion.[5]

Separation from the centres of Russian culture could not, of course, halt Dostoevsky's personal evolution. His arrest, the ordeal of his mock execution, penal servitude, and exile proved not unnaturally to be a watershed in his moral and artistic development. Dostoevsky's biographers have pointed out that even during his most radical period in the 1840s he had remained a utopian and not a revolutionary socialist.

Socialism represented to Dostoevsky and his contemporaries an idealistic humanitarianism which they hailed as the natural successor to Christianity. It was a universalistic doctrine which had as its ultimate goal the brotherhood of all men irrespective of their social and national origins. In the broadest sense, Dostoevsky had never repudiated the Christianity of his childhood, but during his prison years his faith had deepened and become more sure. In spite of the unveiled hostility with which his fellow prisoners greeted him, a hereditary noble, and the revulsion he felt for the depths of their depravity, he nevertheless discovered in these simple people an underlying nobility. In prison he became aware for the first time that the cosmopolitan, socialist dreams of his youth were remote from and even contrary to the nationality newly revealed to him through his contacts with the oppressed Russian people.[6] Dostoevsky did not jettison his faith in universal humanitarianism, but now combined it with the patriotic notion of 'one's own place' (*svoe mesto*). He began to think in terms of the primacy of national cultures in the advancement of universal culture.[7]

The shift in his thinking from the universal to the national focused Dostoevsky's attention on the specific problems of Russian nationality. The alienation of the educated and the uneducated, of the upper and lower classes, had already been painfully impressed on him during his years of penal servitude. The idea of overcoming this alienation in a higher national synthesis, which would liberate Russia and prepare it for its special role in world history, became an obsession with him from this time. The concept of a 'synthetic culture' could hardly have been new to him; it had been advocated by Belinsky in 1841 and by many others before Dostoevsky's arrest[8]; and like Grigor'ev, Dostoevsky turned to Belinsky for inspiration but, again like Grigor'ev, to only one side of Belinsky, the side that stressed the organic nation and Russian nationality in literature and life. It was this common allegiance to Belinsky's patriotic idealism that was soon to draw Dostoevsky and Grigor'ev together.

Dostoevsky's transformation from the socialist cosmopolitanism of his youth to the Christian humanism of his last years was a gradual process. Throughout his life, he clung to some form of universalism. When, therefore, in exile he rejected cosmopolitanism for nationality, he did not relinquish the idea of pan-human unity. In the 1860s, the middle phase of his intellectual development, he was the advocate of a romantic humanism which aimed at the unity of mankind in the name of a single ideal without at the same time sacrificing national individuality. In the years immediately following his return from exile, he had not yet begun to identify Russian nationality exclusively with Orthodoxy or to ascribe to the Orthodox faith a universal mission as he was to do during his final creative period. In the early 1860s Russian nationality meant to Dostoevsky an emerging synthesis of the ideas of Russia and the West, a synthesis in which Orthodoxy played a part as a manifestation of the Russian spirit but not its sole determinant. It is illustrative that he was once accused by Grigor'ev of underestimating the importance of Orthodoxy in Russian nationality and history. The time had not yet come when Dostoevsky was convinced that Russian unity was impossible outside of the universal triumph of Orthodoxy.

There is little evidence to suggest that during his term of exile Dostoevsky's thoughts along these lines had progressed beyond a number of vaguely defined sentiments. But even these few vague thoughts made him receptive to Grigor'ev's ideas about reconciliation when at last he encountered them. Grigor'ev's interpretation of the universalizing effect of the Petrine reforms on Russia's educated stratum and of Pushkin as the artistic embodiment of that universality provided Dostoevsky with the framework he was already seeking to attach universal significance to Russian nationality.

The novelist and the critic approached one another on other points as well. As a necessary corollary to the idea of a synthetic national culture, Dostoevsky was also convinced, as he wrote to A.N. Maikov in 1856, that Russia's destiny was to complete the tasks begun by Europe. Perhaps even more important for his future relationship with Grigor'ev was his acceptance, expressed in the same letter to Maikov, of the 'great political ideal of Peter the Great.'[9] Their respective views on art were also beginning to coincide. Dostoevsky had long believed that the aesthetic idea formed the basis not just of all creative thought but also of the entire historical process. In an article written in exile, but not now preserved, on the place of Christianity in art, Dostoevsky argued that tendencies in literature were useless and even detrimental to art, a theme also likely to endear him to Grigor'ev.[10] Strangely enough, he was not enthusiastic about Ostrovsky's plays which, he felt, lacked an ideal.[11] Under the influence of Grigor'ev, he was later to revise his opinion drastically.

It is unlikely that Dostoevsky came across Grigor'ev's organic criticism before the middle of 1859. He complained in March that he had not yet seen a copy of Russkoe slovo, and it was there that Grigor'ev's 'course' in organic criticism was going forward.[12] In the following month, A.N. Pleshcheev, a poet, a veteran of the Petrashevsky circle and friend of Dostoevsky since the 1840s, wrote to him that Grigor'ev was speaking of

Dostoevsky 'with great sympathy.'[13] The news should have piqued Dostoevsky's curiosity sufficiently to ensure that he read Grigor'ev's articles with attention when they finally fell into his hands.

Pleshcheev was also the first to suggest to Dostoevsky the idea of publishing a literary journal with Dostoevsky himself as its central personality.[14] The plan came to nothing, but the idea was not lost on Dostoevsky's older brother, Mikhail, to whom Fedor had reported the suggestion. On 19 July 1858, Mikhail applied to the authorities for permission to publish a weekly political and literary journal called *Vremia* (Time).[15] Apparently he did not inform Fedor of his intention until after the application had been submitted. Only on 13 September did Fedor record his enthusiastic approbation, and it is evident that he was astonished. 'Can it really be,' he exclaimed, 'that you will publish a newspaper!'[16] By early November Mikhail had received the permission of the censorship committee to proceed with his new enterprise.

In August 1859, Dostoevsky was allowed to return to European Russia, though permission to live in the capitals was denied. He temporarily settled at Tver from which he worked feverishly to obtain authorization to move to St Petersburg.

Another event in August further conspired to bring Grigor'ev and Dostoevsky together. *Russkoe slovo* had not long remained open to Grigor'ev as a medium for his ideas. When the journal had begun publication in January 1859, its editor had been the poet Ia. P. Polonsky, while Grigor'ev was put in charge of literary criticism. Polonsky, it soon transpired, did not agree with many of Grigor'ev's critical ideas, and in the ensuing clash Polonsky resigned in April 1859. On Grigor'ev's recommendation a major reorganization of *Russkoe slovo* took place, and in July, A. Khmel'nitsky became the new editor. Unfortunately for Grigor'ev, Khmel'nitsky soon exhibited a mind of his own and, in an attempt to make the journal more radical, began to excise the names of the Slavophiles from Grigor'ev's articles. In August Grigor'ev, too, resigned in anger and once more found himself without an outlet for his ideas. Both a plan by A.F. Pisemsky to take over *Biblioteka dlia chteniia* on behalf of the former 'young editors' and Grigor'ev's own repeated efforts to revive *Moskvitianin* also failed.[17]

It was during this hiatus in his mercurial career that Grigor'ev drifted into the Miliukov circle. A.P. Miliukov, a teacher and literary historian, had been a close friend of Dostoevsky in the 1840s when both had been involved in the radical Durov circle. On his return from exile in Siberia at the end of 1859, Dostoevsky naturally re-established his friendship with

Miliukov and so entered into close contact with the group Miliukov headed. The members of the circle were all writers and journalists who for the most part could be numbered among the socially unattached intelligentsia. N.N. Strakhov (1828–1896), a budding philosopher, who was introduced into the circle early in 1860, recalled that the majority of its members were interested primarily in political and social questions.[18] Most of the active members of the Miliukov circle were also contributors to the journal *Svetoch* which was published from 1860 to 1862. The publisher was the printer D.I. Kalinovsky and the editors were Miliukov himself and D.D. Minaev.

Svetoch almost perfectly embodied the broad movement of co-operation among the intelligentsia that flowered after the succession of Alexander II, and its contributors were exemplars of the movement of social reconciliation within the intelligentsia. The editors of *Svetoch* were committed to forging from a wide range of publicists and intellectuals of diverse views a broad alliance with progressive and humanitarian aims. In his 'introductory word' to the first issue, Kalinovsky deeply regretted the 'adolescent quarreling of various journals which restricted the advance of truth and hindered national development.'[19] *Svetoch* stood for the reconciliation of East and West, Slavophiles and westernizers, old and new. The two main camps in Russian intellectual life, which had been necessary aspects of the national evolution, Kalinovsky explained, had by now outlived their usefulness. By encouraging the free clash of ideas on the pages of their journal, the editors hoped to effect the reconciliation of the Slavophile principle of love for the people with the westernizers' concept of progress.[20]

Literature, which had always taken the leading role in solving the problems raised by Russian life, was upheld in *Svetoch* as the principal instrument for national reconciliation. The editors of the journal adopted Grigor'ev's contention that literature was linked by internal ties to society and so responded to the most pressing social needs. They went beyond Grigor'ev, however, and moved nearer the utilitarians, in arguing that literature should consciously serve social ends. The task of the artist was to demonstrate the influence of the social milieu on various character types.[21] Strakhov later pointed out that Dostoevsky did not fully agree with the view of art propounded in *Svetoch* because he refused to place service to society ahead of artistic integrity as the criterion of literary creativity. There can be little doubt that on this point Grigor'ev must have sympathized with Dostoevsky.

In a comment on Slavophilism in *Svetoch*, Miliukov remarked that history had shown that Russia could not live in isolation from the advantages of Western knowledge and science. Recent history had just as clearly exposed, however, the inadequacy of Western principles alone to produce a full and satisfying life. With the coming of Emancipation, the period of transition begun by Peter the Great had ended. For the first time, the peasantry was entering into full participation in the nation's affairs, bringing with it the age-old principles of Russian nationality. As education advanced among the peasants, and as they came into closer contact with the educated upper classes, a synthesis of Western science with the national principles would occur, which would effect a transformation of Russian social life.[22] The manifesto for 1862 declared: 'Svetoch was founded with the purpose of promoting that tendency which began in Russia in recent years when people began to understand that if much yet remains to be learned by us from educated Europe, much, on the other hand, should be developed from our own national and purely Russian principles. The joining of Russian elements [with] the fruits of western civilization – here is the basis of our future.'[23]

The gradualist and humanistic optimism of Svetoch was buttressed by the hopes its supporters placed in education, which they looked on as a panacea for most of Russia's ills. 'With the introduction of the great reform,' wrote one contributor, 'with the opening of schools for women and with the universal extension of the Sunday Schools, our society has awakened from a heavy, lasting and lethargic sleep and has set out on a new path, the path of national ... life and progress.'[24]

Svetoch stood for the introduction of such Western, technological advances as the railway into Russia and spoke of adopting certain Western fiscal practices; but its editors nevertheless insisted that the proletarianization that had resulted from industrialization in the West should be avoided in Russia by the retention of the communal system of land tenure. In spite of their self-proclaimed role as mediators between Slavophile and westernizer tendencies, the supporters of Svetoch viewed the peasant commune primarily as an economic and not as a moral entity.[25] This position drew them closer to Chernyshevsky than it did to the Slavophiles. Svetoch also championed the artel or industrial commune, as the most rational method of industrial production in Russia. It is evident that in its view Russia's economic and social future lay primarily with associationism and not with private ownership.[26]

One of the more interesting articles to appear in Svetoch was Mikhail Dostoevsky's review of Ostrovsky's play Groza (The Storm). It was the first expression in print by one of the Dostoevsky brothers of ideas that were to take on fundamental importance in *Vremia* a year later. The older Dostoevsky agreed with Grigor'ev that Ostrovsky was neither a westerniz- er nor a Slavophile but an artist who, in his dramatic creations, expressed the plenitude of Russian life. Adopting Grigor'ev's terminology, he argued that Ostrovsky had said a 'new word' – 'nationality.' It consisted of the recognition of the many-sidedness of Russians, their capacity to grasp and absorb all ideas and to see full and not merely partial truth.[27] It may be argued that Mikhail wrote this review in 1860 under the direct influence of his younger brother. It is, however, more probable that he was expressing the general feeling of the *Svetoch* group, a feeling that in turn owed a great deal to Grigor'ev's conception of the universal synthesizing qualities of the Russian personality.

The Miliukov circle and the journal to which it gave birth continued the work begun by the young editors and Grigor'ev but under much different circumstances. Like the previous group, the socially unattached *intelligen- ty* of the Miliukov circle were responding, in a more open climate, to the intellectual and social tensions of the period and to their own uncertainty about their place in the new order. In *Svetoch* may be seen the same impulse that had been at work in *Moskvitianin*: the desire to discover a principle or set of principles that transcended class or ideological loyalties and to speak for the whole nation rather than for particular social or sectional interests. Certain elements were added in *Svetoch* to Grigor'ev's original conception. Grigor'ev had not, for example, stressed as did the *Svetoch* group the need for universal education or turned his attention to the economic future of the country. The weakness of Grigor'ev's thought was, and remained, his failure to develop a concrete program for the realization of his ideals, a failure that *Svetoch* and later *Vremia* sought to redress. Nevertheless, it should not be overlooked that the idea of the reconciliation of the educated with the 'native soil,' the idea of the Russians' capacity for synthesizing all previous ideas, and the idea of the primacy of literature in solving moral and social issues were rooted in organic criticism and owed more to Grigor'ev than to any other Russian thinker.

On his return to St Petersburg, Dostoevsky was determined to pursue the plans for a journal which his brother had initiated. In May 1860 he wrote to A.I. Shubert that he and Mikhail were anxious to undertake some substantial enterprise in literature and were much occupied with planning it.[28] Strakhov, in his recollections of Dostoevsky, recorded that the brothers were busy during 1860 soliciting a body of contributors for a journal. Strakhov himself met Dostoevsky early in 1860 through Miliukov who was teaching literature at the school where Strakhov was an instructor of natural history. Dostoevsky had already shown an interest in Strakhov's articles on natural philosophy and asked him to take part in the new journal.[29] Strakhov, along with a circle of young friends, had for some time past greatly admired Grigor'ev's work, and Grigor'ev reciprocated by his interest in one of Strakhov's early articles. They met in the fall of 1859 and became fast friends.[30]

It was not entirely clear how Grigor'ev and Dostoevsky were finally brought together. Evidently, they did not meet in the Miliukov circle since Grigor'ev at the time was in Moscow trying, unsuccessfully it proved, to win a position on Katkov's *Russkii vestnik*. A number of entries in the diary of Prince V.F. Odoevsky indicate that on his return from Moscow, Grigor'ev visited Odoevsky in a horribly impoverished state and presented him imploringly with one of his articles. Odoevsky, impressed by the article and moved to pity by Grigor'ev's plight, recommended him to Mikhail Dostoevsky, who hired him as *Vremia*'s chief literary critic.[31] Strakhov, however, maintained that when the editors of *Vremia* tried to enlist Strakhov as literary critic, he suggested that Grigor'ev be approached instead. Dostoevsky apparently replied that 'he, himself, very much loved Grigor'ev and very much desired his participation.'[32] In any event, the invitation was extended though too late for one of Grigor'ev's articles to appear in the first number of the new journal.

These four men, the Dostoevsky brothers, Strakhov, and Grigor'ev, made up the central core of the editorial board. The rest of *Vremia*'s contributors were, for the most part, pirated away from *Svetoch*. Of this unlucky journal's principal contributors only D.D. Minaev refrained from publishing in *Vremia*.[33]

Mikhail Dostoevsky's original request had envisaged a weekly publication. On 18 June 1860, he asked for permission to publish instead a political and literary monthly with the same name and program that he had proposed in 1858. His petition was again granted, and in September 1860 *Vremia*'s first manifesto appeared in a number of St Petersburg and Moscow journals. Strakhov later testified that to the best of his knowledge the manifesto was written by Fedor Dostoevsky himself. He went on to deny, somewhat disingenuously, that he personally had much to do with the formulation of questions of tendency in the journal. His interest in the idea of a 'new direction,' he claimed, arose only because of Grigor'ev's enthusiasm for it.[34]

Although Fedor Dostoevsky was without a doubt the leading personality in *Vremia*, he was much influenced by those around him. It has been suggested that his older brother's part in the formulation of editorial policy was much more important than has previously been supposed.[35] Mikhail had first raised the idea of *Vremia*, had sold his cigarette factory to finance it, and was not, moreover, a man without definite views of his own. His letters indicate that, apart from management decisions, which he handled alone, he dealt also with matters concerning content on his own initiative, although he tried to consult his brother whenever possible. M·DOSTOEVSKY There is also a good deal of evidence that he disapproved of many of the ideas of Strakhov and Grigor'ev. Of the two brothers, Mikhail was the more liberal, and his influence constantly pulled *Vremia* towards a greater tolerance for, though not complete agreement with, such radical journals as *Sovremennik*. Other habitual contributors reinforced Mikhail's more liberal inclinations. A.E. Razin, for example, who wrote the political review section of *Vremia*, was the constant butt of Grigor'ev's mordant outbursts against the journal's minuet with Chernyshevsky. Grigor'ev was implacably hostile to *Sovremennik*, and the emphatic nature of his views tended to counteract Mikhail's more liberal influence on Fedor. The tensions within the editorial board accounted at least in part for a certain ambiguity that plagued *Vremia* from its very inception. Such disagreements should not, however, be exaggerated. Mikhail had almost certainly arrived at his 'native soil' convictions before Fedor's return from exile. On most questions the brothers were in near perfect accord. Strakhov also asserted that on literary questions and matters of tendency in general, Grigor'ev's opinions were solicited and listened to by Fedor with attention and sympathy.[36] In most instances, sincere efforts were made to conform to the testy critic's wishes.

Pochvennichestvo, as it emerged in *Vremia*, was the product not only of the able minds of Dostoevsky, Grigor'ev, and Strakhov, but also of a group of men who produced anonymously the regular monthly features of the journal. Of these contributors, Razin who wrote the political review, A.U. Poretsky who was in charge of the home affairs section, and I.G. Dolgomost'ev who concerned himself principally with questions of education were the most important. They shared Dostoevsky's interest in social and political concerns to a greater extent than did Grigor'ev or Strakhov. Grigor'ev was frequently critical of parts of the program of *Vremia*, although he agreed with its general tendency and later commented that Dostoevsky's journal had 'completely correct beliefs.'[37] Strakhov, in contrast, did not specifically identify himself with the 'men of the soil.' Though he accepted many of the specific tenets of *pochvennichestvo*, and gave some of them their clearest formulations, he nevertheless preferred to concentrate on the more general task of creating a broad nationalistic and idealistic front in order to counter the growing forces of materialism and utilitarianism in Russia.

The original tensions within the editorial board were to surface in the subsequent careers of its members. For the moment, however, their differences were concealed, and all was optimism and harmony when, in January 1861, the first number of *Vremia* appeared under the banner of universal reconciliation.

5

Native Soil

[handwritten margin notes: EDUCATED · UNEDUCATED / WESTERN ↑ · TRADIT. PEAS. / MUSCOVITE · PETRINE / SLAVOPHILE · WESTERNIZER]

Pochvennichestvo, as it unfolded in the pages of *Vremia*, was the culmination of the ideological process that began with the young editors. Behind the strivings of Grigor'ev and his sympathizers lay the profound sense of alienation experienced by the Russian intelligentsia in the 1840s and 1850s. Alienation is the product of a serious discrepancy between the ideal and the real, and it was precisely to the problem of reconciling thought and life that the young editors and Grigor'ev turned. They *[handwritten margin note: ALIENATION]* approached the problem, as has been seen, through the metaphor Russia and the West. (It will be recalled that the polarities of the metaphor included the separation of the educated, westernized classes from the uneducated, traditionalist peasantry, or the mind from the body of Russia; the tension between the ideals of Muscovite and Petrine Russia; and the intellectual conflict between the Slavophile and westernizing tendencies in Russian thought.) To overcome these antinomies was, in their minds, to overcome the discrepancy between thought and life. It is not surprising, then, that in *Svetoch* the reconciliation of Russia and the West was elevated to the central task of the day and that it retained its priority in *Vremia*.

The literary expression of the alienated *intelligent* was the 'superfluous man.' The young editors conveyed the same notion in their writings in the *[handwritten margin note: SUPERFLUOUS MAN]* theme of 'wandering,' a theme that persisted in *Vremia*. During the Emancipation period, when the scope for practical activity had enormously expanded, the intelligentsia subjected the superfluous man to a harsh critical examination. Among the radicals, N.A. Dobroliubov, in his essay 'What Is Oblomovitis?,' and D.I. Pisarev, in 'The Realists,' countered the image of the superfluous man with the image of the realist who spurned abstract speculation and vain talk and buried himself in practical activity. Among the conservative *intelligenty*, the realist of the radicals found an equivalent in the superfluous man or wanderer who at last overcame his alienation by returning to the native soil.[1] In the return to the soil, which emerged as the central idea of *Vremia*, lay the solution not only to the tensions contained in the metaphor Russia and the West, but to the discrepancy between thought and life, the ideal and the real, as well.

Dostoevsky saw it as the task of *Vremia* to analyse the 'nature of our time ... and, particularly, the nature of the present moment of our social life.'[2] The analysis included an examination of Russian history and the principles governing the historical life of the Russians and of the debates that had animated and divided the intellectual life of the country since the beginning of the nineteenth century. These topics took the *pochvenniki* over ground already covered by the Slavophiles, and it will be interesting to compare the analysis and solutions put forward in *pochvennichestvo* to those offered in Slavophilism.

The analytical tools employed in *Vremia*, which are already familiar from Grigor'ev's organic criticism, were part and parcel of the European conservative response to the philosophies of reason. The four cornerstones of the conservative ideology of the *pochvenniki* were philosophical nominalism, relativism, immanentism, and organicism, which they systematically applied to Russia's unique historical conditions and peculiar social arrangements.

1 The *pochvenniki* were consistent antirationalists. They insisted on the primacy of life and experience over theory and abstraction and rejected the imposition of rationally deduced, a priori ideas on life. In this sense, Dostoevsky wrote, 'idealism stupifies, captivates and kills.'[3] His phrase is reminiscent of Grigor'ev's earlier response to Stankevich's Hegelianism: idealism was the sickness of the age because it stultified the natural development of life by forcing it to conform to ideals external to its innate nature. 'The naïve theoretician,' Strakhov wrote in 1861 under his favourite pseudonym N. Kositsa, 'looks at reality and sees with astonishment that life does not resemble his concepts.'[4] The *pochvenniki* numbered among the theoreticians in contemporary Russia both the nihilists and the handful of liberals who were seeking to impose alien and abstract forms and institutions on the native tradition.

The dismissal by the *pochvenniki* of abstract theorizing as a valid source of knowledge bore a close resemblance to the distinction drawn by the early Slavophiles between rationalism (*rassudochnost'*), which was based on logic and analysis, and reason (*razumnost'*), which rested on the integrated activity of all the faculties of cognition.[5] Dostoevsky was also alert to a tendency in philosophy and social thought to substitute theoretical formulas for reality: 'The mistaking of incomplete thought for complete reality – here is the root of all the errors of mankind.'[6] Reason alone then provided an inadequate basis for knowledge. Thought, Strakhov concluded, was efficacious only when it was linked to 'life itself, to reality.'[7]

2 Closely related to the antirationalism of the *pochvenniki* was their theory of relativism. They pointed out that the process of abstract reasoning consisted fundamentally of combining individual objects under general formulas. 'Abstract thought is, therefore, always levelling thought, which sets differences aside and deprives phenomena of their colour.'[8] In its drive towards centralization, theory overlooked local diversity, ignored dissenting opinions, and tyrannized over thought and action, reducing everything to the monotony of its own narrow vision. The theoreticians, who espoused a comprehensive formula, ignored the fact that life advanced many contending theories, each of equal validity, and failed to perceive what the romantics referred to as the 'irony' of life. The defence of diversity by the intelligentsia conservatives in Russia was rooted in an aesthetic appreciation of life, which valued variety and colour as desirable in themselves.

In particular, the *pochvenniki* directed their criticism of the centralizing tendencies of rationalism against the idea of universal humanity. 'Humanity!' Grigor'ev exclaimed, 'this abstract humanity of a badly understood Hegelianism, a humanity which does not exist; for there are only organisms which grow, age and are reborn, but which are eternal – nations.'[9] Dostoevsky echoed Grigor'ev's opinion. There was, he wrote, no reality in the concept man; there were only particular men. These relativist strictures were, of course, aimed at the Russian nihilists who, in the estimation of the *pochvenniki*, supposed that they could reduce the lives of highly complex national and human organisms to a handful of general impulses and needs.

It should be pointed out that the *pochvenniki* were not turning their backs entirely on human universality. 'The general,' Dostoevsky wrote, 'exists as *potential* but not as reality.'[10] Like Herder, Dostoevsky was convinced that the destiny of man was universal, but that the common goal could be effected only through the separate efforts of individual nations. In his notebook for 1863 he remarked: 'We do not consider nationality to be the last word or the final goal of mankind. Only universal mankind can live a full life. But mankind will attain it in no other way than by *emphasis on the unique nationality* (*natsional'nost'*) of every people. The idea of the soil, of nationalities, is the fulcrum, *Antaeus*.'[11]

NATIONAL
EXCLUSIVENESS

There was no suggestion of national exclusiveness in Dostoevsky's formulation, just as there was none in Herder's. Herder was defending German culture against the universalistic claims of French civilization. Similarly, the *pochvenniki* were seeking to liberate Russia from the related idea that the universal human ideal had already been discovered in western Europe and had only to be disseminated the world over. Instead, they maintained that the European ideal represented only a partial expression of the universal ideal which would not be complete until all nations had added their own unique contributions to it.

IMMANENCE

3 The third element of *pochvennichestvo*, the idea of immanence, followed directly from its adherents' view of the role of nations in universal history. Since every nation made some special contribution to the totality of human experience, each must be governed by a particular ideal or principle. The fate of a nation, therefore, was contained in its essence. At first the national ideal lived only unconsciously in the life of a people. But during the course of the nation's history, it gradually attained consciousness. The intellectual, social, and political forms and institutions of the nation at any given moment reflected the national ideal at its current level of development.

Unlike the early Slavophiles, the *pochvenniki* generally preferred to speak of the soul (*dusha*) of a nation rather than its spirit (*dukh*). One commentator has pointed out that what the *pochvenniki* meant by the soul was the unexpressed ideas which were strongly felt and which dwelt unconsciously in the life of the people.'[12] It was these fundamental ideas that they designated the 'native soil': 'Under the term soil are meant those basic and distinctive powers of a people which are the seeds of all its organic manifestations. Whatever the phenomenon is ... be it a song, story, custom, or a private or civil form, all these are recognized as legitimate, as having real meaning, in so far as they are organically linked to the national essence.'[13]

PAST

4 Strakhov's definition of the soil points to the fourth major component of *pochvennichestvo*, organicism. Since every manifestation of the historical life of the nation was the product of its people's unique genius, the history of the nation formed an organic whole, and every stage of its development was necessary to the whole. No aspect of the past could be dismissed as merely a preparation for the present. As the manifestation of a single ideal each past event or achievement was intrinsically valuable.[14] This aspect of the thought of the *pochvenniki* was directed at the disciples of infinite progress who reduced the past to an instrument of the present.

Like most conservatives since Burke, the *pochvenniki* judged the

immanence: [1] remaining or operating only w/in a domain of reality or realm
of discourse: INHERENT. specif ~ having existence/effect only w/in mind or consc.
compare: TRANSCENDENT.

legitimacy of contemporary institutional, cultural, legal, and social arrangements by their rootedness in the past. Men and nations could not ignore their past because for all intents and purposes they were their past. 'To a certain degree,' Strakhov observed, 'human life has already become firmly established, has worked itself through and taken shape; it is no longer simply life; it is historical life. Mankind forms for itself a soil, a firm foothold, history. At the present time, man can no longer reject history, cannot be separate as was the first man, cannot sever his ties with the general world of humanity.'[5] The *pochvenniki* concluded that the normal development of a nation depended on strict adherence to its traditions and to the roots of its unique existence. All legitimate change was organic change, and alien impositions were inimical to normal growth.

The idea of immanence and the organic conception of national development committed the *pochvenniki* to a kind of determinism. In this context, determinism simply meant the conviction that everything that had been and now was represented necessary aspects of the unfolding of the national ideal. The *pochvenniki* therefore excluded violent breaks in the continuity of the historical life of the nation. The whole of the past was contained in the present and would direct the future.

The organic view entailed a final consideration. Just as the history of a nation formed an organic whole so did its society. Individuals, classes, and interest groups were fundamentally united in a common endeavour, the fulfilment of the national ideal, which transcended temporary divisions and antagonisms. Since the attainment of the ideal rested on a co-operative social effort, it could be realized only through the fullest possible growth of every individual and each social grouping. The self-realization of the individual was the prerequisite of national fulfilment. The immersion of individuals in society with the resulting loss of individualism subverted the complete growth of the ideal of the nation. Not surprisingly, therefore, the *pochvenniki* attached an overriding significance to personality and were deeply suspicious of anything that imposed restrictions on the development of the individual. In order to realize his full creative potential the individual had to be rooted in the concrete, historical reality of his own time and place. 'To return to the soil,' Dostoevsky confided to his notebook, 'no one can be *anything* or achieve *anything* without first being himself.'[6]

The *pochvenniki* examined Russian history and the state of society in the Emancipation period in the light of these four major concepts and within the general philosophical framework of which they form a part. The debt that the *pochvenniki* owed to the memory of *Moskvitianin* was never more

DEBT 2
MOCKBИTИЯ
HИH

D's ARTICLE

apparent than in their attitude to Russia and the West. The same ideas that Pogodin had popularized in the 1840s were resurrected in *Vremia*. In his 'Series of Articles on Russian Literature,' Dostoevsky argued that Russia had never been divided into two classes, conquerors and conquered, as had the nations of western Europe. Every political, social, and cultural achievement of the West had been the product of a fierce class struggle, whereas in Russia peaceful co-operation among the various social strata was a fundamental characteristic of the national soul. In spite of external and temporary disagreements, a neutral soil existed in Russia on which all classes merged into a whole and co-operated in peaceful and fraternal creativeness.[17]

DOSTOEVSKY'S
FRATERNITY
————→

After his brief visit to western Europe in 1862, Dostoevsky returned to Russia highly critical of the bourgeois-capitalist society he had for the first time encountered face to face. The root failing of the West, in his view, and the cause of its dilemma stemmed from the fact that the principle of fraternity was absent in Western life. Inequality was, therefore, endemic. Western socialists had uncovered the weakness of their society, but their attempts to generate a feeling of brotherhood, where it was naturally absent, by reason and artifice would inevitably result in the diminution and eventual eradication of individual liberty in the socialist anthill.[18] In default of an internal unifying force, social cohesion in western Europe could be achieved only through some form of external compulsion. The West, then, lacked the qualities necessary to deliver it from its spiritual predicament.[19] Not so Russia, where the innate sense of fraternity guaranteed inner unity and social harmony. 'The Russian nation,' Dostoevsky wrote, 'is an extraordinary phenomenon in the history of all mankind. The character of the Russian people does not resemble the characters of all the contemporary European people.'[20]

SLAVOPHILE
FRATERNITY
THROUGH
ORTHODOXY

The early Slavophiles had arrived at a similar conclusion by a slightly different route. They agreed with the *pochvenniki* that Russia was different from the West by virtue of its Slavic fraternity or communality (*sobornost'*). But the Slavophiles worked out a more intelligible and consistent explanation of these differences than did the *pochvenniki*. According to the Slavophiles, the distinguishing mark of any culture was the religious faith that underlay it. The culture of western Europe was the product of Roman Catholicism which had fallen prey to the one-sided rationalism of Roman philosophy and law. Russia, to its great good fortune, had eluded the Roman tradition, and in Orthodoxy had preserved the inner wholeness of Christ's love. The West had experienced the separation of life and thought, whereas Russians were blessed with the special capacity for integrated knowledge. The separation of life 思 + 生 and thought in the West had, in turn, fostered the atomization of Western society and produced the bourgeois individualism that Dostoevsky had so deplored in his *Winter Notes on Summer Impressions*.[21]

The explanation of Russian uniqueness by the *pochvenniki* was less specific than that of the Slavophiles. They attached far less significance to Orthodoxy, preferring instead to think in terms of national psychological types that were assigned their originality by Providence. They regarded the Orthodox faith only as one manifestation of Russia's distinctiveness. The vagueness of this account proved in the future to be unsatisfactory to the *pochvenniki*. Grigor'ev later criticized *Vremia* for underestimating the role of Orthodoxy in Russian cultural life, and Dostoevsky, too, was soon to find in the Orthodox religion the clue to Russian originality. In *Vremia*, however, the religious motif remained suppressed.

It was on the significance of Peter the Great's reforms that the *poch-* PI'S *venniki* differed most profoundly with the Slavophiles. The Slavophiles REFORMS were far from being unanimous in their views about Peter. As usual, Konstantin Aksakov adopted the most extreme and abrasive position. In his view, Russia stood in imminent danger of losing its 'Russianness,' for that, he argued, 'is where Peter's system of government is leading it.'[22] Most of the remaining Slavophiles avoided Aksakov's uncompromising position. Kireevsky and Khomiakov had identified the fault of the West as the separation of life and knowledge. It was precisely this fault, they believed, that Peter in his reforming zeal had introduced into Russian intellectual development. Peter's reforms, they were agreed, had not been entirely false or unnecessary. Before the reforms, Russians had been P'S culturally too narrow and had unquestionably needed to be brought into CONFUSION the mainstream of civilization. Peter had, however, confused form with OF FORM & content and had laid waste the Muscovite content of Russian civilization in CONTENT the name of empty Western forms. As Khomiakov wrote in 1857: 'The rational development of the human individual consists in his elevation to universal human dignity in accordance with those peculiarities by which nature has distinguished him. The rational development of a nation consists in the elevation to universal human significance of that type which is concealed at the very root of its national being.'[23] Peter's reforms, on the contrary, had trampled roughshod over the national type and had set in motion the prevailing fashion against everything traditionally Russian.

In the years following Peter's death, the Slavophile argument contin-ued, Western education and the forms of Western culture had developed rapidly among the upper levels of the Russian population. Of itself, education was beneficial to Russia. Again with the exception of Konstantin Aksakov, all of the Slavophiles, particularly Khomiakov and A.I. Koshelev, were insistent on this point.[24] But education was not enlightenment. Since the content of learning (*nauka*) was universal but the forms it assumed were always national, education was transformed into true enlightenment only with its complete integration with the national principle. In imposing Western education on the service classes, Peter had also imposed its forms, thus excluding in Russia any possibility of a native science or art. Only the peasant class had been spared Peter's reforming zeal as well as the subsequent dissemination of Western learning. The native way of life and the principles of old Muscovy had, therefore, been preserved in the peasantry. Consequently, Khomiakov concluded in his 'To the Serbians' of 1860, a complete state of inner disunity existed in Russia between the educated and the uneducated.[25] As a result of the reforms intellect and body were separated; knowledge and life had no points of contact.

The *pochvenniki* took a somewhat different view of Peter's reforms and especially of their consequences. In their view, the reforms had been absolutely necessary to Russia's development. Their analysis was surprisingly sensitive to what had actually been taking place in seventeenth-century Muscovy. In the years immediately preceding the reign of Peter the Great, they contended, Russians had sensed a need for spiritual and intellectual expansion. The cause of their restiveness, according to Dostoevsky, lay in the second inherent characteristic of Russians, which along with fraternity governed their development. This was that universality which Grigor'ev had already identified in Pushkin. Russians, said Dostoevsky, 'spoke all languages, understood all civilizations and sympathized with the interests of every European nation.'[26]

Peter had responded, consciously or not, to the Russian yearning for the universal, had moved Russia into the orbit of universal civilization and enabled Russians, as destiny had decreed, to absorb the ideals of western Europe.[27] The *pochvenniki* conceded that for all of this a price had to be paid. Although Peter was correct to lead Russia into Europe, the forms that he chose to impose on his empire were not national. The common people repudiated the reforms, separated themselves from those classes that had followed Peter, and declared their moral independence. Peter's idea, said Dostoevsky, was profoundly national since it was a response to the aspirations of the people for renewal and greater scope; but the fact of Peter, the actual reforms that he carried out, were anti-national because they were rejected by the people.[28] Left to themselves, the common people, far from passively preserving the old, pre-Petrine traditions, as the Slavophiles supposed, actively sought to produce their own independent view of life. Much of what they created was monstrous, but they, too, changed and advanced, and their faith in themselves remained constant.

The *pochvenniki* disagreed with the Slavophiles also about the effect of Peter's reforms on the educated. The Slavophiles distinguished sharply between the people (*narod*), which was national, and the 'public,' a broad spectrum ranging from courtiers through bureaucrats, to novelists, which was westernized and alien to Russian nationality. The *pochvenniki* were equally aware of the enormous gulf that separated the educated from the uneducated in Russia, but they denied that there was any fundamental distinction between the two groups. It was true, they admitted, that the upper strata of society, in temporarily accepting the anti-national forms that Peter had imposed on them through the sheer force of his character, had forfeited the trust of the people and incurred their suspicion and at times hatred. Exposure to European civilization infinitely widened the outlook of the Russian educated class. Its members adopted the European way of life but 'did not become Europeans.' At first they reproached themselves for their inability to do so, but at last they realized that it was impossible. European forms were the product of European nationality which was distinct from their own. Russians had to create a 'new form, our own native form, taken out of our soil, taken out of our national spirit and our national principles.'[29]

What, then, was the purpose of Peter's reforms, which had taken such a toll on national unity? It was, replied the *pochvenniki*, to enable Russians to meet with and absorb the national aspirations of the people of Europe, to awake in the consciousness of Russians the fact of their universality which had dwelt within their unconscious lives from the beginning, and to foster in Russians the realization that 'we are, perhaps, destined by fate to bring about the universal-human solidarity of the world.'[30]

Yet throughout this process, the *pochvenniki* insisted, Russians had remained Russians. They were as convinced as Belinsky had been in 1841 that a people could not lose its nationality by exposure to diverse national life-styles.[31] In his influential biography of Dostoevsky, Nikolai Berdiaev argued that the fundamental weakness of Slavophilism, and later of populism, was the tendency to identify Russian nationality with the common people. The fallacy was, he went on, one of the cardinal causes of the tragedy that overtook Russia in 1917. Among the offenders he included Dostoevsky.[32] There is little evidence, as will be seen, that

Dostoevsky ever held such a view. He clearly did not hold it in the early 1860s. Instead, he fully concurred with Grigor'ev's definition of nationality as an organic whole made up of elements drawn from all classes of society. It was wrong, he argued in his article 'Pedantry and Literacy' in 1861, to equate nationality exclusively with the common people:

Why should nationality belong only to the common people? Does nationality disappear when the people develops? Are we, the educated, not really the Russian people? To us the opposite appears to be the case; with the development of the people, all of its natural gifts, all of its wealth develops and strengthens and the spirit of the people shines through more brightly ... We only know that we were divided purely by external circumstances. These external circumstances did not permit the residual mass of the people to follow us, thus including *all* the forces of the national spirit. We only know that we are a too separate and small part of the people and that if the people do not follow us, we will never be able to express ourselves completely ... not as we would have expressed ourselves had the whole Russian people been with us. But it does not follow from this that we have lost our national spirit, that we have degenerated.[33]

Unlike the Slavophiles, the *pochvenniki* refused to believe that educated Russians had somehow defaulted on their nationality and become aliens in their own country. The reforms of Peter had precipitated no such fundamental contradiction in the nation. The common people had continued to develop after Peter, and the educated had not discarded their nationality but merely tempered it in the clash with other nationalities. The two parts represented the embodiment of the two major aspects of Russian nationality: fraternity in the common people, universality in the educated. Only in their reconciliation would Russian nationality attain its full and conscious expression.[34] The *pochvenniki*, therefore, set out to promote a community of interests between educated and illiterate.

The metaphor Russia and the West had still another side which captured the attention of the *pochvenniki*. The ideological analogue to the historical gulf that separated Russia and the West and divided the educated and the people in the time of Peter was the intellectual rift between the Slavophiles and the westernizers. In a series of what amounted to leading articles in the early numbers of *Vremia*, Grigor'ev explored the origins and implications of the schism in Russian intellectual life. His remarkable and original analysis of the growth of the conflicting intellectual trends in Russia during the first half of the nineteenth century exhibited an insight into the psychology of Russia's intellectual development that was almost entirely unknown in Slavophilism. Grigor'ev's articles provide invaluable insight into the way the conservative *intelligenty* perceived themselves in relation to other intellectual groups in Russia and into the place they occupied in the evolution of Russian thought; they merit examining in detail.[35]

After Peter's reforms, Grigor'ev began, there was a rapid transformation of the external forms of Russian political and social life. Despite these changes, however, eighteenth-century writers never doubted the integrity and worth of Russian nationality. While the rest of Europe slavishly imitated Enlightenment France, 'with us there was still none of this – neither a negation by us of our nationality nor a struggle on its behalf.'[36] It was only with the great historian Karamzin that the separation of old and new appeared both in Russian life and literature. Karamzin, said Grigor'ev, was the first complete representative in Russia of European ideas. He was also the first real talent in Russian literature and was the first to exercise a powerful moral hold over society. Until 1812 Karamzin was a westernizer. It therefore fell to him to introduce the ideas of the Enlightenment into Russia and bring part of society under the spell of European ideals.[37]

Karamzin was to Russian intellectual life, Grigor'ev continued, what Peter the Great had been to Russian political and social life: he was the first European among educated Russians. He approached Russian reality with the European ideal and deceived both himself and the reading public by subjecting Russian history to the abstract and rationalistic standards of the West. Karamzin viewed Russian history exactly as contemporary historians in the West viewed their own history. He wrote of Russian events and characters not in a tone proper to them but in a tone derived from their supposed analogues in the West. Russian self-consciousness, Grigor'ev pointed out, was built on Karamzin's *History of the Russian State*.[38]

Grigor'ev suggested that Karamzin was also the chief source of all the false attitudes towards Russian nationality in literature. Under the influence of the Western interpretation of the Russian past in Karamzin's *History*, novelists such as M.N. Zogoskin and dramatists such as Pogodin easily fell prey to the charms of Walter Scott, whose works introduced into Russian art the Western understanding of history. Works of historical fiction were produced in Russia in the style of Scott; they had nothing in common with Russian reality.[39] By the early 1830s began the period that Belinsky in 'Literary Reveries' had called romantic-national. A whole spate of historical novels, which Russians supposed fully represented their nationality, appeared. No one except Pushkin suspected that this flurry of historical fiction was due to the influence of Walter Scott and of Karamzin's false historical forms. These novels, in fact, said Grigor'ev, depicted Russian historical characters as no more than copies of their descendants' coachmen. A whole portrait of Russian nationality was painted. When it proved to be false, a crisis occurred among intellectuals in which not only the false picture but Russian nationality itself was rejected.[40]

It fell to Chaadaev to expose the essential falseness of Karamzin's representation of the Russian past. At the time he wrote his 'first philosophical letter' in 1829, Grigor'ev argued, Chaadaev was seduced by the magnificence of the Roman Catholic conception of human unity. Thus, when he failed to find in the real Russian past the parallels with Western history that Karamzin had claimed for it, Chaadaev was intellectually and emotionally unprepared to search in Russian history for the particular laws and attributes on which the positive differences between Russia and the West could be enumerated. Instead, he came to regard Russia as a helot set aside by fate as an example to the rest of the world of the inevitable destiny of a nation cut off from humanity and from the sources of salvation.[41]

Grigor'ev pointed out that there were two possible answers to Chaadaev's disclosure that Russia did not fit into Western forms as Karamzin had supposed: either 1) Russians were not completely human and so should sever themselves from their past, which had deprived them of full humanity, and seek to become western; or 2) Russian life was completely different from Western life, though no less human. The westernizers opted for the former, and the Slavophiles chose the latter. 'The Westernizers,' Dostoevsky took up Grigor'ev's argument, 'having adopted the theory of west European, universal life and meeting in Russian life phenomena entirely dissimilar from this theory, condemned Russian life.'[42] Westernism failed to distinguish between the false nationality conjured up by the writers of the romantic-national period and true nationality and so 'took false forms for the idea itself.'[43]

At first the westernizers were aware only of the differences between Russian life before and after Peter's reforms. Having assured themselves that with Peter Russia had set out on the Western path and having incorrectly understood the Hegelian dictum that the 'real is rational,' Belinsky and the other westernizers were able to reconcile themselves to Russian reality under Nicholas I. But soon they became conscious of the disparity between the Russia of their own day and western Europe and rejected everything Russian in the name of the European ideal. Aggravated by the extremes of the westernizers, the Slavophiles, too, fell into extremes. An apparently irreconcilable gulf opened between the two schools.[44]

Grigor'ev's analysis of the origins of the Slavophile-westernizer controversy prepared the ground for a comprehensive critique of both camps. The downfall of Slavophilism, according to the *pochvenniki*, was its idealism, which imposed on its adherents an abstract, theoretical view of Russian reality. Late in 1861, Dostoevsky addressed the Slavophiles: 'You are Russians, honourable men, you love the fatherland; but your idealism is your undoing, and sometimes you made terrible blunders even in understanding the most basic elements of Russian life.'[45]

Their idealism, the *pochvenniki* believed, had led the Slavophiles into a number of errors. Pride of place among them belonged to their idealization of Muscovite life. Muscovy represented for the Slavophiles the normal condition of Russian nationality from which subsequent generations had deviated. 'The Slavophiles,' Dostoevsky claimed, 'taking the old Muscovite ideal as the norm ... condemned *at a stroke* everything in Russian life that did not fit into their narrow framework.'[46] The accusation is hardly fair. Khomiakov was far from idealizing the lives of his Muscovite ancestors. It is not, however, the accuracy of the critique of Slavophilism by the *pochvenniki* so much as their own view of Muscovy that is of interest here. The Muscovite period, Dostoevsky went on, was distinguished by the falseness of its social relations. It was a time in which shame, affected humility, and slavery were supreme, a time of apathy towards religion and of brutality in family life.[47] In short, Grigor'ev concluded, Muscovy was a narrow shell and one which, moreover, was Byzantine-Tartar and not national at all.[48] Dostoevsky went even further. If any model for national life existed, he asserted, it was not to be found in the sixteenth and seventeenth centuries, 'when centralization had already seriously encroached upon the truth and freedom of the land,' but in the first six centuries of Russian history, when the free land lived a broad and open life.[49]

The *pochvenniki* found in the *Raskol* or schism further evidence for their view that Muscovite nationality was false. The church schism of the seventeenth century represented to them the rejection by the common people of the life of Muscovy. The *pochvenniki* took a great interest in the schism and viewed schismatic writings as one of the best sources for the study of Russian nationality in their own day.[50] If the people had reacted so violently to Muscovite life, it was vain to search in Muscovy for evidence of the true Russian character. Even if Russian nationality were hidden beneath the beards and caftans of Muscovy, both Grigor'ev and Dostoevsky were fully aware of the impossibility of turning back. Grigor'ev wrote: 'To return to pre-Petrine Rus', little as Rus' would want to do so, or to the Rus' of the twelfth century, even though we might wish it, cannot be done, at least with respect to forms. The life we lived after the reform cannot be eliminated: it *was*, and to deny as false the forces at work within it is quixotic fun, innocent, of course, but not a little amusing.'[51]

The second major error of Slavophilism, so the *pochvenniki* believed, was its idealization of the peasant as the only remaining embodiment of Russian nationality. This myth prevented the Slavophiles from discerning the true nature of their times. They remained the victims of a proud and stubborn immobility at a time when all of Russia was in a state of flux. The Slavophiles failed to grasp that nationality was not a static entity, monopolized and preserved by one social group. Rather it was a process of continuous creation from the strivings of separate individuals and groups, ever advancing towards complete and conscious expression. The Slavophiles had played a significant part in their time, but in the general return to the soil 'Slavophile influence played scarcely any role.'[52] Enmeshed in its own theory, Slavophilism had proved incapable of correctly interpreting Russia, either past or present, and retained merely historical interest. Grigor'ev pronounced an obituary for the Slavophiles: 'Slavophilism, which is by now already the same kind of historical phenomenon as Westernism, did not take the people as it was in life but always searched for its own ideal people and trimmed the shoots of the great, organic life according to a ready-made pattern.'[53]

Westernism was also subjected to a penetrating analysis by the *pochvenniki*. Grigor'ev's earlier critique of the baleful influence of the Hegelian idea of universal spirit on Russian intellectual development in the 1840s formed the framework of their analysis. Russians, Grigor'ev maintained, had not understood Hegel because they had taken his theory too literally. In the aftermath of Chaadaev's letter, the westernizers had applied the German romantic ideal to Russian history, but having in time noted the discrepancy between the ideal and the real Russian past had rejected the history of their nation as a false path. Belinsky, who exercised enormous influence over his contemporaries, was instrumental in fostering what Grigor'ev called the 'historical view.' Grigor'ev believed that in placing the ideal or goal of humanity at the end of history, the historical view, by which he meant Hegelian historicism, reduced individuals and nations to mere instruments of universal spirit. Men were seen as conforming, whether willingly or unwillingly, to the demands of the final purpose. The inevitable result of this cosmopolitan notion of human progress was the elimination of individual differences and local peculiarities and the centralization of human attributes under the general rubric of abstract humanity. The westernizers, therefore, denied Russia's uniqueness and, rejoicing in Peter the Great as the hero who had brought the nation into the current of universal human progress, insisted that Russia too must pursue the path of Western development. For the sake of a theory imported from the West, the westernizers ignored the true facts and real needs of the national life.[54]

Both Grigor'ev and Dostoevsky believed nevertheless that westernism represented a necessary facet of Russian development. Westernism was, Dostoevsky affirmed, the last spark of the Petrine reform and represented the innate capacity of the Russian for self-analysis and self-criticism.[55] Having searched for truth abroad, the westernizers inevitably concluded that the European ideal of humanity was partial and inadequate for Russia:

But having recognized the necessity of the soil, Westernism became convinced, by its previous life and development, that it was not a question of maledictions but of reconciliation and union, that the reform had outlived its time but, nevertheless, had introduced us to the great element of universal humanity, had forced us to comprehend it and place it before us as our main purpose in the future, as the law of our nature, as the most important goal of all the strivings of Russia's vitality and spirit. And take note: the great mass of society in Russia always sympathized with the Westernizers.[56]

The merciless analysis by the westernizers had, therefore, pushed society forward. They were, Dostoevsky was convinced, the 'beginning of consciousness, the beginning of will power, the beginning of new forms of life.'[57]

Having unravelled the metaphor Russia and the West and set out its polarities – Russia before Peter and Russia after Peter, civilization and the Russian ideal, the educated and the people, Slavophilism and westernism – the *pochvenniki* turned to the more challenging task of resolving the conflicts which it contained. The solution, like the metaphor itself, was comprehensive. The ultimate goal that the *pochvenniki* had in view differed little from that proposed by the Slavophiles. Both were seeking to overcome the gap between the educated and the masses and reintegrate Russian society. They differed, however, about the means by which the desired end would be attained. Whereas the Slavophiles were voluntarists, the *pochvenniki*, as has been seen, were determinists. To the static national ideal of Slavophilism, which the educated had to retrieve by means of a conscious act of will, the *pochvenniki* opposed an evolving, organic synthesis of indigenous elements with universal civilization. The former were most evident among the common people but were also strongly felt among the educated; the latter was the gift of the educated to the people. The Slavophile analysis of Peter's reforms precluded an evolutionary solution. The reforms had, in their view, interrupted the natural development of Russian history and divided the consciousness of the nation into two irreconcilable camps. Only one camp, that of the people, had retained Russian nationality; the other had surrendered itself entirely to alien ideals. 'The restoration of our specific intellectual powers,' Khomiakov wrote in 1847, 'fully depends on a living union with the ancient but, nevertheless, to us fully Russian life, and this union is possible only by means of sincere love.'[58] Imbued as they were with the alien, Western principles, the Slavophiles believed, the educated had forfeited their nationality. Only by a conscious act of the renunciation of westernism, an act culminating in sincere and profound love for the people, could they regain their nationality. It was not reconciliation that the Slavophiles offered but renunciation, repentance, and humble submission.

The *pochvenniki* took quite another view of the matter. Since nationality was not a fixed entity, but rather, as Herder had demonstrated, a continuous development in which all classes participated, there was not and never had been a rift in the national consciousness. Russian nationality belonged to neither the educated nor the people but transcended and subsumed both in an organic whole. Since Peter's reforms had been a necessary part of Russian national development, the continuity of Russian history had never been broken. Russia before Peter and Russia after Peter were organically joined. The *pochvenniki* refused to view the reforms of Peter, as did the westernizers, as the real beginning of Russian historical life, or as did the Slavophiles, as a break with the national character. Rather, they accepted Russian life as history made it. In the manifesto for *Vremia* of 1862 Dostoevsky wrote:

We do not go to ancient Moscow for our ideals [Slavophilism]; we do not say that first everything has to be transformed in the German manner and only then can we consider our nationality to be suitable material for a future, eternal edifice [westernism]. *We have worked directly from what is and only wish to permit the greatest freedom of development to what is.* Given such freedom of development, we believe in the Russian future; we believe in its independent potential.[59]

By the middle of the nineteenth century, the *pochvenniki* maintained, the Petrine reforms had achieved all of their objectives. Russians had been introduced to civilization; and they at last understood that the 'character of our future activity must be in the highest degree universal and that all the ideas of the separate nationalities of Europe would perhaps find reconciliation and further development in Russian nationality.'[60] Unlike the Slavophiles, who ultimately opposed European to Slavic civilization and advocated withdrawal and internalization, the *pochvenniki* wanted to build on European culture, to revitalize it, and not to retreat into a narrow nationality. 'We know,' Dostoevsky wrote, 'that civilization only brings new elements into our national life, not in the least harming it, *not in the least deflecting it from its normal course,* but, on the contrary, widening our horizon, clarifying our goals and providing us with a new tool for future achievements.'[61]

Once civilization had been savoured and absorbed, educated Russians had come to the realization that further progress necessitated a return to the native soil, to the fundamental sources of the national character, the great reservoir of which was the common people. Without calling on the reserves of strength in the people, the educated would remain suspended in the air of abstraction. Thus the journey into civilization begun by Peter had ended in the return to the concrete reality of the Russian soil.[62]

Before the new life could begin, the reconciliation of the followers of the reforms and the common people was essential. Dostoevsky continued:

Here we are not talking about the Slavophiles or Westernizers. Our era is completely indifferent to their domestic quarrels. We are talking about the reconciliation of civilization with the national principle. We believe that both sides must finally come to an understanding of one another, must clear up all the misunderstandings which have amassed in such incredible numbers between them and then advance in concord, with uncompromisingly combined forces, along a new, broad and glorious path. Union at all costs, in spite of all sacrifices and as quickly as possible – that is our motivating idea, that is our motto.[63]

Ultimately, the *pochvenniki* resolved the conflicts inherent in the metaphor Russia and the West by denying that they existed except in the minds of the 'theoreticians.' They were simply abstractions that had no existence in the concrete reality of Russian life and history or, at most, were temporary aberrations on the surface of the otherwise unruffled inner unanimity of Russian culture and society. The first guiding principle of Russian nationality ⟨fraternity⟩ guaranteed internal social harmony. But by itself, fraternity had, during the Muscovite era, proven incapable of creating a free and full life for the people. Hence the significance of Peter's reforms. For Russians possessed yet another quality ⟨universality⟩ or the capacity to assimilate the collective achievements of the ages and to create a harmonious whole from the conflicting principles of other nationalities. To this universal synthesis, the Russians would add their own principle of fraternity. The Russian experiment, therefore, was an experiment on behalf of humanity and represented the next phase in the development of universal civilization.

The obvious eclecticism of *pochvennichestvo* permitted it considerable flexibility in the formulation of a program. The whole concept of an integrated culture presupposed an amalgam of widely diverse components. But the tendency to borrow extensively from a wide variety of sources also impeded the exposition of a clear and concise statement of beliefs that the reading public could readily assimilate. The vagueness of *Vremia*, which contemporaries noted and criticized, was by no means mitigated by the editors' insistence that only life could determine the course of Russian development. The principles guiding the evolution of a nation could not be known in advance of their revelation in life itself. As Dostoevsky pointed out, a tendency 'is attained through experience, through time and life, and takes shape in direct relationship to the development of society itself. An abstract formula is not always appropriate.'[64] For all their professed commitment to the lessons of experience, however, the assessment of the *pochvenniki* of Russia's potential rested far less on a detailed and accurate evaluation of the forces at work in the past and present than it did on a utopian vision of the future. This vision, which was rooted in the romantic-idealist concepts of national types and national destinies, coloured their view of Russian history and blinded them to the real significance of the events taking place around them.

In spite of its limitations, *pochvennichestvo* nevertheless represented a significant change from Slavophilism. Slavophilism was originally conceived in a still relatively stable social and economic environment. The Slavophiles, as land-owning members of the Russian gentry, were rooted in the modes of traditional life in Russia. They therefore placed their ideals in the past and hoped to recapture it by an act of will. The conservative *intelligenty*, in contrast, had no such links with the past; their future was inextricably bound up with the future of their country. The *pochvenniki* therefore located their ideal in the future. All that was needed was to permit the present to evolve naturally for their ideal to be realized. In the changed circumstances of the Emancipation period, which held at least the promise of a more open social and political life, conservative nationalists required a more dynamic and egalitarian conception of nationality than the early Slavophiles had provided. *Pochvennichestvo* provided such a conception. It furnished conservatives with a coherent doctrine that stressed the organic unit of society and armed them with a weapon against the ideologies of class divisiveness. In a time of dramatic change, the idea that nationality was not a fixed entity but an ideal in the process of becoming enabled conservatives to account for and even welcome change while still preserving the framework of tradition. The evolutionary conservatism set out in *pochvennichestvo* was better adapted to a society experiencing economic and social modernization than were the static conservative forms of an earlier generation.

6

Native Soil and Social
and Political Culture

Intelligentsia conservatism and intelligentsia radicalism in Russia were similar in that both were responses to the ominous advance of modernization in the specific forms it was taking in the most developed nations of western Europe. Both camps feared and vilified the egoism and acquisitiveness and the specialization and mechanism that they identified with Western bourgeois society. Their own political and social objectives were shaped to a marked degree by the characteristics of Western life that they opposed. They directed their efforts to halting the atomization of Russian society and to reinforcing the moral bonds between the individual and the community. At the same time, they wished to preserve the free activity of the integrated personality as the primary creative force in society and culture. The whole endeavour was profoundly humanistic. In their opposition to the spread of liberal bourgeois values in Russia *intelligenty* of the right and left discovered common ground on a significant number of humanitarian social and political aims. The *pochvenniki* shared many of these aims. It is not, therefore, surprising that names and ideas usually associated with the radicals appeared in *Vremia*, or that the journal sided with the radicals on several important issues. With their commitment to the idea of reconciliation, the editors of *Vremia*, especially Dostoevsky, were anxious to forge links among the rival factions in Russian journalism. Such agreement on specific matters, though it initially appeared to foster reconciliation, could not for long conceal the larger philosophical and ideological issues that divided the right and left.

The transitional nature of the Emancipation period was particularly favourable to the *pochvenniki*. It was a time when the gentry uneasily contemplated a future of diminished social and economic status, when the peasantry hovered near the brink of full citizenship, and when the more open society promised by the reforms held out to the intelligentsia previously unheard of opportunities for social and state service. The endemic uncertainty about the direction the reforms were leading enabled the *pochvenniki* to draw believable links between their visionary hopes and the practical, everyday concerns of a society in flux. They were able to project a semblance of realism that eluded them only when the new elements created by the reforms settled down and solidified into new social arrangements. The heyday of *pochvennichestvo* was the fluid era of the early 1860s when everything was yet to be settled.

No blueprint for the future of Russia appeared in *Vremia*. Although there was no lack of hints about what the editors hoped the country would become, much more was said about what it should not become. The *pochvenniki* did, however, suggest concrete ways by which Russians should go about building their future. They also took it upon themselves to criticize and oppose the 'abstract' plans proposed for Russia by the 'theoreticians.' The tactic naturally involved them in all the important debates of their day, and it is from their involvement that their social and political philosophy must be pieced together.

One of the memoirists of the period, a man who had been an ardent supporter of Grigor'ev, recalled that another name sometimes applied to the *pochvenniki* by their contemporaries was the *postepenovtsy* (gradualists).[1] The name was appropriate because it signified the conviction of the *pochvenniki* that a sudden and rapid transformation of the life of the country would inevitably lead to the eradication of everything that was quintessentially Russian. They believed, on the contrary, that the national ideal needed scope to unfold naturally, step by step along an unhurried and normal path. ' Every society,' Dostoevsky wrote, 'can accommodate only the level of progress to which it has developed and which it has begun to understand.'[2] As the Emancipation reforms went forward, the ideal, which was gradually attaining consciousness in the collective mind of society, would progressively find more perfect embodiment in the concrete forms of the social and political organization of the country, thus slowly closing the gap between the ideal and the real.

The *pochvenniki* did not oppose change. Progress and life, they avowed, were preferable to stagnation and sleep. But revolutionary change was anathema to them because it imposed ideas and institutions on a society unprepared to receive them. Revolutions invariably destroyed more than their results justified.[3] They found in unreasoning opposition to legitimate change one of the principal sources of revolution. As a living organism, society generated within itself the forces necessary for its own measured transformation. To thwart this evolution was to court the catastrophe of revolution. 'Therefore, God grant,' Dostoevsky implored, 'that this force be given some legal and normal outlet.'[4] The safe course of politics lay somewhere in the vast expanse between reaction and revolution.

Contemporaries were understandably confused about the political complexion of *Vremia*. On many issues, it took its place in the camp of the progressive journals. Apart from its enthusiasm for the changes being brought about by the autocracy, a fact which in the circumstances of the times betrayed little about its political coloration, *Vremia* embraced an impressive list of progressive causes. It advocated the abolition of corporal punishment, agitated for sweeping hospital and prison reform, and recommended that Jews be granted the full rights of citizens. The editors entered a lively debate with the conservative journals *Russkii vestnik* and *Vek* over the woman question and joined the radical organs *Sovremennik* and *Russkoe slovo* on the side of female emancipation. During the demonstrations at St Petersburg University in 1861, *Vremia* supported the protestors, and a beef dinner complete with wine was sent from the editorial offices to some of the students imprisoned by the authorities. In the summer of 1862, when St Petersburg was swept by an epidemic of fires, the journal undertook a stout defence of the nihilists against official and semi-official charges that they had turned to arson.[5]

Dostoevsky genuinely believed that *pochvennichestvo* was a progressive force. When in October 1862, Nekrasov, the editor of *Sovremennik*, declined to make further literary contributions to *Vremia* because he feared to compromise himself in the eyes of his radical supporters, Dostoevsky was stunned and sent off the agonized reply: 'Is our journal really retrograde ... ? But I am convinced that the public does not consider us to be retrograde.'[6] Yet Nekrasov's reluctance was understandable. In spite of a wide area of agreement on specific issues, stemming from a shared humanitarianism, the *pochvenniki* and the nihilists were poles apart in their analysis of the contemporary Russian scene and the needs of state and society. As the discussion about the Emancipation reforms dragged on, the differences between the two sides became more pronounced.

The reading public was not deterred from subscribing to *Vremia*, whatever it may have thought of its tendency. In 1863 the police compiled the circulation statistics of the major journals. The number of subscribers to *Vremia* was set at 4,000, a figure roughly corresponding to Dostoevsky's own account of 4,200. *Sovremennik* and *Russkoe slovo* were assigned 7,000 and 4,000 subscribers respectively and Katkov's *Russkii vestnik* 5,700. Although the police attributed some 7,750 postal subscribers to the Slavophile journal *Den'*, the editor, I.S. Aksakov, privately estimated that *Den'* had 3,500 subscribers from October 1861 to October 1862 and only 2,500 in the next subscription year.[7] In comparison to its rivals, therefore, *Vremia* enjoyed a more than respectable following. Much of its appeal lay no doubt in Dostoevsky's own literary contributions. Both the *Notes from the House of the Dead* and the *Insulted and Injured* were serialized in *Vremia*. But only two years later, in 1864, even the intriguing *Notes from the Underground* failed to bolster either the appeal or the subscription list of *Epokha*, the successor to *Vremia*. There can, therefore, be little doubt that the journal was read for its program; it probably exercised considerable influence on its readers.

Pochvennichestvo was in part a product of the enthusiasm generated among the intelligentsia by the abolition of serfdom. For the *pochvenniki*, Emancipation represented an event greater than the reforms of Peter the Great and was equivalent in significance to the conversion of Russians to Christianity.[8] The end of serfdom signalled the beginning of the gradual unification of the nation into a self-conscious, harmonious, and organic whole and made possible the moral rebirth of Russian man on a higher plane of integrated national consciousness. Peter's reforms and Emancipation represented two facets of the same process. The *pochvenniki* believed, as has been seen, that the reforms liberated the service class from the narrow ideal of Muscovy and placed it in the mainstream of Western civilization. Having mastered Western ideals and Western knowledge, the educated had recognized the inadequacy of those ideals not only for Russia but also for civilization itself. They experienced a profound need to admit their 'Russianness,' to return to the roots of Russian organic life and seek there the key to the future advancement of humanity.

The educated had, however, exhausted their spiritual reserves in attaining their present level of consciousness; they were impotent to go forward without unleashing and tapping the native resources still slumbering in the unconscious mind of the common people. At this critical juncture, the young tsar destroyed serfdom, which had posed the last political obstacle to the peaceful union of the educated and the people. With his act, he released the national principle of fraternity, which was best exemplified in the institutions of peasant association. The reconciliation of the educated with the national principle and the transformation of the peasants into citizens, as well as their introduction to civilization, would henceforth proceed together.[9] Neither side need relinquish the ideals that formerly had guided it. The end of the process was the 'merging of the principles of education and their representatives with the national principle and the participation of the whole of our great Russian people in all the events of our current life.'[10]

The *pochvenniki* did not view class rivalry as an obstacle to concord within Russian society. They believed that in Russia there was no class stratification in the Western sense. The position of the individual on the social scale was defined instead by his educational level and general moral qualities.[11] Russian nationality transcended class interests and hostilities. Dostoevsky wrote: 'Let us grant that we have rather well-defined social strata. But in all of our strata there are many more points of unity than of disunity, and that is the essential. It is the guarantee of our universal peace, tranquillity, brotherly love, and prosperity. Every Russian is first of all a Russian and after that he belongs to a class.'[12]

Besides facilitating the reconciliation of the educated and uneducated, Emancipation had cleared the way for the intellectual and moral development of the people. 'Our new *Rus*',' Dostoevsky proclaimed, 'understands that there is only one cement, one link, one soil on which everything will come together and be reconciled – that is universal, spiritual reconciliation, the source of which lies in education (*obrazovanie*).'[13]

Like *Svetoch*, *Vremia* championed education as the solution to most of Russia's problems. There was in the attitude of the *pochvenniki* towards the lower classes a hint of repentance and of debt to the people, characteristic of the intelligentsia in the 1860s and 1870s. As the most advanced segment of the population, the educated were obligated to take the initiative in going to the people and educating them. The responsibility for the ignorance of the common people rested squarely on the educated who had failed in the past to plead for their development.[14] But the educated had a better reason than guilt for helping the masses to overcome their ignorance. They, themselves, could advance no further without the resources of the people behind them. The instrument for the release of these resources was education. The educated had everything to gain by the enlightenment of their ignorant brothers because the 'spread of education in an intensified form and as soon as possible is the main task of our time, the first step to any activity.'[15]

The gradualist and humanistic approach of *Vremia* to social change was typified in its attitude to education. The first step towards universal education was, in its view, literacy (*gramotnost*'): 'For our part we are completely convinced that literacy will improve the people morally and give them a sense of their own worth which in its turn will eliminate many abuses and disruptions, will eliminate even their possibility.'[16] Apart from the moral maturity with which only education could endow the people, the dissemination of enlightenment also held the key to economic and social progress in Russia. In October 1862, a paean of praise to the salutary effects of education appeared in the home affairs section of the journal:

The question of the level of the moral development of a particular segment of the public leads directly to the question of education, of enlightenment, of intellectual development. We must now take decisive action to advance education. This is essential for economic reasons as well. Our interest, quite apart from our worth as human beings, demands it. The transformation of the judicial sector requires lawyers in enormous quantity; agriculture has been so placed by the force of circumstances that it must take a new, national direction ... ; in various mills and factories there is an extreme need for chemists, technologists, mechanics and mineralogists; the universal shortcomings of the roads require engineers; finally the spirit of the times demands honest and morally developed citizens, and who can control the spirit of the times? Let no one even try: it cannot be controlled.[17]

In the eyes of the *pochvenniki*, the function of education was to develop the moral independence of the individual fully. They were especially critical of the Slavophile view that education should aim at subsuming the individual personality in the immutable values of the community. Grigor'ev complained as early as 1858 that the 'idea of the annihilation of the individual in the communalism of our Russian soul is precisely the weak side of Slavophilism.'[18] *Vremia*'s defence of the autonomous personality was consistent with the understanding of the *pochvenniki* of nationality. Since nationality was not a static entity but an evolutionary process involving the whole nation, the national ideal could achieve its complete expression only when every member of the nation contributed to it. Only education could release the full moral potential of each individual. With the establishment of complete moral equality through education, there would remain in Russia neither classes, nor rich and poor, but only citizens. This was, for the *pochvenniki*, the true meaning of democracy: a society of educated moral equals, individually motivated by a common national purpose. Grigor'ev captured the essence of the idea, especially its apolitical character, when he wrote to Strakhov in 1861 that he was neither a conservative nor a revolutionary but wished only to be a citizen.[19]

In nationality the *pochvenniki* discerned a bulwark against the devaluation of moral and cultural standards threatened by mass democracy. 'The idea of nationality (*natsional'nost'*),' Dostoevsky wrote, 'is a new form of democracy.'[20]

The *pochvenniki* neither doubted the eagerness or capacity of the peasant to learn, nor feared that civilization would be degraded or diluted by exposure to him.[21] Like the Slavophiles, they believed that although science (*nauka*) was general and its laws were universally applicable, its forms were always national.[22] Science, according to the *pochvenniki*, had so far been imitative in Russia because learning had not yet been integrated into the national principle. The reconciliation of the educated with the people would result not in the destruction of science in Russia, as some of the critics feared, but in its flowering. The people were not merely to accept civilization passively but were to judge it, to discard whatever was false in it, and to invest its useful and true products with a new legitimacy and purpose. In so doing they would not only revitalize civilization but also give new life to the exhausted intellectual world of western Europe.[23]

Since the *pochvenniki* attached so much importance to education, it was to be expected that they would have a great deal to say about how it should be conducted. In this area, at least, they were modernists. They rejected outright the traditional Russian school system which, they argued, suppressed individuality by forcing students into a common mould and subjecting them to preconceived rules of action. Under the existing régime, they pointed out, a student was taught to live life exactly as his father had lived it. The school authorities regarded innovation with suspicion and even horror.[24] Church schools were not spared either. Although the *pochvenniki* agreed, despite reservations about the morals of the Russian clergy, that the spiritual upbringing (*vospitanie*) of the people was the responsibility of the church, they emphatically denied that literacy and, more broadly, education (*obrazovanie*) were also the exclusive province of the clergy. Freedom of conscience in Russia was to them too precious to be squandered by the establishment of a clerical monopoly on education.

If the *pochvenniki* repudiated the traditionalist modes of education they were equally critical of the more up-to-date utilitarian approach. The utilitarians, in their view, did not require a student to develop the human side of his character but only asked of him that he grow up a practical person performing a task useful to society. Such functionalism in education, in the opinion of the *pochvenniki*, stunted the natural human development of the student. It also hindered progress because what was considered useful for the future was always defined in terms of the present needs of society. The circumstances of life altered too rapidly, however, to make such prediction practicable.[25]

The *pochvenniki* discovered their ideal of education in Lev Tolstoy's pedagogical journal, *Iasnaia-Poliana*, which Tolstoy published briefly in the early 1860s. Tolstoy's articles were reviewed enthusiastically in *Vremia* and his ideas were adopted by the journal as its own. Tolstoy's philosophy of education was based on the idea of the removal of all constraint on the student. Since every human being naturally sought knowledge, Tolstoy argued, no external motivation was required. It was only necessary to provide the facilities needed for learning and to permit the student the time and liberty to develop his unique abilities. Creativity and imagination were not to be curbed but, on the contrary, encouraged to flower. Only in an atmosphere of complete educational freedom would the people be able to select a curriculum entirely natural to it.[26] It was for this reason that the *pochvenniki* opposed a major reform in the curriculum of the universities, which was being debated at the time, as premature. Only when a fully national curriculum had been worked out on the initiative of the people, at the lower levels of the educational structure, they believed, should the form and content of university education adjust itself accordingly.[27] Given their views on the importance of personality in the making of nationality, it is understandable that they embraced an educational philosophy based on individualism and freedom.

Of more immediate concern than the education of children was the question of literacy for the adult peasantry. For this purpose, the *pochvenniki* regarded the newly founded Sunday schools as particularly effective. The Sunday schools were established by young intellectuals and social activists, as well as by some of the more progressive members of the gentry, to teach reading, writing, and arithmetic to any peasants willing to devote part of their free time to learning.[28] Dostoevsky was impressed by the large number of peasants who attended the schools. He interpreted their dedication as a sign of the innate instinct of the peasant for truth and his respect for learning and looked forward to the day when the Sunday schools extended to every corner of the nation.[29]

Since literacy was the primary element of education, the *pochvenniki* were anxious to attract the peasants to reading. They were not alone in their concern. Popular education became a vogue after Emancipation, and books for the masses were rushed into circulation. Dostoevsky disapproved of most of the new textbooks for popular reading. In their crude efforts to teach the peasants the rudiments of civilized behaviour, these works, in his estimation, succeeded only in patronizing their readers. Their authors treated adult peasants like small children with vacant minds. The textbooks contained not what the peasants wanted to know but what their educated benefactors supposed they should know. Dostoevsky believed that education should be linked to the soil and to life and not to the latest, Western pedagogical theory. He deemed special readers for the peasants to be useless. The peasant, who was quick to realize that he was being treated as an object for moral improvement, was almost certain to reject the readers in order to preserve his autonomy and dignity. All that was required was to give the peasants good books that interested them. Once the taste for reading was acquired, more concentrated teaching methods would be feasible. Love for the people, Dostoevsky concluded, if manifested in a spirit of guardianship and not in an exchange of ideas in mutual respect, would not be reciprocated. Each side had to learn from the other before their final reconciliation was possible.[30]

The intense humanism of the *pochvenniki* was never so evident as in the means they proposed to effect social change in Russia. They advocated neither severe social constraint nor revolutionary licence. Rather, they placed their faith in the individual, in the moral worth of the autonomous personality. In their view, social cohesiveness and historical continuity were the products of the free creativity of individuals, standing in an organic relationship to their own time and place. It was the individual who, breathing the air around him, to use Grigor'ev's metaphor, created the values of society, and not society that imposed its conventional values on the individual. Here was the essence, for the *pochvenniki*, of moral progress and so, too, of nationality. For nationality (*natsional'nost'*) was the reflection in art, social attitudes, and political and social institutions of the conscious moral level of a nation at a given time.

Dostoevsky's humanism was a strange amalgam of that abstract, but deeply felt, humanitarianism of his youthful period of utopian socialism and the almost irrational, but very real, love he felt towards his ignorant tormentors in prison. It reached out not abstractly to the aggregate but concretely to real persons. Grigor'ev, who in poverty and dissipation had plumbed the lower depths of St Petersburg life, was no less sensitive to his own humanism. In 1861 he wrote to Strakhov, 'But you know I am really creating a whole world for myself, a world in which I live as a kind of prophet and champion of humanism.'[31] And it was as the champions of humanism that the *pochvenniki* turned to questions of society and politics.

The political theory of Slavophilism was indelibly imprinted on *pochvennichestvo*. In a letter to Strakhov in 1861, Grigor'ev stated: 'In my politics, as you know, I was and remain a Slavophile. The *narod*, the *zemskii sobor* ... that is what I believe in.'[32] The foundation of Slavophile politics was the sharp distinction between the state (*vlast'*), or the sphere of politics, and the land (*zemlia*), or the sphere of society. The Slavophiles regarded political authority as a necessary evil which guaranteed the nation from external force and threats. At most, the state was an outward symbol of the inner unity of the nation. The proper activity of the land was with internal order and moral perfection. Relations between the state and the land were governed by independence, respect, and mutual non-intervention. The land represented the sphere of public opinion embodied in a *zemskii sobor*, which the state was morally, but not legally, obligated to consult. Since the Slavophiles considered the participation of the land in the exercise of political power to be an evil, they rejected any form of constitutional or representative government. The best form of government, they believed, was hereditary and unlimited monarchy. Although the land was protected neither by constitutional nor legal guarantees against tyranny, the right to interfere in the independent life of the land was not among the prerogatives of the autocrat.[33]

Given the clear separation of state and society, of the political sphere and the moral sphere, that the Slavophiles envisaged, it was quite possible to see no contradiction between autocracy on the one hand and the most sweeping social and humanitarian progressivism on the other. The *pochvenniki* at least evidently failed to see any incompatibility. The state remained, for them, a constant, the symbol of external order and unity, whereas the land, in their view, continued to grow organically in the form of an autonomous and increasingly more perfect moral and social order. Consequently, they set politics aside and turned to the ethical restructuring of society.

The integrity of society, the *pochvenniki* believed, lay in its capacity to control its own fate. Society had to take responsibility not only for its own administration but also for its moral self-improvement. During the debate on education the *pochvenniki* consistently opposed state control of the schools. The schooling of the people was the duty of society and not of the state. The forceful intervention of the state in education, or in any other sphere of social competency, served only to undermine the moral commitment of the society.[34] The extension of bureaucratic authority into local affairs, which had reached its zenith during the reign of Nicholas I, was detestable to them for the same reason.

The *pochvenniki* did not suppose that society could manage its own affairs spontaneously; it required institutions for discussion and control.

The commune, which was the traditional body of peasant self-adminstra-tion, was the institutional embodiment of the Russian principle of fraternity and best met the real spiritual and material needs of Russians: 'The free commune has from time immemorial been the Russian people's preferred form of community, and its restoration in its original guise will not in practice be a difficult or unrealizable task.'[35] Freed by Emancipation from bureaucratic controls and the interference of the former serf-owners, the commune could resume its traditional role in local self-government and re-establish the spontaneous, free, and fraternal relations that had distinguished Russian life in earlier times.

If the *pochvenniki* looked backward to Russian tradition for one institution of social control, they looked forward for another to the newly planned district councils or *zemstva*, which came into existence only in 1864. They maintained that the *zemstvo* should be democratically elected and operate completely free of bureaucratic interference. Local officials, too, should be elected by unrestricted universal suffrage, since elected officials enjoyed a goodwill and authority generally denied to state appointees.[36] Dostoevsky and his supporters were well aware that Emancipation had abolished serfdom only legally. Psychologically its effects and the habits instilled by centuries of bureaucratic caprice would linger on in society for many years. Nevertheless, they were confident that the full participation of the peasantry in local administration as well as in such prerogatives of the citizen as jury duty would in time overcome the ill effects of landlord and bureaucratic tyranny.

The separation of the commune and the *zemstvo* from the central state authority served, in the opinion of the *pochvenniki*, not only to guarantee the independence of society but also to preserve local diversity. The idea of localism (*mestnost'*) was particularly dear to Grigor'ev who, as has been seen, had waged a struggle against the subordination of the life of the regions to the centralized Moscow ideal of the Slavophiles since the beginning of his career. Grigor'ev's localism was a reflection of the romantic's love for colour and diversity and was dictated more by aesthetic than by political considerations. Grigor'ev directed his arguments both against S.M. Solov'ev and the statist school of history and against the Slavophiles whom he suspected of wishing to turn all Russia into Moscow. For some time, he was able to carry the rest of the *pochvenniki* with him. When in 1861 A.P. Shchapov, the Siberian historian of the *Raskol*, developed his conception of regionalism (*oblastnost'*), Grigor'ev, ever on the lookout for allies, insisted that *Vremia* open its pages to him. Shchapov argued that the history of Russia was not one of a central idea or

MOSCOW
VS.
REGIONS

region, but one of a wide variety of local groups. He interpreted the schism as a democratic defence of the 'lands' or regions against Muscovite centralization.[37] Dostoevsky appears to have been intrigued by the idea, and several other articles which viewed the *Raskol* as the rejection by the common people of Muscovite life were printed.[38] Grigor'ev also admired the works of the Ukrainian historian N.I. Kostomarov, who asserted the existence of a separate Ukrainian cultural-historical tradition.[39]

Traces of Grigor'ev's localism lingered on in *Vremia* and in its successor, *Epokha*. But Dostoevsky gradually grew suspicious of regionalism, which he feared would culminate in separatism. As the Polish crisis deepened in 1862 and 1863, his dislike of Kostomarov and other advocates of regional diversity increased, and articles defending local diversity appeared less frequently in his journals.

The political theory of *pochvennichestvo* was most succinctly encapsulated by Strakhov. In his memoirs of Dostoevsky he wrote of the *pochvenniki*:

In the practical field, we stopped at *pure liberalism*, that is, at that doctrine which least of all agrees with the idea of forcible upheaval and, if it insists on any changes in the social order, seeks to secure these changes by means of conviction and persuasion only. Pure liberalism, as is known, is the faith that the absence of compulsory measures leads to the best results in social authority, that under these conditions the interests of all are more correctly understood and mutually balanced. In a word, it is those principles which the advocates of freedom of thought, freedom of speech, freedom of trade, etc. support, principles which, it is obvious, may far from attain their objectives but which must be supported in the majority of cases where there are no clear foundations for other forms of action. Therefore, the liberal message is feasible and useful under any form of government although it does not provide a complete and defined theory of society. Other principles, which have greater force and urgency, should rule over these [liberal] principles.[40]

Strakhov's conception of liberalism represented the extreme application of the idea of laissez-faire to social development. The *pochvenniki* viewed life as a process of the free realization of ideals. Their rejection of state intervention to preserve or revolutionary compulsion to transform society reflected their desire to secure the individual and society from the interference of reactionary authoritarian governments on the one hand and the ravages of revolutionary theory and practice on the other. Since they believed that legitimate progress resulted from the unimpeded unfolding of the national ideal in the consciousness of the people, publicity (*glasnost*'), by which they meant freedom of speech, of the press, and of conscience, was essential.[41]

The 'pure liberalism' of the *pochvenniki* was far removed from liberalism as it was generally understood in the nineteenth century. The *pochvenniki* were harsh critics of Russia's own liberals whom they accused of trying to impose alien, Western forms of government on the Russian people. Dostoevsky once observed in his notebooks: 'We have always hated the vulgar liberal because he leads nowhere.'[42] Russian liberalism in the 1860s was, in fact, a model of moderation. Early Russian liberals such as B.N. Chicherin, K.D. Kavelin, and E.F. Korsh were endowed with a lively sense of the organic nature of political development. They believed that Russia was not yet ready for a constitutional order but looked forward to the day when a truly Russian form of constitutionalism, based on the historical traditions of the nation, would emerge. They hoped at best to lay the foundations for liberal constitutionalism in Russia. To this end, they advocated the creation of a corporate social structure and the gradual establishment of the rule of law. In particular, they opposed the communal system of land tenure, which hindered the growth of private property. Even on this point, however, their position was moderate. Kavelin wrote to Herzen in 1862 that he personally was opposed to private property as an exclusive form of landholding and preferred to see communal and private property coexist in Russia. He went on, however, to say that the 'absence of private property, its abolition, is the greatest nonsense, the truest path to Orientalism and to the sacrifice of the principle of individuality and freedom.'[43]

Chicherin led the liberal attack on the peasant commune. He contended that the commune was not an ancient institution as the Slavophiles maintained but an innovation introduced by Peter the Great for administrative and fiscal reasons. The implication was that since the state had brought the commune into existence it had every right to abolish it and replace it by a system of small, private landholding. And since the commune was a relatively recent creation, it could be dispensed with without fear of violating Russian tradition.

The *pochvenniki* opposed the liberals on every point. The major failing of liberalism, according to the *pochvenniki*, was its tendency to confuse the sphere of the land with the sphere of the state. The liberals held that society had a political as well as a moral nature. The *pochvenniki*, like the Slavophiles, were convinced, on the contrary, that the Russian character was profoundly apolitical. The involvement of society in political affairs through the introduction of constitutionalism violated the very nature of Russians and deflected society from its proper ethical goals.

Since the *pochvenniki* regarded society as a voluntary moral union, they LAW
rejected the liberal conception of law as the basis of social relations.
Reconciliation, for the *pochvenniki*, constituted a moral revolution, the
voluntary rejection of class prejudices and egoism and the intermingling
of the social strata on the basis of the innate capacity of Russians for
brotherhood. A regulatory society was the antithesis of their conception.
The intrusion of law into social relations resulted, in their view, in the
mechanical organization of society which was characteristic of the
bourgeois West. Such a society deprived social life of its dynamism
because change could no longer be incorporated without first breaking
down the rigid forms that legalism imposed on the political and social
organisms.[44] Law was for the *pochvenniki*, as for the Slavophiles, merely
custom, the formal expression of traditional social arrangements, which
had no autonomous status or validity but was subordinate to morality.
Correct civil relations were, therefore, the result not of correct laws but of
correct human relations.[45]

The *pochvenniki* found a working example of their conception of law COURTS
and the courts in the arbitration courts set up after the Emancipation edict
to mediate disputes between landlords and peasants over the allocation of
the land and the conditions of sale. The courts were composed of
members of the contending sides themselves. Their decisions were not
binding but depended on the mutual goodwill of the parties involved.
The *pochvenniki* maintained that such courts set a precedent for voluntary
agreements between former lords and serfs, helped to advance class
co-operation and trust, and familiarized the peasants with the finer points
of civil affairs.[46]

The *pochvenniki* opposed a legal order also because it threatened to CORPORATE
legitimize the very class structure that they hoped to overcome. Wherever ORDER
they encountered it, the *pochvenniki* repudiated the corporate mode of
social organization. During the debate about the future of the universities
in Russia in the early 1860s, Kavelin and Chicherin advocated turning the
universities into corporate bodies. Dostoevsky strongly opposed such a
scheme on the grounds that it would set the universities apart from the
people. 'The corporate mode of life,' he argued, sounding for all the
world like Rousseau, 'always leads to the diminution and suffocation of
life. In every corporation there is a particular sphere of honoured ideas
and accepted points of view on subjects. In such a milieu, the individual
has difficulty in preserving himself intact: he is despotically required to
look out for corporate interests only because chance has thrown him into a
corporation.'[47]

Opposition to the corporate ordering of society brought the *pochvenniki*

gENTRY

also into the debate over the future of the Russian gentry. Deprived at least in part by the Emancipation reforms of their economic and social privileges, many members of the gentry began to search for a new, distinctive role to play. The most extreme expression of gentry unrest originated in Tver where the local assembly of the nobility petitioned the tsar for a kind of gentry constitutionalism. The government squelched the movement by exiling the petitioners to their estates. But the idea of a special place for the gentry died hard. For a time in the early 1860s, M.N. Katkov, editor of the *Russkii vestnik*, advocated special rights and functions for the Russian gentry akin to those enjoyed by the English gentry. Chicherin and Kavelin, too, considered it essential that the gentry consolidate and expand its corporate structure. In the absence of a strong middle class, the guarantee of legal rights to the gentry, in Chicherin's view, was a necessary prerequisite for the preservation and extension of a legal order in Russia.

To the proponents of a separate status for the gentry, the *pochvenniki* replied that there was no foundation for a distinct gentry class either in Russia's present condition or in its history. The gentry did not now and never had enjoyed rights exclusively its own except the right to own serfs, a right that the Emancipation had swept away.[48] To Chicherin's argument that the gentry had, since receiving corporate status in the reign of Catherine the Great, acquired the habit of legal authority, the *pochvenniki* retorted that it had, in fact, learned only the taste for personal authority that rested not on law but on caprice.[49] The entire history of Russia had militated against the formation of separate estates in the Western sense. And there was no need to create artificially a separate gentry class that would serve only to stratify society and render it immobile.

As there was no basis, either historical or legal, for the separate existence of the gentry class, and as its creation from nothing would endanger the integrity of the social fabric, the *pochvenniki* maintained that the gentry should cease to think of itself as an independent caste with rights and privileges distinct from those of other Russian citizens.[50] Reconciliation meant the complete obliteration of class lines: 'There is no hidden meaning in our words about union. One must understand them literally, yes literally, and we are still sure that we have expressed ourselves clearly. We have said frankly and we say again that it is necessary to unite fully with the people morally and as closely as possible; that it is necessary to merge with them completely and to become as one with them morally.'[51]

Dostoevsky's protestations notwithstanding it is not clear exactly what the union of the gentry with the people entailed. The *pochvenniki* believed communalism, as the social expression of Russian fraternity, to be the mode of existence most natural to Russians. They objected also to the patriarchal nature of Slavophilism, which was intended, in their view, to preserve a distinction, though not one of privilege, between the gentry and the peasantry. It is not obvious, however, that moral union with the people meant for them the communalization of all property. There is even some suggestion that they expected a sphere of private property to continue in their new ideal order.

It is clear that the *pochvenniki* required that separate gentry institutions be merged with the *zemstva*. The gentry was to enjoy neither legal nor institutional distinctions. It could, however, for some time exercise a special moral influence, not as a class but as a group of individuals. As the group most favoured in the past, the gentry was morally obligated to take the initiative in breaking down class barriers, to further the education of the masses, and, most importantly, to reject the arrogance of learning. 'As the educated part of the *zemstvo*,' Dostoevsky wrote, 'the gentry will stand at the head of the people, not in the capacity of an unacknowledged estate but as the acknowledged *best men*, the people's elders (*narodnye startsy*).'[52]

The idea of the gentry as the 'best men' was a powerful one for Dostoevsky. Later it reappeared in 1876 in his novel *A Raw Youth*. The main character, Versilov, repeats Dostoevsky's idea from more than ten years before:

Our gentry, having lost its rights, could now regain the highest estate in the guise of the preserver of honour, light, science and the highest idea, and, here is the main point, not shutting itself up as a separate caste, which would be the death of the idea. On the contrary, the gates to the estate were opened a long time ago; now the time has come to open them completely. Let any feat of honour, science and valor among us give anyone the right to join this high rank of people. In this way, the estate will of itself turn into a meeting of the best men only ... and not a privileged caste.[53]

What Dostoevsky had in mind was a moral order, composed of men of intellectual distinction and special virtue from all backgrounds. They would represent the most advanced and most self-conscious segment of society and the most complete expression of nationality at its latest stage of development.

The *pochvenniki* were warm advocates of the autocratic ideal. Autocracy, they believed, best answered the real needs of the national character

AUTOCRACY and guaranteed the separation of state and society. They did not, however, accept the bureaucratic form autocracy had taken in Russia during the reign of Nicholas I. The strength of the autocracy, in their view, rested neither on the bureaucracy nor on the gentry but on the peasants, who constituted the only truly conservative force in the nation.[54] The direct union of the tsar with the whole of the people, united in the name of the Russian ideal, represented to the *pochvenniki* a bulwark against revolution. The autocracy, consequently, should seek to become more national by sinking its roots in the people and its traditions. A government based on an abstract idea was inevitably non-national, whereas a 'living, organic state is always national.'[55]

The conservatism of *pochvennichestvo* by no means forced its advocates into a static mould. In an interesting article that first appeared in *Nachala* in 1899, P.B. Struve suggested that Russian conservatism of the nineteenth century was divided into two camps. He differentiated the idealistic and mystical conservative romantic, who demanded the full realization of his cultural-social ideal in life, from the realistic conservative formalist, who conceived of life in its particulars and tried to work from its practical data. Struve placed the Slavophiles in the first category and Katkov in the second.[56] The *pochvenniki*, too, belonged in the first camp. They were guided by the belief that the proper way to 'conserve' the national essence was to remove all obstacles to its free and natural development. Dostoevsky's assertion, therefore, that the *pochvenniki* believed in the fullest possible development for what already existed was an expression of what Grigor'ev called 'conservatism in the best possible sense.' Dostoevsky himself deplored that conservatism which ignored the CONSERVATISM pressing demands of life, blindly adhered to outmoded forms, and defended injustice in society simply because it was old. Such conservatism only hastened social disintegration and fostered revolutionary discontent. In March 1862 he defined true conservatism as fidelity to the spirit of the nation: 'The state needs the kind of conservatism which is based on national traditions, which defends everything reasonable in the past – the spirit of the people and its interest, which examines and criticizes every new need in social life. This conservatism will be a truly conserving force.'[57] True conservatism for the *pochvenniki* was the perfect balance between change and continuity. Change was inevitable and desirable but was legitimate only when it took place within the constraints of tradition.

The economic expression of Russian fraternity, the *pochvenniki* maintained, was associationism. The common people had preserved the principle of association in the commune and *artel'*, but were themselves unable to build a viable economic or social system on it. Such a system would emerge only when the educated classes infused the forms of association with knowledge and the highest goals.[58] Here in the most practical terms was what Dostoevsky meant by the reconciliation of civilization with the national principles. The result of the union would be the flowering of Russian science and technology, the establishment of an individualistic, yet equal and federated, society, and the relative prosperity of all. Here also was the justification for the idealism of *pochvenni-chestvo*. If the real spiritual needs of Russians were first met and their traditions honoured, their material well-being was also assured.

The spirit of anti-capitalism was common to both socialists and conservatives in Russia in the second half of the nineteenth century. Often in the case of conservatives, Grigor'ev and Konstantin Leont'ev are good examples, anti-capitalism was sponsored by an aesthetic impulse, a revulsion for *poshlost'*, an untranslatable word that conveys banality, vulgarity, coarseness, drabness, and monotony with overtones of corruption and decay. Russian conservative romantics despised capitalism as much for its bourgeois values and life-style as for the suffering it visited on the working man in the West. Most of the *pochvenniki* shared this impulse, and a number of articles were published in *Vremia* which deplored the egoism and narrowness of the bourgeois ideal.[59]

The antipathy felt by the *pochvenniki* for capitalism arose from the conviction that not only capitalism but also the socialism which, in their view, it inevitably spawned were based on mechanistic, exploitative principles that were antithetical to the organic principles governing Russian life. This attitude derived less from their perfunctory acquaintance with the West and its ways than from a study of Western socialist writings. Although the *pochvenniki* were certain that some socialists had correctly analysed the roots of the Western malaise and had recognized the need for association in their social organization, they were inherently incapable of realizing it except in a mechanistic and theoretical way.

The *pochvenniki* were particularly attracted by the individualist libertarianism of P.-J. Proudhon. His 'philosophy of misery' served as the apologia, at least in part, for their own economic analysis. Their sympathy for Proudhon was not unnatural. He was an idealist, though an atheist, who spurned idle dreams of untold wealth in an earthly paradise and advocated an ethic of work and moderation. He emphasized the need for spontaneity in social organization, a view that accorded well with Dostoevsky's faith that Russian social life would evolve naturally and immediately from its own internal sources.[60] In his *La Guerre et la paix*, Proudhon argued that man's destiny on earth was purely spiritual and moral. Men were condemned to daily labour but also to perpetual poverty since their labour could never do more than satisfy their needs. But man, trapped by his idealism and seduced by tantalizing wealth, refused to recognize the law of poverty, and his efforts to overcome it ended in gross inequality, wars, and revolutions.[61] It was imperative that men seek their glory elsewhere than in the satisfaction provided by the accumulation of luxuries. 'Work, sobriety and moderation; the liberation of the feelings and of the ideal: this is our law.'[62]

A lengthy review of *La Guerre et la paix* by P. Bibikov appeared in *Vremia* in December 1861 and a translation of part of Proudhon's *Théorie de l'impôt* in January 1862. Most of the political review section for October 1861 was devoted to an exposition of Proudhon's ideas and their application to Russia.[63] Man, the anonymous commentator began, was fated to work. But the majority of men produced only enough to satisfy their barest physical and spiritual needs. The experience of the industrial nations, where increased labour resulted in ever-growing poverty, proved that poverty was a law of nature. It was characteristic of man to work no more than he need to meet his wants. This, the commentator hastily added, did not imply that Russia need not increase the amount of its labour. As the moral level of individuals increased so did their fundamental physical needs. Thus the Englishman, who was more advanced than his Russian counterpart, needed money for newspapers and books whereas the Russian felt no equivalent need. An increase in the amount of labour was indispensable not only for the moral well-being of the people, but also for the security and standing of Russia internationally. The author drew a distinction already made by Proudhon between poverty (*bednost'*), which was natural, and destitution (*nishcheta*), which was unnatural and destructive. Russians should not be charmed by the allure of wealth but devote themselves to quiet industry and voluntarily submit to the law of poverty. 'If humanity could live in such tranquil poverty, then perfect order would reign on earth. There would be no vices, no crimes, people would comprise a society of sages. But now this cannot be and never will be because of the infraction of the two great laws, poverty and moderation.'[64] The inevitable result of transgressing these laws was war, revolution, and destitution. The lesson for Russia was that the proper end of man was spiritual satisfaction and not material prosperity.

COMMUNE

The best instrument for the equitable distribution of the products of labour, according to the *pochvenniki*, was the Russian commune. Since in the commune every peasant possessed a plot of land, he was secured against the pauperization that had overtaken the proletariat in the industrialized nations of western Europe. The commune was not to remain in its backward condition. The *pochvenniki* advocated the application of the latest scientific advances to agricultural production in order to increase the overall productivity of the land and supplement the meagre share of each individual. Like the populists of the next decade, they did not believe that capitalism was the indispensable vehicle of scientific and technical progress. They understood, of course, that the gentry was in a better position to take advantage of science in agriculture, but the *pochvenniki* did not despair of its eventual extension to the communal lands.[65]

In spite of their hostility to capitalism, the *pochvenniki* wished to encourage the industrialization of Russia:

> Without industry which changes the condition and form of raw materials and adapts them to the satisfaction of various needs, without industry which meets all the most important demands, the country will always be purely agricultural and will forever remain poor, and consequently, ignorant. These two qualities, gradually enforcing one another, will eventually reduce the country to a state of sheer savagery in comparison with the progress which in the meantime will inevitably be made by other, more naturally developed countries.[66]

This attitude reflected, in part, the fear of the realist that without industry Russia could not survive the pressures of the modern world and would be reduced to a colony of Europe. In keeping with their emphasis on roots, the *pochvenniki* were drawn to the historical school of German political economy, the chief contemporary exponent of which was Bruno Hilde-brand. Hildebrand argued basically that the economic organization of a nation could not be divorced from its historical origins or rationalized on the basis of purely abstract formulas.[67] On Hildebrand's authority the *pochvenniki* argued that since the historical form of production in Russia was association, the natural form for Russian industrialization was the *artel'*. In order to assist the formation of the *artel'* they came out flatly against the determination of the government to tie the peasants to the land by the terms of the Emancipation settlement. Instead, they argued for the introduction of the principle of the free movement of labour in order to release workers from agriculture to work in communal industrial enterprises.[68] The *pochvenniki*, therefore, did not insist that all factories should necessarily be industrial adjuncts to the agricultural commune. They were confident that the co-operative character of the new city-based, industrial enterprises would compensate the workers for their displacement from the land and spare them the misery that dislocation entailed under capitalism.

In order to protect nascent Russian industry from world competition, the *pochvenniki*, again drawing on contemporary German economic theory, opposed free trade and opted for moderate tariff protection.[69] ECONOMIC They were also acutely aware of the pressing need for improved MODERNISM communications in Russia and were leading advocates of an accelerated program of railway construction to facilitate exports.[70] These policies, along with the advocacy of other modern innovations such as universal fire insurance, suggest that the *pochvenniki* were the exponents of a far-reaching economic modernism.

COTTAGE INDUSTRY Apart from industrialization by means of the *artel'*, the *pochvenniki* also supported the growth of cottage industry. Cottage industry was an economical form of production because it required little machinery and a minimum of tools. And, as a secondary activity of the worker, it did not detract from his primary economic function, agricultural production. Cottage production was particularly useful at a time when there was little capital available for investment in factories. The *pochvenniki* rejected the view that cottage production represented the lowest level of industrial development and would inevitably be replaced by the highest – factory production. They maintained that the two forms should coexist. Improved means of communication would provide direct access to the market for the home producers. This would result in the elimination of the middleman who made excessive profits at the expense of the peasants and secured monopolies on distribution. *Vremia* urged the government to extend credit to cottage enterprises and to encourage the co-operative purchasing of raw materials and distribution of finished products through village associations.[71]

Vremia was not primarily an economic journal, and the *pochvenniki* made no effort to detail a comprehensive scheme for Russian economic development. They were more concerned with the ethical implications of economic organization than with practical economic planning. The contributions on economic matters were submitted by a variety of authors and were not always consistent. Nevertheless, the general tenor of their economic ideas was clearly discernible. They rejected both industrial capitalism and industrial socialism in favour of more libertarian forms of associationism, and co-operativism in agriculture and industry. In these forms they believed they had found the means for the democratic sharing of production in a world where men were destined for honourable impoverishment. While other countries longed for association, as the strivings of Western socialists proved, but lacked the means to attain it, associationism was an innate article of faith in Russia. There were no Luddites among the *pochvenniki*. Science and technology were positive values if harnessed to the correct forms of social and economic organization. It was here that their foresight failed them, however. Although they had discerned that the economic needs of men would grow more complex with the advance of civilization, they, along with most of their contemporaries, could not envisage the incredible degree of technological and human specialization that was required to meet those needs. It was this complexity of demand that ultimately shaped modern industrial society and not the potencies of national character.

In retrospect, *pochvennichestvo* appears naïve and even woolly minded. The *pochvenniki* had hoped to take advantage of the special features of Russian economic and social development, which they interpreted as national originality, to infuse the traditional forms of social cohesiveness with the latest advances of science and technology. They believed that the best way to conserve the values of the nation was to give them the fullest scope for expression and development both in the present and the future. They also recognized that the politicization of society threatened social disharmony and sought, by idealizing autocracy, to exclude politics from what was to them the essentially moral activity of society. [SEP OF POLITICS/SOCIETY]

The attempt was destined to fail. Like the Slavophiles earlier and the populists later, the *pochvenniki* mistook backwardness for originality. This misapprehension prevented them from understanding the true significance of the Emancipation reforms. Rather than fostering the organic unity of society, as the *pochvenniki* believed, these reforms were a symptom of the breakdown of medieval corporate social forms that had begun with the reforms of Peter the Great. The organic model of social organization was inadequate in a world where functionalism, professionalization, and increasing social heterogeneity were the prerequisites of national survival. The primitive forms of association, on which the *pochvenniki* wagered the future of Russia, did not prove to be an adequate defence against the universally dehumanizing potential of industrial technology and organization. The scientific and technological civilization that they welcomed served only to sap the remaining sources of Russian originality from within. [PROBLEMS OF (P) THEORY:]

The endeavour to shield society from the demoralizing effects of politics proved equally futile. Society could not pursue its independent ends separately from the state, and the state could not function in the modern world without organizing society to respond to its needs. The tension in Russia between the autocratic state and an increasingly complex society could be resolved only when society was sufficiently organized politically to seize control of the direction of the state. Such a solution was too slow in coming, and the *pochvenniki*, in fostering the chimera of a conservative-autocratic utopia, significantly contributed to its delay.

7

Native Soil and literature

The full complexity of *pochvennichestvo* cannot be appreciated apart from the aesthetic theory from which it sprang. The entire conceptual framework of the native soil movement had originated with the organic criticism elaborated by Grigor'ev in the 1850s and was still sustained by its links with literature. The organic interpretation of Russian literature served the reciprocal functions of first revealing to the *pochvenniki* the hidden content of Russian nationality and then verifying the social and political theories that they constructed from the original revelations of literature. The aesthetic underpinnings of *pochvennichestvo* plainly betrayed its romantic roots. The romantics viewed the universe as an aesthetic creation and tried to make sense of reality in terms of an aesthetic idea. The *pochvenniki*, as we have seen, believed that the ideal developed through the history of a nation, and they looked to literature as the main vehicle of this development. Literature mediated between the national ideal, which dwelt potentially or unconsciously in the life of the people, and the self-conscious manifestations of the national ideal that were realized in the ever-changing life of society. In a parallel process, literature also served as the primary instrument for the reconciliation of universal Western civilization with Russian fraternity. It is not surprising that the *pochvenniki* who lived by literature should have stressed the importance of the writer in national development, but their exaggerated faith in the efficacy of literature in the shaping of the nation illustrated the severe limitations imposed by the authorities on other more direct means of influencing social development even in the relatively liberal period of the reforms.

The aesthetic theory of *Vremia* and later *Epokha* was virtually indistinguishable from Grigor'ev's organic criticism. There can be little doubt that Dostoevsky's ideas about art, which leaned heavily on Schelling's aesthetics, <u>were borrowed from Grigor'ev.</u>[1] Not only were the general conclusions of the two men almost identical, but the vocabulary Dostoevsky employed and the arguments dearest to him were also often the same as those used by Grigor'ev in his pioneering articles of the 1850s. There were some differences of temperament between them. Dostoevsky never surrendered himself wholly to aesthetics as did Grigor'ev. Whereas <u>Grigor'ev held that thought entered conscious life only through art</u>, <u>Dostoevsky looked on art as one among several agents of human consciousness.</u> Although both stressed, as had the Slavophiles, <u>the superiority of intuitive knowledge over conventional logical thought,</u> Grigor'ev interpreted intuition more narrowly than did Dostoevsky. For Grigor'ev intuition was artistic intuition which was to him inseparable from religious intuition. He maintained that science, which as the product of the rationalistic activity of the intellect was lacking in the vitality of life, was inferior to art, which was organically linked to concrete reality. Art was the spontaneous product of life; science was the product of abstract reasoning from the categories of the mind. Dostoevsky would have disavowed little of this. He, nevertheless, believed that science, too, if it were rooted in practical life, was endowed with creative intuition.[2] These minor differences did not, however, imperil his essential agreement with Grigor'ev on the meaning and function of art in human life.

The *pochvenniki* were interested principally in the role of the writer in the development of the nation. Although a few articles on the plastic arts and a series on music appeared in *Vremia*, most of the articles that raised aesthetic questions concerned literature. Since the *pochvenniki* assumed that the <u>sources of life and literature were identical, literature was, in their</u> view, the <u>spontaneous expression of reality. The writer was the organic</u> <u>product of the time and place in which he was born and wrote. His work</u> <u>was never entirely personal but contained the essence of the social milieu</u> <u>in which it was created</u>. Literature was, therefore, always true to life and always contemporary. Dostoevsky wrote:

The important thing is that art is always faithful to reality to the highest degree, its deviations are fleeting and temporary; art is not only always faithful to reality but cannot be anything else but true to contemporary reality. Otherwise it would not be real art. The mark of real art is that it is always contemporary, urgent and useful ... Art which is not contemporary and does not answer contemporary needs cannot exist. If it does exist it is not art, it becomes shallow, degenerates, loses its power and all artistic value.[3]

Since the essential characteristics of a given time and place were ultimately joined to nationality, literature was, as Grigor'ev held, always profoundly national: 'The truly essential power of the manifestations of art in general and poetry in particular consists in their organic unity with life, with reality, of which they serve more or less as intelligible expressions cast in artistic forms. And since any life, any reality, is meaningless without its popular (*narodnaia*), that is, national (*natsional'naia*), envelope, it would be more correct to say that this power consists in an organic link with nationality (*narodnost'*).'[4]

For the *pochvenniki*, then, literature was the direct, spontaneous, and positive expression of the life of the nation. It re-created the national life in artistic forms not as the writer wished it to be, in order to accord with some preconceived theory, but as it really was.[5] In this way, literature penetrated the unconscious workings of the national life and bestowed on them a conscious existence. In their turn, these ideas, now consciously expressed in a work of literature through the intuitive genius of the writer, gradually became an imperative for the whole of society.[6] Literature was both the conscious expression of the national ideal at its most advanced level of development and the agent of its future development.

The *pochvenniki*, particularly Grigor'ev, believed that art directed life in a way rational thought could never do. Rational thought was grounded in conscious, or past life. But life moved too rapidly for thought to contain it for more than a fleeting moment. Grigor'ev echoed Tiutchev's line from the poem 'Silentium,' 'A thought once uttered is a lie,' and continued: 'Consciousness can explain only the past: artistic creativity hurls, so to speak, its clairvoyant views into the future, often very distant, and flings out sketches which only subsequent development fills in with colours.' The organic view, Grigor'ev concluded, 'embraced not only mind with its logical requirements and the theories to which these requirements inevitably give birth, but mind and its logical requirements – *plus* life and its organic manifestations.'[7] Such views on the superiority of art to rational thinking and the propheticism of artistic creativity were common to contemporary idealists. Schelling had given them their clearest formulation in Germany, but they gained supporters throughout Europe and America as well as in Russia. Balzac and Proudhon in France, Coleridge and Carlyle in England, and Emerson in America shared Grigor'ev's faith in the almost mystical qualities of art.

The insistence of the *pochvenniki* that contemporary literature faithfully reflected Russian nationality contrasted starkly with the Slavophile view that most of the literary output of Russians was alien to the native soil.

Although Konstantin Aksakov among the Slavophiles had, with characteristic extremism, advocated a frankly utilitarian approach to literature,
he was not typical of the Slavophiles. Kireevsky, Khomiakov, and Samarin
believed that under normal circumstances art was the product of the
national spirit. In 1847 Khomiakov wrote that 'everywhere and in all
times the arts were national. By analogy alone, it is impossible to suppose
that the law has changed for Russia.'[8] But, he continued, 'the spiritual
power of a people creates through the artist' only when the internal life of
the nation was whole. 'With us,' Khomiakov concluded, 'because of the
division between life and knowledge, art is impossible.'[9] Kireevsky had
already remarked on the unoriginality of Russian literature in 1845. The
classes from which most Russian writers originated, he contended, were
in the thrall of Western ideas and forms and so were separated from the
real life of the nation. Until the gap between knowledge, which was
contained in the educated classes, and Russian life, which dwelled in the
peasant class, was bridged, Russian art would remain imitative.[10]

The Slavophile view of Russian literature had not changed substantially
from the 1840s. After the deaths of Kireevsky in 1856 and Khomiakov
and K.S. Aksakov in 1860, I.S. Aksakov emerged as the leading Slavophile
ideologist. In an anonymous article in *Den'*, with a note appended by
Aksakov in which he expressed his agreement with the author, it was
argued that Russian literature reflected not Russian nationality (*narodnost'*) but an independent gentry nationality (*natsional'nost'*) that was
grounded entirely in the western European experience of the gentry after
the reforms of Peter the Great. Its significance lay only in the satirical
works it produced which exposed the despair and uselessness of the
Russian public.[11] In a later article, Aksakov himself wrote that the true
function of Russian literature since the time of Lomonosov had been to
protest on behalf of life and nationality against Europeanization. In his
view only Boltin, Fonvizin, Griboedov, and Gogol' had actually met this
function. Their protest 'disturbed the spiritual and moral complacency of
fashionable society which was comforting itself with a lie.'[12]

The *pochvenniki* had no patience with such views. Grigor'ev had long
ago denied that the mind and body, or thought and life, of Russia had
ever been divided, and his long-standing denial that nationality could be
fragmented in the way the Slavophiles supposed was reasserted in *Vremia*.
Nationality embraced the ideals of all the strata of a society in an organic
whole. There could be no such thing as, for example, peasant drama,
because literature always expressed the ideal of the whole nation. In this
sense, the *pochvenniki* believed literature to be profoundly democratic.[13]

Although the *pochvenniki* believed that literature expressed the national ideal, they did not feel that it was confined by nationality. It will be recalled that it was their conviction that the national contained some aspect of universal humanity and so participated in universality. 'We are joined,' wrote Dostoevsky, 'both by our historical and our inner spiritual life to the historical past and to universal humanity.'[14] Artistic talent consisted in the ability of the artist to convey universal ideals through the national idiom: 'Of course, in every talent there is something universally human, otherwise it would not be a *talent*; but even this universally human element is expressed in the colours of time, place and people.'[15] The closer the ties of a nation with history and with the universal life of humanity, the richer was its own life and the better could it cope with progress and with intellectual and spiritual growth.

With his superior intuitive powers, the artist divined the simple, universal truths of human life. These truths gave character and significance to his work and constituted his point of view. An artist could not merely reflect reality passively or mechanically: 'A true artist cannot do this: he will inevitably reveal himself, be it in a painting, a story or a musical composition; he will mirror himself unwittingly, even against his will, he will declare himself with all his views, character and level of his development.'[16] The *pochvenniki* were critical of what they called simple realism. The simple realist held a mirror up to life but soon discovered that he was incapable of distinguishing the essential from the contingent in the reflection. Without a universal ideal, he fell easy prey to conventional ideals and preconceived, a priori ideas. The inevitable result of such servility to the mundane was scepticism.[17]

The *pochvenniki* rejected both the utilitarian definition of art and that of the school of art-for-art's sake. In terms similar to those he had used in the 1850s, Grigor'ev wrote in 1862:

Poetry is not the simple reflection of life, a process which is indifferent and unselective in its attitude toward the eternally diverse manifestations of life, but is the comprehension, the rationalization, the generalization of phenomena. In this is its meaning, importance, legitimacy and eternality – in spite of the doctrine of the theoreticians [utilitarians] who in the present condemn it to slavish service to theory and in the future to final annihilation as something unnecessary and useless, and also in spite of the doctrine of the literary gastronomes who turn it into a kind of *sauce piquante* of life.[18]

Grigor'ev was certain that only an autonomous art, free from the

limitations of conventional ideals and preconceived goals, truly served
society. Under these conditions art was a moral force that bridged the gulf
between the ideal and the real.

ART
serving
society

The most complete expression of Dostoevsky's aesthetic views was his
'Mr – bov and the Question of Art,' a withering outburst against the
utilitarian theory of art of which Dostoevsky believed Dobroliubov to be
Russia's leading exponent. He began his analysis with the remark that in
recent years Russian criticism had become pettier and increasingly more
vulgar. The cause was, he suggested, the growing misapprehensions
among literary critics about the nature and function of art. Like
Grigor'ev, Dostoevsky disavowed any sympathy for either of the two
existing trends of criticism. In the school of art-for-art's sake he located
those critics who held that art was an end in itself and was justified only by
its internal content. There could be no question of the utility of art, in the
view of these critics, because it was as much a part of man as were his arms
and eyes. Art grew out of itself and was constrained by no external
purpose. In the utilitarian school he put those critics who argued, on the
contrary, that art should serve man directly in accordance with the
demands of external social circumstances. If a society faced a particular
problem it was the duty of artists to apply themselves to its immediate
solution. Dostoevsky granted that some utilitarians regretted such wilful
constraint on art, but nevertheless they regarded it as necessary in the
interests of a good cause. To them, art must first be of immediate use to
society.[19]

DOSTOEVSKY
ON ART :

The weakness for Dostoevsky of the utilitarian view was that in
subordinating art to short-term social ends, the utilitarians, in his opinion,
undermined the true utility of art. For in the long run, unconstrained art
was useful not just to a single society but to the whole of mankind.[20] Since
time alone could determine what in art was truly useful, the prescription
of the goals of art beforehand was destructive of its real purpose.
Dostoevsky did not deny that it was right to 'urge, wish and ask' that a
work of art deal with current problems but maintained it was wrong to
'demand' that it should do so.[21] The utilitarians, he continued, dispensed
with the requirement that a work of art be of artistic value, provided it
possessed a clear and useful aim. But an inartistic work, he asserted, never
attained its aims and usually harmed the cause in the interests of which it
was conceived. Dostoevsky defined artistic value as the ability of the
writer, for example, to 'express his idea in the characters and images of
the novel so clearly that the reader, on reading the novel, completely
understands the idea of the writer exactly as the artist understood it when

he created his work.'[22] If the work lacked artistry it remained an artificial construct, divorced from reality and convincing no one.

In order to convince, a work of art had to be real; in order to be real, it had to express its ideal in conformity with the spirit of its time and place, through recognizable characters. The greater was the artistry of the work, the greater its utility: 'The fact is that art is the best, the most convincing, the most indisputable, the most intelligible means for presenting to the masses precisely that cause about which you [Dobroliubov] are so concerned, the most businesslike way if you will, you who are a business-like man. Consequently, art is to the highest degree useful and useful precisely from your point of view. Why do you despise it and victimize it when it should really be given precedence over all other demands?'[23] To abandon art, Dostoevsky believed, was to surrender the most useful weapon in the struggle for truth and social contentment. But to demand that art be useful was to violate its inherently free nature and deprive it of its real utility.

From the beginning of time, Dostoevsky went on, art was inseparable from man and responded to his needs and ideals. Since art was the catalogue of the inherent creative capacities of man, it could not have aspirations other than those of man. If unconstrained by preconceived aims, art remained loyal to the ends of man: 'The more freely [art] develops, the more normally will it develop and sooner will it find its true and *useful* path. And since its interests and aims are the same as the aims of man whom it serves and with whom it is inseparably allied, then the freer its development, the more use will it bring to humanity.'[24] The *pochvenniki* therefore defended the autonomy of the artist while at the same time asserting the utility of his creations.

The logical extreme of the utilitarian view, the *pochvenniki* believed, was the complete eradication of art. If it were to be judged only on the basis of its usefulness to the cause, its function would be eliminated if a better, alternative means for serving the cause could be found. 'In essence,' Dostoevsky addressed Dobroliubov, 'you despise poetry and art; ahead of all else, you have to have a cause, you are practical men.'[25] Strakhov later took up the same argument. The materialists, he said, at least recognized the existence of art, although they subordinated artistic forms to real objects. But the nihilists had gone a step further. They refused to acknowledge art at all. Their only question about art was what does one need it for? Nihilism and art, he concluded, were mutually exclusive: 'Nihilism in art means simply the pure and naked negation of art and its phenomena as things absolutely unnecessary in life, as unworthy to live. In a word – art is no more. It has died, has become obsolete.'[26]

The *pochvenniki* warned that the annihilation of art would be catastrophic for mankind. Apart from its leading, prophetic role in national development and its usefulness in representing the truth in living images to the masses, art performed a still more essential function in the world. For the *pochvenniki* believed that truth and beauty were inseparable: 'Beauty alone can embody truth, and such an embodiment communicates to us a vital confidence in the reality, the properties and the movement of truth. Naked thought obtained from the cerebral process alone, only through the path of logic ... always remains something alien to us.'[27] Since art was man's link with the ideal, it was deeply moral; literature was the conscience of society, the source of its ethical notions.

ART = INTEGRAL 2 MAN

Schelling maintained that artistic creativity arose from a sense of inner spiritual disharmony. Man's need for harmony drove him to search for beauty because the essence of beauty was perfect harmony. Dostoevsky fully accepted the view that art met man's longing for harmony and was necessary to his spiritual well-being:

And perhaps it is in this that the greatest secret of artistic creativity lies, namely that the image of beauty which art creates at once becomes an idol which is worshipped *without any conditions*. And why does it become an idol? It is because the need for beauty is more strongly developed when man is in discord with reality, in disharmony and conflict, that is, when he is *most alive*, because man is always alive precisely at that moment when he is searching for and trying to get something; then he experiences a most natural desire for everything that is harmonious, for tranquillity, and in beauty there is both harmony and tranquillity.[28]

BEAUTY AS SALVATION OF THE WORLD

The penetration of beauty into life through art acted on man morally, imperceptibly transforming his spiritual world. The evocation of beauty as the salvation of the world was not a metaphor for the *pochvenniki* but represented to them a real spiritual process of reconciliation and harmonization. The romantic tendency to identify the aesthetic with the religious ideal was at work among the *pochvenniki*. Grigor'ev, as has been seen, had already associated Beauty with the Russian Christ in the 1850s. Dostoevsky had not by 1863 yet linked Beauty as the saviour of the world to Christ as the image of Beauty. It was, however, a powerful formula to which he was not for long to remain indifferent.

Literary criticism was Grigor'ev's chief intellectual preoccupation. It was therefore not surprising that he should have defended its independent role. But Dostoevsky also stressed the important functions of criticism: 'Art assists human development by its strong and powerful form, acting on man in a plastic and image-forming fashion. But criticism is as natural and has as legitimate a role in the question of human development as has art. It consciously considers what art has represented to us only in forms. The whole force and lifeblood (*sok*) of social assumptions and convictions at a given moment are expressed in criticism.'[29] Whereas criticism did not, apparently, deprive thought of its spontaneity and contemporaneity, scholarly writing and journalistic popularization did. They were derivative because they synthesised ideas already consciously expressed in literature. History, according to the *pochvenniki*, occupied a position midway between artistic creativity and scientific synthesis. Grigor'ev did grant, however, that at its best, history moved entirely into art.[30]

The resemblance between Dostoevsky's and Grigor'ev's theories about the process by which artistic types were created is equally as striking.[31] The process encompassed three phases; copying, typification, and idealization. Realism, or naturalism, was the product of the first. To the *pochvenniki*, naturalism was the lowest form of artistic activity since only an immature aesthetic sensibility could be stimulated by mere copying. Rather, it was necessary for the artist to separate the inessential and untypical features of the character he was portraying from the essential and typical. The function of art was to reduce the character or phenomenon to its essence, thus typifying it. Far from copying reality, the artist reflected, and so transformed, reality through the prism of his ideal:

If [the artist] unconsciously describes only the object, we learn nothing; but the artist comes and conveys his views about the object to us, tells us what this phenomenon is called and will name for us the people participating in it, and sometimes name them in such a way that these names are transformed into a type and finally, when everyone believes in this type, its name becomes the household word for all people who are related to this type. The more powerful the artist, the more truly and profoundly does he express his thought, his opinion about a social phenomenon, and the more he serves social consciousness ... The duty and calling of art are contained in this, and along with this, the role which art plays in social development is clearly defined.[32]

The actual process of idealization took place when a character began to 'live an ideal life in the fantasy and in the work of the artist, to act and to speak in complete conformity to this character.'[33]

Typification was a crucial concept for *pochvennichestvo*. For it was typification that made the identification of literature and life possible. Literature presented ideal or archetypal representations of living people or real phenomena. These representations not only reflected social reality, but, because they were ideal, also conditioned the development of social reality. Literature contained the very essence of the real social processes that were taking place and served as a barometer of impending social change. Consequently, it was in literature that the *pochvenniki* sought and found the traits of the national character and the course of its development, and it was to yet more literature that they turned to validate their previous findings.

PUSHKIN!

They believed that the processes of typification and idealization in modern Russian literature had begun in the works of Pushkin. Dostoevsky made Grigor'ev's earlier idealization of Pushkin his own. Pushkin penetrated the essence of Russian nationality, analysed the duality of the Russian character, and set the limits of the Russian ideal. 'Pushkin was everything,' Grigor'ev wrote, 'the basic component of our spiritual life, the reflection of our moral process, its spokesman, as mysterious as our life itself.'[34] Pushkin had captured the schism in the Russian soul that exposure to Western civilization had caused. In the Byronesque type ① personified by his characters Eugene Onegin and Aleko, he disclosed the plight of Russia's educated man who was cut off from the soil, alienated from life, and tormented by destructive egoism. From the 'predatory' type was descended a whole line of characters, among them Lermontov's Pechorin and Turgenev's Rudin. These types were the ideal reflection of the westernizers and represented, as Grigor'ev argued, the analytical side of the national character.[35] Near the end of his career, Pushkin created Belkin, the other half of the Russian physiognomy. Belkin represented the humble type in Russian literature, a type prepared to yield to life and bow before the wisdom of the soil. Tugenev's Lavretsky was the fullest and most recent example of this type in Russian literature. The humble type, the *pochvenniki* believed, had its analogues in life. Among them were included the young editors of *Moskvitianin*, but not the Slavophiles who, in Grigor'ev's words, remained 'bitterly hostile to the living life and its expression in literature.'[36] The parallel courses of literature and life since Pushkin had gradually prepared the way for the reconciliation of the humble and predatory types in *pochvennichestvo*.

The role of Pushkin was not exhausted by his depiction of the two sides of the Russian character. He represented also Russia's claim to European nationality and to intellectual and spiritual independence within the circle of European nations. Pushkin, according to the *pochvenniki*, synthesised all the conflicting tendencies of Western civilization in his works. Russian nationality did not live in isolation from the rest of civilization but incorporated all the European ideals which it had encountered since the reforms of Peter the Great. Dostoevsky saw Pushkin as conclusive evidence of the universality of Russia:

The phenomenon of Pushkin is proof that the tree of civilization has already borne fruit, and that the fruit is not rotten but is a noble, golden fruit. Everything that we could have found out about ourselves from our acquaintance with Europe we have found out; everything that civilization could make clear for us we have made clear for ourselves, and this knowledge has appeared to us in Pushkin, in the fullest, most harmonious form. We understand through him that the Russian ideal is wholeness, universal reconciliation and universal humanity.

Pushkin's sketch of Russian nationality was progressively being filled in with the colours of life itself, and his 'colossal significance' was becoming ever more apparent.[37]

Faith in the interpenetrability and interchangeability of life and literature was the distinguishing characteristic of *pochvennichestvo*. The *pochvenniki* supposed that literature, taking its lead from reality, incorporated in ideal forms the unconscious processes of life and influenced life by generating awareness of those processes. The study of literature became, in large part, a substitute for the study of life itself. Literature was offered in evidence as proof that certain desired changes in social attitudes and forms were actually taking place. As Dostoevsky wrote in 1861, 'We see in Pushkin the confirmation of all our thoughts ... For all Russians, he is the living exposition in full artistic completeness of the Russian spirit.'[38]

By their analysis of Russian literature after Pushkin the *pochvenniki* reinforced their initial interpretation. Lermontov, they believed, had given the critical and negative side of the Russian character its fullest expression. He had, however, also produced the humble type of Maksim Maksimich. Gogol' had continued the critical trend in his exposure of the vulgarity (*poshlost'*) of vulgar men. In so doing he had unwittingly founded the natural school of Russian literature. Pisemsky, in his earlier works, and Ostrovsky had further elaborated the side of Russian nationality that Pushkin had only sketched in Belkin. Turgenev's whole evolution, which had culminated in the creation of Lavretsky, had been one of movement from the depiction of the predatory to representation of the humble type. And Dostoevsky was the first to enter the soul of the common people in his *Notes from the House of the Dead*. Other writers such as Pisemsky, in his more recent writings, and Goncharov reflected the narrow, suffocating ideals of the conservative gentry, the bigoted merchants, and the Germanized bureaucracy.[39]

The *pochvenniki* were particularly incensed by Dobroliubov's interpretation of Ostrovsky's dramas. In his 'Dark Kingdom' and 'A Ray of Light in the Dark Kingdom,' the latter a review of the play *The Storm*, Dobroliubov portrayed Ostrovsky as a disciple of the accusatory literature of the natural school. In his opinion, Ostrovsky exposed the inhumanity and ignorance of the mechant world, the 'dark kingdom' that was characterized by its 'petty tyranny' (*samodurstvo*).[40] The *pochvenniki* did not deny the accusatory aspect of Ostrovsky's work but believed there was more in the 'dark kingdom' than petty tyranny. They emphasized the dramatist's close links with the native soil. Above all Ostrovsky was national: 'Nevertheless, Ostrovsky's new word was no more or less than nationality, a word which, properly speaking, is already old, because the aspiration towards nationality in our literature did not begin with Ostrovsky, but in reality new because it is defined more precisely, more clearly and simply, though, without doubt, incompletely in his activity.'[41] The types created by Ostrovsky portrayed merchant life as it was, in both its somber and bright guises. Much of what was good and beautiful in Russian life, the *pochvenniki* believed, was emerging through his sensitive pen. In the light of his first unfavourable impression of Ostrovsky's work, Dostoevsky was particularly generous in his private as will as his public utterances about it. In his notebooks, for example, he singled out a number of characters from one of Ostrovsky's plays as brilliant depictions of Russian man and eulogized the directness of Ostrovsky's relationship to his characters.[42]

Grigor'ev believed that the search for roots that had begun with Pushkin had ended with Dostoevsky. Society, of course, lagged behind literature but was gradually squaring itself with the living ideals of which literature had made it aware. The parallel development in social life had seen a movement from westernism and its reaction, Slavophilism, to nihilism and its reaction, *pochvennichestvo*. In this organic transformation creative writing had played the leading part. Dostoevsky wrote in 1861 that Pushkin, Turgenev, and Ostrovsky could do more for Russian development than could the political section of the very finest journal.[43] In the revelation of truth, the poetic manner was the most efficacious because 'poetry could not be opposed to truth.'[44] Literature had not only exposed the roots of the national life, but also revealed the two sides of the Russian ideal. The need for the reconciliation of fraternity and universality had finally been recognized in life and in literature. The future role of literature was to secure their union and lead Russia to its proper destiny.[45]

Art played a decisive role in *pochvennichestvo*. Not only was it the agent of social consciousness, but also it was a moral force that transfigured man's spiritual world through beauty. As the only activity of the human mind that was spontaneously informed by life, art alone contained life's dynamic and multi-faceted activity. The artist was rooted in the soil of his nation, but artistic genius was also linked by intuition to those fixed and eternal ideals that underlay all reality and towards which all life tended. Since the aspirations of the human soul towards the ideal were always constant, the ideal content of art was the same in all times and places. But art always came dressed in national costume and concerned itself with the contemporary forms in which the eternal questions presented themselves. Aesthetic creativity was inherent in human nature and was inseparable from men's hopes and fears. As the product of its time and place, art could not but treat those hopes and fears in the context of contemporary reality. Though free from prescribed aims, art served both society, in its quest for the ideal, and humanity, in its search for harmony and tranquillity.

If aesthetics is the key to the understanding of the theory of *pochvennichestvo*, as the source from which it sprang, it is equally the key to the understanding of its limitations as an account of reality. By interpreting Russian social development through the prism of literature and by projecting their findings into an idealized future, the *pochvenniki* created a closed system that had almost no points of contact with reality. Grigor'ev was oblivious to the dangers. Dostoevsky, who once remarked that Grigor'ev, too, was only a theoretician, was more cautious. He felt compelled to refute the charge that the *pochvenniki* indulged in indiscriminate aestheticism. He asserted that *pochvennichestvo* interpreted society not entirely through literature but through literary criticism and science (*nauka*) as well. His protestations were, however, disingenuous. The *pochvenniki* discounted all criticism that did not accord with their own view of literature and refused to countenance any philosophical or scientific doctrine that did not support their ideal of Russian nationality, the nature of which they had predetermined by the interpretation of literature. The *pochvenniki* looked in literature and found what they yearned for; but so did the nihilists. Literature is not a transcript of reality, but a catalogue of human attitudes to reality. In this, Russian literature was faithful to life, but it could not be confined to a single interpretation.

The loyalty of the *pochvenniki* to literature, for all of its shortcomings as a guide to reality, is not difficult to understand. In periods of rapid transition, when the ideals that unite society are disintegrating and disagreements over new standards are pervasive, the search for some unifying principle is intensified. The romantics looked at human feelings and found them good; the *pochvenniki* looked at human feelings and found them not only good but also constant in their idealism. Literature was the realm of human feeling writ large, where men, with all their weaknesses showing, aspired together towards noble and worthy ends, and where even heroic and tragic failures proved the value of the enterprise. Like idealists elsewhere in Europe, the *pochvenniki* reacted against what in Russia was called 'accusatory literature,' which in their view mocked and debased man by portraying only his lower nature. It was not the affair of art to conceal the worst sides of man, but neither was it its business to ignore human worth and idealism. For it was in the latter that men became one and the differences between them were erased. The *pochvenniki* therefore turned to a 'higher realism' that discovered in even the basest of characters the aspirations that bound man to man.

8

Native Soil and its rivals

The emergence of public opinion during the reform period as a significant force in Russian history was accompanied by a flowering of Russian
journalism. The burgeoning journals and newspapers played the leading
role in focusing and expressing the long-suppressed feelings, interests,
and grievances of society. Once the euphoric days of co-operation in the
immediate post-Emancipation era were over and the limits of the government's plans were revealed, the number of controversial issues grew. The
transitional character of the times was, in any event, conducive to debate,
but specific events in the early 1860s also encouraged disagreements. The
year 1862 was particularly troubling for Russian society. Severe peasant
disturbances, unrest in the universities, the summer outbreak of fires in St
Petersburg, and the ominous overture to the Polish revolt of 1863 frayed
Russian nerves and sharply divided public opinion.

The idea of reconciliation placed *Vremia* in an ambiguous relationship
with its journalistic competitors. The attempt to encompass nearly all
sides while self-righteously pointing to the failings or naïve short-
sightedness of each appeared patronizing in the extreme to rival editors
and exposed *Vremia* to criticism from many quarters. Inevitably, the
editors of *Vremia* were drawn into the arguments that raged among the
journals. They were forced not only to choose sides on specific issues, but
also to define more clearly their attitude to the factions within the
intelligentsia. Although *Vremia* maintained an independent position
throughout its brief history, it had soon to abandon its lofty pose as arbiter
and descend to the field of battle.

Vremia sparred with several important Russian journals at one time or
another. Such incidents were mostly brief exchanges over matters of
passing significance. But the debates with *Sovremennik, Russkii vestnik,* and

Den' bore on fundamental issues. Each of these journals represented a defined tendency in Russian thought. In debating with them the *pochvenniki* were forced to defend and at times to rethink their own position.

The clash with the radical journal *Sovremennik* was surprisingly slow in coming. The idealism, particularism, and gradualism of the *pochvenniki* were patently at odds with the materialism, universalism, and revolutionsm of the so-called nihilists. Yet during 1861, the first year of its existence, *Vremia* was not involved in a single serious confrontation with either *Sovremennik* or *Russkoe slovo*. Their arguments were restrained and at times even cordial, and *Vremia* more than once supported the nihilists against the attacks of other journals. In some respects, the Dostoevsky brothers bent over backwards to appease the radicals. Years later Strakhov recalled that in 1861 Fedor often exercised his prerogative as editor to insert complimentary adjectives before the names of leading westernizers mentioned in Strakhov's articles.[1] Mikhail went so far as to forbid Grigor'ev to place not just flattering modifiers but even initials in front of surnames of the Slavophiles discussed in his contributions.

Only in the early months of 1862 did the editorial policy of *Vremia* begin to change from a more to a markedly less sympathetic attitude towards the nihilists. It was not that the *pochvenniki* agreed initially with the philosophy and methods of the radicals and then changed their minds; they were critical of nihilism from the beginning. Dostoevsky deliberately adopted a policy of restraint towards the radical journals; it is obvious that at first he did not see the differences between Chernyshevsky and himself as irreconcilable. As naïve as it may now seem, Dostoevsky took the idea of reconciliation very seriously, far more seriously than most modern commentators allow. He was well aware of the vast philosophical distance between *Vremia* and *Sovremennik*. None the less, he believed that even nihilism, extreme as it was, represented a necessary side of Russian nationality that would soon be engulfed in the general return to the soil. In that optimistic year of 1861, Dostoevsky's hopes were high that a period of ideological reconciliation and social co-operation was beginning. Consequently, he chose to emphasize the common ground between *Sovremennik* and *Vremia* and to ignore the profound gulf separating them.[2]

He discovered common ground in the humanitarian goals shared by the two journals. As has been seen, Dostoevsky returned from prison and exile with the humanist views of his more radical youth still intact. On humanitarian questions, therefore, he frequently found himself in sympathy with the nihilists. It was not the goals of the nihilists that he rejected, but the extreme theoretical, by which he meant revolutionary, means he believed Chernyshevsky and his followers were willing to employ to achieve their ends. 'We want the same thing as you,' he addressed Chernyshevsky in his notebook for 1862, 'exactly the same thing, but only on condition that it be done more sensibly.'[3]

A number of factors combined finally to convince Dostoevsky that he had misjudged nihilism. Pressures for a clean break with the radicals built up within the editorial board of *Vremia* from the beginning. Neither Strakhov nor Grigor'ev agreed with the Dostoevsky brothers that the nihilists could be conciliated or should be pampered. In June 1861 Grigor'ev departed for Orenburg in order to teach in a military school. There were several reasons for his 'flight,' but it is clear from his letters from Orenburg that one of them was his conviction that *Vremia* could not honestly support nationality and idealism and at the same time consort with *Sovremennik*. He particularly resented the contributions of Razin. Not only were Razin's more liberal views suspect to Grigor'ev, but he also disliked him personally. The critic was outraged when Razin remarked that Grigor'ev should simplify his articles so that Razin's wife could understand them. The crowning insult was Mikhail Dostoevsky's jest that Grigor'ev was saving all his best work for *Svetoch*.[4] Strakhov, too, was dissatisfied with Dostoevsky's restraint towards *Sovremennik* and had done what he could to provoke the nihilists in a series of articles signed 'N.K.'

On their side, the editors of *Sovremennik* found it hard to resist pointing to the self-satisfaction of *Vremia*. Chernyshevsky had greeted the first number of *Vremia* in 1861 amiably enough, but he concluded his review by pointing out: 'As far as we can judge by the first number, *Vremia* diverges from *Sovremennik* in its ideas about many of those questions on which there can be a difference of opinion in the good part of society. If we are not mistaken, *Vremia* intends to be as little in agreement with *Sovremennik* as with *Russkii vestnik*.'[5] But no matter how much *Sovremennik* welcomed the 'honourable and independent opinion' of *Vremia*, the editors could not but be piqued by Dostoevsky's sarcastic assault on the aesthetic views of Dobroliubov and Chernyshevsky in his article 'Mr –bov and the Question of Art' in February 1861.

In August, *Sovremennik* made public its own attitude to the tendency of *Vremia*. An article, written by I.A. Piotrovsky, pointed out that those journalists who sought a rapprochement with the people had an extremely abstract conception of *narodnost'* or the historical soil. The article continued: 'It must be said that in taking this path, our journalism falls into vague ideals, interprets Westernism and Slavophilism and, trying to catch *something* common to them, finds nothing solid on which anything could be based, and uncovers nothing living or useful which could be followed up.'[6]   ANTONOVICH

Piotrovsky's article, in which *Vremia* was not even mentioned specifically, was only the harbinger of a much more direct and purposeful blast by M.A. Antonovich in December 1861. Antonovich, who emerged as the principal in the dispute between *Sovremennik* and *Vremia*, was without doubt the most fractious member of the *Sovremennik* group. In his December article he took great pains to associate *pochvennichestvo* in the minds of the public with the reactionary tendencies of the past. The history of the 'soil,' he said, may be traced back to the obscurantist 'official nationality' of the notorious reactionary journal *Maiak* of the 1840s. Since the demise of *Maiak*, the retrogressive view of nationality had passed through Slavophilism and finally found a new home in *pochvennichestvo*.[7]

Having categorized the *pochvenniki* to his own satisfaction, Antonovich launched into a systematic critique of their doctrine. Like Piotrovsky, he found the idea of the soil to be vague and undefined and could detect in *pochvennichestvo* no specific means for getting back to the soil.[8] He deplored the particularism of *Vremia's* conception of nationality and proclaimed the universality of civilization. In the eighteenth century, he argued, science had been transplanted from England to France and had borne fruit in France just as later it was to bear fruit in Germany.[9] He advised the *pochvenniki* to dream a little less about Russia's 'future great historical role' and to busy themselves with matters 'closer to us.'[10] And finally he rejected *Vremia's* panacea of 'literacy' as totally inadequate to meet the real needs of the peasantry. Literacy, he said, was an 'indifferent tool, a force which was valuable not in itself but for the effect which it produces.'[11]

Antonovich's attack on the idea of literacy in *pochvennichestvo*, which went straight to the heart of the differences between *Sovremennik* and *Vremia*, highlighted the fundamental divergence between the conservative and radical conceptions of how change occurred in society. The conservatives contended that the inner life of the spirit was prior to the external forms of social organization and that the independent personality was the sole creative force in human life. The radicals asserted, on the contrary, the primacy of the forms of social life that shaped and determined the individual personality. The radicals, therefore, believed that since man was the product of his environment, it was necessary to improve the environment in order to alter human nature for the better. The conservatives believed that since society was only as good as the individuals it comprised, it was necessary to improve men morally in order to alter society for the better.

The *pochvenniki* and nihilists divided on this issue as might be expected. Early in 1863, Dostoevsky wrote in his notebook: 'Man changes not for *external* reasons but for no other reason than from *moral* change.'[12] The *pochvenniki* held that a materially advanced society could very well be intellectually and morally backward and politically and socially immature, whereas an intellectually and morally developed nation would sooner or later attain a satisfactory level of material well-being and social and political maturity. Their gradualist program was, therefore, grounded in the idea of the moral self-improvement of the citizen through education.

Antonovich was outraged by what he regarded as the callous indifference of the *pochvenniki*. While they prated about educating the people, he stormed, they ignored the simple right of the peasants to their daily bread. The moral depravity of the peasantry was the product of its poverty and could be overcome only by first alleviating its economic condition. 'No matter how you praise literacy, no matter how eloquently you prove the great superiority of spiritual food to material, nevertheless, one wants to eat, both you and those to whom you recommend your diligent teaching ... The hungry man above all desires and seeks bread, and can set to learning only when he has satisfied his hunger.'[13] Behind Antonovich's strictures lay the conviction that the determining factor in politics was the struggle between competing social or economic classes. The improvement of the economic condition of the peasant was contingent upon the overthrow of the gentry class and the removal of the autocracy that supported the gentry. Chernyshevsky had arrived at this position as early as 1859 or 1860 when he saw how little the peasants would benefit from the Emancipation reform. The ideal of class reconciliation held out in *Vremia* appeared to him and to Antonovich a reactionary subterfuge on the part of the *pochvenniki*, designed to keep the poor in their oppressed state.

At stake in the growing conflict between *Sovremennik* and *Vremia* was one of the most crucial issues in the intellectual history of nineteenth-century Russia. In 1909, P.B. Struve wrote in *Vekhi*, the testament of twentieth-century Russian idealism, that the intelligentsia had failed completely to grasp the importance of personality or to understand that social progress was the result of the moral improvement of man. Consequently, they had neglected the moral education of the people and reduced education to an instrument merely to inspire popular unrest against authority.[14] Struve and the other *Vekhi* contributors surveyed the havoc caused by this neglect during and after the revolution of 1905. The *pochvenniki* contemplated the origins of the same neglect. The radicals of the 1860s hoped to use education as a tool to ignite a revolutionary spirit and to effect a rapid transformation of society. They valued education, to repeat Antonovich's words, 'not in itself, but for the effect which it produces.' The *pochvenniki* anticipated the dangers of this view and saw in education the means for the gradual and non-violent liberation of the people through moral self-improvement.

Antonovich's assault, which he reiterated in another article in April 1862, must have gone a long way to convince Dostoevsky of the futility of placating the nihilists. It is, however, evident that he still did not object to their aims as much as their methods. As late as 1863, he wrote in his notebook:

EXPERIENCE

One can say to the theoreticians and nihilists: you preach socialism, but you yourselves believe in *experience*. Understand that you will never convince anyone of socialism by means of an unfounded conviction. Experience is necessary. And consequently it is necessary to strive only for the strengthening of and progress in the present-day life which you despise, and through that strengthening you will attain more and more experiences by which the people themselves will arrive at socialism if only it is true that it is a universal cure for the whole of society.[15]

Dostoevsky may have doubted that socialism was a universal cure, but he particularly doubted that the nihilist approach could effect anything useful in society.

Dostoevsky's notebooks for 1861–2 testify that the so-called 'Pirogov affair' did much to confirm his doubts and to precipitate his break with the radicals. At the end of the 1850's N.I. Pirogov, a notable figure in Russian educational circles, was appointed trustee first of the Odessa and later of the Kiev school districts. In 1859, he published an article in which he discussed the general undesirability of corporal punishment in schools, but with the reservation that in some cases it was a necessary corrective. Dobroliubov attacked Pirogov vigorously in *Sovremennik* for this vestige of inhumanity. He explained to his readers that even an authoritative figure such as Pirogov, seemingly a liberal man, could fall prey to reactionary views. A year went by without a response to Dobroliubov's admonitions. In the spring of 1861, when Pirogov retired, however, the incident was revived. A student at Kiev University published an article praising Pirogov's tact in handling the issue of corporal punishment in the schools. This article prompted *Otechestvennye zapiski* to take up the cudgel against

Dobroliubov, accusing him of undermining Pirogov's authority for the sake of an abstract humanitarian objective. In his reply in August, Dobroliubov reiterated his original objections to Pirogov.[16] *Vremia* made no comment about the affair until April 1862, after Dobroliubov's untimely death. Then, in an anonymous review of Pirogov's pedagogical articles, the editors declared that although Pirogov had been wrong to retain corporal punishment in the schools even if only in special cases, he was, nevertheless, an honourable and noble man who had fought stoutly for the liberalization of the school régime and did not deserve the opprobrium poured on him by his enemies.[17]

The Pirogov affair had evidently been troubling Dostoevsky for some time before April. In his notes late in 1861, Dostoevsky asked the radicals, 'Why do you demand of Pirogov more than he can give?'[18] Society, in Dostoevsky's opinion, was not yet ready for the advanced humanitarian ideals of *Sovremennik*. Those would be accepted gradually through a process of education, assimilation, and compromise and not through coercive journalistic invective: ('And the fact that public opinion is nevertheless not for you but for Pirogov means that Pirogov has served society and that it is heartily committed to him – but not you. Your path is false. To whistle and to whistle – apparently that is the essential! You have little love for the cause! And little humanity!'[19])

Dostoevsky's private response to the Pirogov incident suggests that by the end of 1861 his gradualism had won out over the need he had felt to conciliate the nihilists. The nihilists, he was now convinced, neither knew the people nor understood the organic nature of the historical process. Their radical theories presented an obstacle to the eventual realization of the very humanitarian goals which they shared with the *pochvenniki* and posed a threat to the normal and peaceful evolution of Russia. The humanitarianism of *Sovremennik*, Dostoevsky concluded, was the product neither of love for the people nor of understanding for their organic needs but of naked theory.

The direction taken by Dostoevsky in 1862 must have been gratifying to Grigor'ev. His old enemy Razin stayed, it is true, but the minuet with *Sovremennik* gradually ceased. Humanism remained an integral part of *pochvennichestvo*, but Dostoevsky no longer saw it as a bridge between *Vremia* and *Sovremennik*. Convinced that Grigor'ev and Strakhov had been right all along in opposing the radicals, Dostoevsky joined them in their condemnation of nihilism. 'You began it first,' he wrote: 'We did not want to begin although we hummed and hawed for a long time. But you were dear to us, we sympathized with you and decided it was better to be silent, although I cannot tell you really how our hearts sometimes ached to read your buffoonery ... But now you have begun, and now we very much want to tell you everything, not partially as before.' And he concluded, 'At base we agree with you, but on this base you build only nonsense.'[20] This passage leaves little room for doubt about Dostoevsky's state of mind regarding nihilism in 1861 and the early months of 1862. His own fundamental beliefs remained unchanged throughout; but the growing doubts he experienced about the methods of the radicals and the validity of their convictions ultimately compelled him to repudiate them despite his sympathy for some of their humanitarian objectives.

The struggle that developed between *Sovremennik* and *Vremia* was not a mere difference of opinion over minor matters. It was a contest between two mutually exclusive points of view for the minds of the reading public and especially of the young. In this confrontation, *Sovremennik* ultimately proved the more successful. The polemic in which the two sides became entangled was not unique to Russia, but was part of a continuing European debate between the proponents and opponents of philosophical materialism. The man among the *pochvenniki* most sensitive to contemporary trends in Western philosophy was Strakhov, who led the offensive against *Sovremennik*. The weapons had, however, been supplied by Grigor'ev several years previously in the debate with the Russian Hegelians.

The *pochvenniki* interpreted nihilism as an extreme manifestation of NIHILISM westernism. The same bold humanitarianism and cold rationalism sustained both. Like westernism, they held, nihilism personified the critical side of the Russian national character. It was a necessary development and served the useful function of destroying many cherished Russian illusions. But nihilism, like its predecessor, had practically outlived its usefulness. The adherents of *pochvennichestvo* asserted that, in part, their own movement had been spawned from the negation of the nihilists. The rise of *pochvennichestvo* was evidence that the time for negation had ended and that of construction had begun.[21] There was a measure of truth in this contention. The intelligentsia conservatives had defined many of their most cherished views in opposition to the materialism, scientism, and utilitarianism of the radicals.

Since the nihilists had inherited the rationalist tradition of the westernizers, they were, in the view of the *pochvenniki*, likewise theoreticians. They did not know Russia or Russians. Their ideas were not rooted in the firm soil of Russian nationality but were hollow repetitions of the most advanced social ideals of the West, which were detached from Russian reality. The *pochvenniki* defined ultra-westernism as the idea of extreme centralization in the name of abstract humanity coupled with the

VLTRA-
WESTCENISM

fanatical belief in an infinite progress that endlessly devoured its offspring.[22] In the cosmopolitan fantasies of the radicals, nationalities merged and individuals were reduced, in Dostoevsky's words, to 'effaced copper coins.'[23]

The eagerness of the 'theoreticians' to sacrifice nationality, traditions, and individuality, the analysis of the *pochvenniki* continued, arose from their obsession with the notion of universal material well-being. A naïve faith in science and progress was the source of materialism. The radicals had deluded themselves into believing that science had cleared the way for the endless extension of material progress and that the problems of mankind, material and moral, would one by one submit to the soothing caress of the scientist.

MATERIALISM

The essence of the idealist critique of materialism was that science was too narrowly based to encompass the totality of human thought and actions, and materialism was unable to account for a free will that defied both the laws of nature and, at times, human self-interest. Under one of his more pessimistic pseudonyms, Grigor'ev diagnosed the disease of progress and proclaimed a manifesto of idealism:

Because of a profound sympathy for progress, the dreariest faith in the infiniteness of progress has been implanted to a point of incurability; in us, the unnecessary people, above all dwells the forlorn conviction that the human soul with its multi-various strings remains and will always remain the same, that the moon will never unite with the earth as Fourier hoped; neither will the variegated colours of nationalities and individuals coalesce into a common, tidy, robust and mundane mass of humanity; nor will the human passions be reduced to mathematically determined and voluntarily acceded to needs; nor will art, that eternal hymn and eternal howl of the human soul, dry up and disappear.[24]

Grigor'ev made it clear that the *pochvenniki* declined to accept the materialist proposition that men were merely atoms in a universe of like atoms, all equally subject to the scientific laws of matter. The natural sciences, they argued, were only one aspect of intellectual activity and not the centre of gravity of historical life. As Strakhov wrote, 'Human life is shaped and guided by other, more profound principles.'[25] Man could transcend his environment and rise above the laws of nature because he alone among living creatures was able to decree laws and form ideals for himself that contradicted the laws slavishly followed by nature.

The mindless application of the principle of natural selection to social development, in which early Social Darwinists indulged, particularly distressed Strakhov. In a review of Mlle Clémence Royer's notorious introduction to the first French edition of Darwin's *Origin of Species*, Strakhov insisted that man was distinguished by his capacity to will against nature and was, therefore, distinct from nature; he concluded: 'One thing is perfectly obvious: we cease to understand human life, we lose its meaning as soon as we fail to distinguish man from nature, as soon as we place him alongside its other products and begin to judge him from the same point of view from which we judge plants and animals. The secret of human life is contained in life itself.'[26]

The *pochvenniki* attacked the utilitarianism of the radicals, along with their materialism. They maintained that utilitarianism was untenable as an explanation of human motivation. The primary concerns of men in life were not exclusively linked to their material comfort. 'They constantly want to make life a very serious profession,' Strakhov declared, 'to turn it into a matter more important and gratifying than the simple absence of suffering.'[27] On the contrary, men were by nature idealists who struggled towards a higher purpose than the mere winning of their daily bread. Idealism ruled the world and, though it was the source of most human suffering, could not be destroyed.

The *pochvenniki* believed that the nihilists were not only wrong but also a threat to the survival of civilization. As men of art and of not inconsiderable learning, the *pochvenniki* were profoundly aware of the agonized struggle through which civilization had passed to attain its present level of sophistication. They were far from believing that the achievements of Western culture in art, philosophy, and theology were false or superfluous to the needs of modern man. But the theory of progress deceived men into supposing that the accomplishments of the past were at best but instruments, now useless, of the higher attainments of the present or at worst obstacles to a rationalist reordering of social and intellectual life. The *pochvenniki* were dismayed at the cavalier treatment accorded history, philosophy, and art by the nihilists. In a controversial article about Dobroliubov, Dostoevsky compared the young critic with Belinsky. Belinsky, he maintained, had grown up under the best influences of European intellectual life. Dobroliubov, while an honourable man, had acquired as a seminarist a narrow, distorted education. His sole aim was to demonstrate to his readers that intellectual authorities were unnecessary, and that long study and profound thought were superfluous. Whereas Belinsky constantly raised the level of Russian culture and education, Dobroliubov deliberately diminished it.[28]

Both Strakhov and Dostoevsky energetically defended history and philosophy against strident attacks by Chernyshevsky and by Antonovich, the self-appointed guardian angel of materialism. Grigor'ev raged against those critics – presumably Pisarev was one of them – who supposed that all worthwhile knowledge was contained in a handful of popular books. The *pochvenniki* were persuaded that although particular authorities were subject to criticism, the general authority of philosophy, science, and art had to be recognized. 'This authority is property acquired throughout the whole life of mankind. The existence of this authority is a sign that there can no longer be chaos and vacillation in human life, that it can no longer disintegrate into atoms.'[29] Art, science, and philosophy were the present fruits and future guarantee of civilization. In undermining their authority the Russian materialists had become the agents not of construction but of a senseless destruction, modern Huns who rode roughshod over the inheritance of centuries.

In June 1862, Chernyshevsky was arrested and eventually exiled, and *Sovremennik* and *Russkoe slovo* were suspended from publication by order of the censor for eight months. When *Sovremennik* resumed publication in 1863, all pretense of cordiality and even sensible argument between *Vremia* and *Sovremennik* was abandoned. In January 1863, the new editors of *Sovremennik*, who now included the novelist M.E. Saltykov-Shchedrin, assessed the tendency of *Vremia* in an unsigned article. *Vremia* was characterized, they wrote, by its 'naïve self-satisfaction.' Dostoevsky and his cohorts, they charged, not without justification, had failed totally to define what they meant by the soil and dashed from one side to another in a series of contradictory articles. Almost all the useful ideas now being published in *Vremia* had already appeared in *Sovremennik*. The evaluation concluded with a resounding denunciation of the *pochvenniki*: 'Your point of departure is false; you constantly state: the theoreticians give themselves up to extremes, they persecute both the good and the bad sides of Russian life, while we hold to the middle, rejecting what is bad and bringing to light and publicizing what is good; this is all nonsense, phrases and phrases as you can see for yourselves; those whom you have called the theoreticians have also recognized the good sides and pointed them out before you.'[30]

Sovremennik's fresh offensive precipitated a merciless round of slanging between the two journals. The exchange, though no doubt highly gratifying to the main combatants, Dostoevsky and Saltykov-Shchedrin, produced scarcely a single constructive idea. The hostilities continued almost unabated until *Epokha*, the successor to *Vremia*, went bankrupt in

March 1865. At the end of the day the *pochvenniki* were no less convinced than before that the nihilists had their feet in the air.

In the furor which followed the publication of Turgenev's *Fathers and* ОТЦЫ и *Children*, the *pochvenniki* seized on the main character, Bazarov, as the дети embodiment of the separation between life and thought in nihilism. Bazarov, Strakhov wrote in an unsigned review of the novel, consciously rejected life. Beneath the external characteristics grafted on to him by his education, however, he lived deeply and passionately. In the face of living experience, he proved incapable of cold, abstract detachment. Life stood above him, directed his actions, and ultimately destroyed him when he resisted.[31] In another context, Dostoevsky had written, 'Life and reality are for us.'[32] Nihilism, the *pochvenniki* were certain, could not for long hold out against the forward flow of life.

The polemic with *Sovremennik* was an education in the ethics and psychology of politics for Dostoevsky. Having descended into the journalistic fray from the detached and dogmatic heights of universal reconciliation, he was forced to meet and to recognize the enemy. He found himself having to choose among alternative programs for social change and to admit the limitations of reconciliation as an instrument for ideological harmonization. From at least the end of 1862, the nihilists became outsiders in Dostoevsky's view, irreconcilable, westernizing aliens, who neither knew nor loved the Russian people. Organicism and gradualism, he realized, had to be fought for rather than being left to flow from the course of events.

His education bore immediate literary fruits in *Winter Notes on Summer Impressions*, written in the winter of 1862–3, following his first trip to western Europe, and published in *Vremia* in 1863, and in *Notes from Underground*, probably conceived late in 1862, written in 1863, and published in *Epokha* in 1864. In these works, especially the latter, Dostoevsky subjected Chernyshevky's utilitarian doctrine of enlightened egoism to a devastating psychological analysis and rejected the very possibility of constructing human life on rational foundations. He found an alternative to utilitarianism in the autonomy of the individual, the absolute need of the personality to develop and assert itself. In Russia, however, the anarchic personality was tempered by the national principle of fraternity. 'The well developed personality,' he wrote, 'completely convinced of its right to be a personality and no longer fearing for itself, cannot put its own individuality to any other use, that is, has no other purpose, except to give the whole of itself to all so that all others too may

SOLUTION
2
CHERNY.

be equally autonomous and happy.'[33] For Dostoevsky, true self-sacrifice, free of the slightest expectation of self-advantage, was possible only in the most advanced stage of individuality. It was in the debate with *Sovremennik* that Dostoevsky developed and honed his conception of the relation between the autonomous personality and the community.

RUSSKII
VESTNIK

In *Russkii vestnik* he met and recognized a related but different enemy: conservative westernism. Like the *pochvenniki*, the editor of *Russkii vestnik*, M.N. Katkov, was steeped in German idealism. He had, however, developed a lively interest in English society and institutions which significantly influenced his social and political views, and his Anglomania had reached the peak of its intensity in the early 1860s. During the first years of his editorship, from 1856 to 1860, Katkov, too, had been caught up in the reconciliatory spirit of the age and had tried to forge in *Russkii vestnik* a broad westernizer-Slavophile alliance that excluded only the radicals around *Sovremennik*. Katkov's idea of reconciliation was scarcely philosophical. It was instead pragmatic and political, an attempt to find some common ground among the individuals and factions within the journalistic fraternity. Katkov himself assumed a pose of aloofness from the sectarian squabblings of the journals and so opened himself to persistent charges of opportunism.

Katkov had, however, mature and clear political views of his own in which he tried to reconcile his English-inspired ideal with the needs and conditions of Russia. He was a monarchist who believed that the safeguard against bureaucratic absolutism lay in an aristocracy. 'Uproot the monarchical principle,' he argued, 'and it will become the despotism of a dictator; destroy the natural aristocratic element in society, and its place will be taken either by bureaucrats and demagogues, or by an oligarchy of the worst kind ... destroy centralization and not its abuse, but its very root, and you will kill the whole nationality, you will destroy the labor of centuries, you will undermine the basis for future development.'[34] Katkov had been highly critical, even in his most liberal period, of the statist principles of Chicherin and Kavelin. He had broken with Chicherin because 'in his [Chicherin's] opinion, the state rises above everything, and everything bows at its feet'[35] and had fallen out with Kavelin over the question whether communal and private property should coexist in Russia, as Kavelin advocated, or whether communal tenure should universally give way to private ownership, as Katkov wished. In Katkov's view, state and society had distinct but complimentary spheres and functions which came together organically through the agency of a *zemskii sobor*, an advisory council of the land. He was not a constitutionalist in any of the accepted meanings of the term. He rejected all legalistic or formalistic contractual relationships and vehemently denied having ever advocated parliamentarianism in Russia.

The organic union of autocrat and society could not be effected, in Katkov's opinion, until society attained economic, social, and moral freedom. He opposed the government's decision to retain the collective fiscal responsibility of the commune because he believed it restricted the peasants' mobility and inhibited their growth as independent producers. Katkov could discern no independent social group in Russia. He did not see in the Russian gentry an equivalent of western aristocracy. The primary characteristic of aristocracy was its autonomy, whereas, to Katkov, the Russian gentry represented a dependent state class. He hoped, however, to create an aristocratic element in Russia through the imposition of a high property qualification in *zemstvo* elections.[36] From this group of wealthy and leisured electors, which he viewed as a kind of English squirearchy, he expected political leadership in local self-government. Although all citizens would enjoy civil responsibility in Katkov's Russia, only the wealthy would be entrusted with political responsibility.

Katkov was genuinely outraged by the continued agitation of the radicals for more concessions after the Emancipation decree in February 1861. He identified a number of enemies of public order, whom he tended to lump together, but most dangerous among them were the nihilists. He, therefore, embarked on a furious anti-nihilist campaign in *Russkii vestnik*. Unlike the *pochvenniki*, Katkov did not distinguish between the means and ends advocated by the nihilists. Consequently, he openly polemicized against several of the more moderate humanitarian goals of Chernyshevsky and his followers. It was in the defence of some of these goals that *Vremia* was first drawn into a confrontation with the editor of *Russkii vestnik*. Katkov had singled out *Svistok*, the satirical supplement to *Sovremennik*, for special abuse. In March 1861, *Vremia* came to the defence of *Svistok*[37]; Katkov replied sarcastically and hostilities got under way in earnest.

The *pochvenniki* objected to the complacency and intolerance of *Russkii vestnik*, its 'conceit, magnificence of Jupiter and childish irritability.'[38] They hastened to add that they did not agree with *Svistok* but found something vital and useful in it in contrast to the morbid pedantry of *Russkii vestnik*. They charged that Katkov made the mistake of most reactionaries of judging the worth of an idea by the people who advocated it. But not all ideas supported by extremists were inherently false. Any idea, *Vremia* pointed out, could be slandered, perverted, and ridiculed; this had, in fact, been a favorite resort of the reactionary Bulgarin in the 1840s.[39] But to reject all ideas simply because they were new was to block the progress of society towards more normal relations.

WOMENS'
EMANCIPATN →

The particular example that the editors of *Vremia* settled on was the question of women's emancipation. By women's emancipation, they explained, they did not mean that a woman should cuckold her husband at every opportunity. Rather, they wanted to urge on society the need for a more loving attitude towards women. *Russkii vestnik*, they continued, had falsely argued that in Russia women were equal in the law. Even if they were, the editors of *Vremia* replied, it was not a matter of law but of customs and beliefs. The moral equality of women was essential so that the feudal ideal of chivalry, lionized by *Russkii vestnik*, would give way to the love and respect of equals. The sense of marital duty would not diminish, and nothing would die out except a few unnatural conventions imposed by men.[40] 'History is surely nothing more than the canvas of this dying out and the gradual drawing near of mankind to legitimate, natural and normal duty ... And surely you know history, you often talk about it.'[41]

Katkov replied sourly that all the feverish talk in *Vremia* about the soil and Russian literature was simply another sign of the cultural rot that was besetting Russia. Later, he lumped the 'notorious teaching about alienation from the native soil' together with nihilism.[42]

D's PLAY

The debate with Katkov about progress towards more normal and humanitarian human and social relations may have contributed to Dostoevsky's reluctance to break entirely with the radicals. As late as October 1862, he wrote a satirical play in *Vremia* in which he sided with the nihilists against Katkov. The setting of the play was an imaginary meeting of the right, the nihilists, and the progressives. Katkov was the main orator at this meeting and the nihilists and others occasionally interjected comments. The intention of the play was to ridicule Katkov's Anglomania and to poke fun at his haughty aloofness. Katkov was portrayed as a man completely enamoured of form and indifferent to substance. Dostoevsky mistakenly accused Katkov of trying to introduce parliamentarianism into Russia in spite of the fact that there was no basis for such a form in Russian reality. The play leaves no doubt that Dostoevsky placed himself among the progressives who in the play had much more in common with the nihilists than with the right.[43]

The differences between *Vremia* and *Russkii vestnik* went well beyond humanitarian concerns. Katkov's whole conception of the future political and social order of Russia contradicted the most fundamental convictions of the *pochvenniki*. In December 1862 *Vremia* turned its attention to

Katkov's hopes for the gentry in local self-government. The editors strongly opposed Katkov's plans to develop an aristocratic element in Russia by assigning the task of local administration to the landed gentry.[44] It was not, said *Vremia*, the intention of the manifesto on the *zemstva* to turn them into aristocratic institutions. Katkov's distinction between an aristocratic element enjoying political rights and a popular element enjoying only civil rights, the *pochvenniki* contended, was alien to Russian traditions. Russia knew only the *narod*, the whole nation (*natsiia*), and the Russian tsar. Within the *narod* there were neither estates nor corporations.[45]

Dostoevsky was suspicious also of the statist elements contained in Katkov's conception of Russian nationality. It smacked, in his view, too much of the official nationality of the reign of Nicholas I. 'Mr. Katkov,' he wrote in his notebook in 1863, 'finds no difference between our official life and the basic Russian national forces. There Mr. Katkov stubs his toe.'[46] To Dostoevsky, true Russian nationality lay outside the state and its functions and resided entirely in the traditions of the land. Earlier he had pointed out that on several occasions in Russian history the state had been annihilated whereas the land remained and had saved and restored the state. 'The nucleus of life will always be the *narod*,'[47] he concluded.

The *pochvenniki* found Katkov's westernism, like the schemes of the nihilists, to be theoretical and detached from the realities of Russian life and needs. Katkov's ideals, Dostoevsky once remarked, had less chance of being realized in Russia than those of Fourier. In *Den'*, the Slavophile journal of Ivan Aksakov, *Vremia* discovered 'theoretical' views of a quite different sort. The Slavophile ideal was not imported from the West but transferred from Russia's own distant past and in many respects corresponded closely with *Vremia*'s own hopes for Russia. The ideological distance between *Vremia* and *Den'* was not, therefore, very great, a fact that probably accounted for the mistrust with which they eyed one another. Both were attempting to defend the orthodoxy of Russian nationality and to occupy the same ground but from different directions.

After the deaths of Khomiakov and Konstantin Aksakov, both in 1860, the younger Aksakov brother, Ivan, had become the chief spokesman for the Slavophile camp. His views as they were expressed in *Den'* represented Slavophilism as the public knew it in the 1860s. The *pochvenniki* were themselves far from unanimous in their attitude towards the Slavophiles. While remaining highly critical of Slavophilism Grigor'ev nevertheless admired its founders and sought to honour their memory whenever possible. Strakhov, whose primary concern was to forge a broad national-

istic and idealistic front against nihilism, was seldom critical of the
Slavophile tendency though he once judged Ivan Aksakov to be a
'fanatic'[48]; Dostoevsky, who in fact rarely hesitated to criticize the
Slavophiles, had little direct knowledge of their writings until the summer
of 1863, when *Vremia* had already been proscribed by the censor. In
September of that year he wrote to Strakhov that the Slavophiles, whose
works he had been reading during the summer, had indeed said a 'new
word.'[49] Before this revelation, however, Dostoevsky was censorious of
Slavophilism in general and of *Den'* in particular.

The mutual suspicion of the two journals was not entirely unfounded.
There were significant differences between the *pochvennichestvo* of *Vremia*
and the Slavophilism of *Den'*. The *pochvenniki* made little distinction
between the earlier Slavophilism of Kireevsky or Khomiakov and the later
Slavophilism of Aksakov. Dostoevsky greeted the first number of *Den'*,
which appeared in October 1861, coldly: 'These are the same Slavophiles,
the same pure, ideal Slavophilism, not a whit changed, whose ideals to this
day are so forcefully entangled with reality; for them there are neither
events nor lessons. The same Slavophiles with the same implacable hatred
for everything that is not theirs and with the same incapacity for
reconciliation; the same violent impotence and petty, completely un-
Russian formalism.'[50] Dostoevsky later conceded, however, that *Den'* and
the Slavophilism of which it was the heir had revealed several sides of
Russian nationality previously concealed and cited the Slavophile emphasis on the commune as an example.[51]

Grigor'ev, as is known, was deeply suspicious of the Slavophile
idealization of Muscovy. He viewed it, in the same way he viewed the
nihilists' admiration for the most advanced Western ideas, as theory that
always sought to reduce the great variety of life to a single, simple
formula. He detected the same tendency in *Den'*. Only a few days before
his death in 1864, he urged on Strakhov the necessity to combat the
centralizing proclivities of *Den'* and to defend the rights of the regions
against the claims of the Moscow ideal.[52] Grigor'ev distinguished between
Slavophilism (*Slavianofil'stvo*), which he regarded as a contrived theory of
Muscovite centralism, and Slavism (*Slavianizm*), which he saw as the living
expression of the Slavic soul in all its many manifestations. He believed
that if Russians severed their links with the latter, they would be cutting
themselves off from their very essence and falling into a narrow
exclusivism.[53] The whole idea of pan-Slavism as a political movement with
Moscow at the head was alien to Grigor'ev, who saw in the Slavs a colourful
family of diverse cultures. At this time, too, Dostoevsky showed little

[margin note: LITTLE INTEREST IN PAN SLAVISM]

interest in pan-Slavism though he never shared Grigor'ev's strong regionalist views with much enthusiasm.

Grigor'ev's fears of Aksakov's Muscovite intolerance were not far wrong. When *Vremia* was closed by order of the censor in 1863, Strakhov wrote to Aksakov to beg his good offices in petitioning for the reinstatement of the journal. Aksakov had no intention of assisting Dostoevsky, however. Instead, he sent a reply to Strakhov in which he gave full vent to his dislike of *Vremia* and its tendency. *[margin note: MUSCOVITE TENDENCIES]* Among the failings of Dostoevsky's journal, he included the damaging fact that it was published in St Petersburg. In his opinion, a journal could not be national and yet emanate from that alien capital. Many years later, in his memoirs, Strakhov made the pusillanimous reply that since both Dostoevsky and Grigor'ev had been born in Moscow and he, himself, was a provincial, the tendency of *Vremia* was not fatally flawed.[54]

Aksakov disagreed also with the whole idea of the reconciliation of the educated with the people. *[margin note: VS. RECONCILIATION]* Like the early Slavophiles, he maintained that the educated ranks of Russian society had betrayed and lost their nationality after the reforms of Peter the Great. He chided 'certain St. Petersburg journalists' for believing that some essential bond still existed between educated society and the peasants. The differences between the two segments of the nation, according to Aksakov, were not quantitative but qualitative. Two separate worlds had developed according to completely different laws. If a peasant, he wrote in October 1861, could hear the educated toadying to Western sources and pouring scorn on everything indigenous to Russia, he would say, 'I do not need you, you are alien to me.'[55] Aksakov, therefore, saw no possibility of the reconciliation of the two worlds. Unlike the *pochvenniki*, who were quick to advocate the fullest participation of the peasantry in all the new reform institutions, Aksakov was dubious at first, particularly about peasant participation in the *zemstvo*. Only later did he adopt *Vremia's* position that such participation was the key to the building of a self-conscious society.[56] It is evident that at this time he was still clinging to the old Slavophile concept of interiorization, or a voluntary withdrawal from the greater world into the national Orthodox spirit.[57]

In the same letter to Strakhov in which he accused *Vremia* of being anti-national, Aksakov also charged it with not openly propounding Christianity. In his opinion, Russian nationality was grounded exclusively in Orthodoxy, and its fate was inextricably bound up with the intensification of national life in the spirit of the church.[58] *[margin note: ORTHODOXY]* It is true, as Strakhov later admitted, that *Vremia* did not express clear views about religion.[59] The *pochvenniki*, particularly Grigor'ev, accepted Orthodoxy as one of the components of Russian nationality, but their conception of nationality was more psychological than religious. The universal reconciliatory powers and the fraternity of the Russian people were characteristics of the national psychological makeup that existed prior to the conversion to Christianity. Orthodoxy was one of their expressions but not their source. The *pochvenniki* and Aksakov disagreed also about the nature of true Orthodoxy. Although Aksakov was critical of the Russian church he, nevertheless, adhered to the Orthodoxy of the Nikonian reforms of the seventeenth century that were the basis of the official church. The *pochvenniki*, on the contrary, believed that the *Raskol*, or schism, was nearer to the original, democratic religious spirit of the people than was the official Orthodoxy that the schismatics had repudiated.[60] It was to this spirit that the *pochvenniki* wished to return.

Aksakov and the *pochvenniki* further differed over the relationship between the individual and the community. Aksakov argued that though the people (*narod*) was comprised of individuals each with his own personal life and separate spheres of action and freedom, such individuals taken separately were not the *narod*. Only individuals taken together made up a new collective personality, the *narod*, in which separate personalities disappeared. As part of the national organism each individual lived not according to the dictates of his intellect but was guided by the collective consciousness. Aksakov believed that morality was defined not by personal convictions but by custom and the collective way of life. Although he advocated the strengthening of the personality to enable it to retain its sense of allegiance even in separation from the *narod*, he did not mean by this the strengthening of individuality, but the reinforcement of the national idea in the personality to the exclusion of individuality.[61] These views on the relationship between the individual and the community reflected the influence of that current of German romanticism that totally subordinated the individual to the collective, seeing in this voluntary subordination the essence of personal freedom. The *pochvenniki*, by contrast, were the heirs of that branch of the romantic school that demanded the fullest possible freedom for the individual development of the personality.

In reading *Vremia* and *Den'* one is struck by the humanitarianism of the former and the intolerance of the latter. This is particularly evident in their respective attitudes to the Jews in Russia. Aksakov argued that since it was impossible to be Russian and not be Orthodox, those Jews who did not wish to convert should be excluded from all national political and social activities.[62] *Vremia* sprang to the defence of the Jews in the name of the Christian spirit of 'peace, love and concord.' *Den'*, the *pochvenniki* argued, was arousing hatred without just cause.[63] A few months later *Vremia* returned to the theme of the Jews. The argument was made that if political restrictions and the laws confining Jews to particular localities were revoked, the Jewish Question would resolve itself: 'When they are given the right to citizenship in the whole of Russia, they will disperse over the whole state, become inconspicuous, disappear and be swallowed up by the majority because there will be one of them to every one hundred Christian souls.'[64] Such an implied policy of assimilation may have been objectionable to most Jews, but it was preferable to the persecution Aksakov advocated. It is unlikely that these views on the Jewish question could have been expressed so consistently in *Vremia* without Dostoevsky's approval. In light of his later anti-Semitism they are all the more remarkable. In any event, the humanitarian note struck by *Vremia* in its attitude to the Jews was illustrative of the difference in tone between *Vremia*, which was compromising and conciliatory, and *Den'*, which was dogmatic and intransigent.

Although *Vremia* and *Den'* differed in tone and were far apart on a number of important humanitarian issues, they were basically in agreement when it came to questions of ideology. Both conceived of Russian nationality and the institutions appropriate to it as exclusively the product of Russia's historical experience and uncompromisingly excluded even the possibility of borrowing social or political forms from the West. Strakhov had already made it clear that his sympathies lay with Slavophilism and was soon to lead *Vremia*'s successor, *Epokha*, in its 'surrender to *Den'*.' As Dostoevsky familiarized himself in 1863 with the work of the early Slavophiles, he too more and more reoriented his thinking towards the religious basis of Slavophilism. Even more significantly, Aksakov was at the same time fundamentally revising the patriarchal notions of his Slavophile predecessors and moving towards the more democratic, evolutionary, and reconciliatory ideas that characterized *pochvennichestvo*.

With the passing of the first generation of the Slavophiles, the younger Aksakov had been faced with the difficult task of forging from the vague cultural idealism of his Slavophile predecessors a political and social doctrine applicable to the radically changed conditions of post-Emancipation Russia. Although he struggled to preserve the essentials of early Slavophilism, Aksakov made a number of important concessions. The most significant was the sacrifice of the idealization of the common people as the sole proprietors of the national spirit. The early Slavophiles maintained that the common people fully embodied the one, true religion, Orthodoxy, and were living a Christian social life in their communes. The national salvation of all Russians, in their view, lay in their voluntary surrender to the people in, as Robert E. MacMaster has written, 'a new degree of interiorization, achieved through more active, dedicated, corporate life in the Church.'[65] It was this new life that would serve as an ideal example of the Christian commonwealth to other Europeans.

Ivan Aksakov, in contrast, denied that the common people were in possession of a secret truth that the educated had somehow lost after the reforms of Peter. Early in his career, he had been impressed by the abysmal ignorance of peasant life and had been unable to detect the image of the saints in the Russian peasant. In the communal mode of life and the naïve religiosity of the peasants he discerned, however, the potential for a Christian nation. By 1862, he concluded that the nation did not exist in actuality in the ignorant masses but only in potentiality. The actualization of the nation took place, according to Aksakov, only when the people had raised themselves to the level of *obshchestvo* (society). 'Obshchestvo,' he explained, was that 'milieu in which the conscious, intellectual activity of a particular people takes place, which creates national self-consciousness by means of national and spiritual forces which have already been worked out. In other words, *obshchestvo* IS the *narod* in its second moment, on the second level of its development, the self-conscious *narod*.'[66]

Aksakov maintained that genuine social activity was the product of national self-consciousness. The creation of national self-consciousness in turn rested on education (*obrazovanie*). By education Aksakov did not mean merely a fund of knowledge or intellectual education. Rather, he had in mind a personal and spiritual development through which the individual personality recognized its identity with the whole nation and expressed the national idea as its own. Aksakov insisted that *obshchestvo* was formed not of a federation of classes but of people drawn from all classes and linked by education. Literacy was, in his opinion, a tool for the creation of *obshchestvo*, but was inadequate in itself. Neither a literate peasantry nor the educated gentry constituted *obshchestvo* unless it was conscious of doing so, that is, unless it was conscious of its common identity in the national ideal. Since the press was the best means for expressing and clarifying the all-national principle and thus creating *obshchestvo*, the realm of free opinion, Aksakov required freedom for the printed word and liberty of conscience.[67]

Aksakov also offered, for the first time in Slavophilism, the broad definition of the people (*narod*) that Kireevsky had called for in 1847. He asserted that the *narod* could be understood in two senses. In the broad sense, it embraced the entire population; in the narrow sense, it included only the common people. The *narod*, which was the unconscious repository of the national idea, constituted a living, spiritual organism. The thought process of the national organism was one of unconscious creativity. Conscious activity took place when separate individuals began to articulate thoughts that the *narod* had only felt in their unconscious. Such conscious expressions gradually formed a stock of national self-consciousness, the culmination of which was the creation of *obshchestvo*.[68]

Aksakov despised the radical intelligensia, in spite of its superior education, because he believed it was totally blind to its own nationality. He accused both the nihilists and the liberals of tampering with history by attempting to impose a preconceived plan of social organization on the people rather than encouraging the free, organic development of the nation from its own principles. For all his hostility to the radicals, it was evident that Aksakov was revising his view of the broader stratum of educated Russian society. The idea of the reconciliation of the people with the educated was by the middle of the 1860s becoming a canon of Slavophilism. In September 1864, for example, M.N. Lopatin wrote to *Den'* 'from the country': '*The educated Russian people* and the *peasantry* are the only two forces which can and must move our *internal* social life forward. While they are divided and, even worse, while they are hostile, internal life stands dumb and immobile. It kills and crushes everything that needs light and freedom. Imagine them united and going hand in hand. This is to imagine an ideal of such social sublimity that before it even an inveterate Fourierist's head would be turned.'[69] Dostoevsky recognized the significance of Lopatin's article for *pochvennichestvo* and made an oblique reference to it in his notebook.[70]

If accommodation with *Den'* seemed possible, even probable, it was unthinkable with *Sovremennik*. Any illusions that Dostoevsky had harboured about the possibility of reconciling the nihilists with the 'native soil' had by now been dispelled. The break with *Sovremennik* and the bitter, though far less traumatic, exchanges with *Russkii vestnik* were indicative of the deep divisions within Russian society and thought. By 1863 the era of harmonious feelings had passed. It was replaced by a period of clashing interests as groups jockeyed for position in the new order. In such a climate hopes for universal reconciliation inevitably faded.

9

Second thoughts

During the polemics between *Vremia* and its rivals, the conservative nature of *pochvennichestvo* became more prominent. Dostoevsky renounced his earlier flirtation with the radicals, and Grigor'ev and Strakhov hardened their anti-nihilist views. In spite of their new-found unanimity about the harmfulness of radical tendencies in Russia, the three principals of *pochvennichestvo* were soon to differ in their approachs to Russian nationality and the question of Russia and the West. All three had always, in any case, retained a certain individuality regarding these matters, and changing political, social, and economic conditions in the decades following the reforms were conducive to second thoughts about Russia and its place in the world.

Dostoevsky's dalliance with Chernyshevsky in 1861 and 1862 had proven a source of considerable vexation to Grigor'ev. He had left St Petersburg for Orenburg in June 1861 and from there had levelled a flood of criticisms against the Dostoevsky brothers and a number of *Vremia's* contributors, making it clear that he regarded himself as the guardian of the purity of Russian nationality. At the beginning of June 1862, he returned from Orenburg, where he had led a lonely and dissolute existence. In spite of his deteriorating health and his state of depression on his return, he settled down to repair his ruined fortunes. He published frequently in *Vremia* and supplemented his income by translating Italian librettos for the Russian opera. By the end of the year, he was living in an orderly flat and, according to Strakhov, was even affecting a certain dandyism in dress.[1]

Grigor'ev was at this time completely absorbed in the operas of Aleksandr Serov and the plays of Ostrovsky. He also exercised extensive influence on a circle, to which Serov belonged, that had formed around

A.A. Potekhin. Grigor'ev had enormous faith in Serov as a national artist, and the critic's death was a severe blow to the composer. Shortly before he died, Grigor'ev in a debtor's cell urged Serov to ignore the sceptics and to write a great national opera that could serve as an example to other composers.

At the beginning of 1863, F.T. Stellovsky, a publisher and music store proprietor, decided to finance a weekly social, literary, theatrical, musical, and artistic journal called *Iakor'* (The Anchor); he appointed Grigor'ev editor-in-chief. Grigor'ev took on the editorship as the 'last serious gambit of my life.'[2] It began badly: on a trip to Moscow to round up contributors, the sight of his home city so demoralized him with nostalgia that he spent all his money and returned to St Petersburg having done nothing for the paper. In spite of this setback, *Iakor'* appeared at the end of March 1863. Grigor'ev at first worked feverishly to make it a success, elated once again to control fully the editorial policy of a journal. He also edited a satirical supplement to *Iakor'* called *Osa* (The Wasp). Neither met with any real success except in the theatrical world, and Grigor'ev soon lost interest in them. Although he remained the official editor of both journals until his death in September 1864, he had virtually ceased to take an active part in their publication by the beginning of that year.[3] For a brief period, however, he took advantage of the opportunity to express his ideas without any editorial constraints.

Grigor'ev conceived of the main tasks of *Iakor'* on two separate planes – negative and positive. He believed that many of the contemporary programs for solving Russia's problems, based as they were on the concept of material progress, were false. The negative, or critical, task of his journal was 'to draw attention to these false notes wherever they are heard, without fear or hesitation: here is our critical, negative and, consequently, defined task, – because with us, in general only our negation is defined.'[4] For this critical function, the satire of *Osa* provided the most useful weapon. Grigor'ev cautioned, however, that satire, unless used carefully, could undermine the faith of the masses in literature and journalism. Satire was effective only when something positive, 'a living faith in the idea of truth, beauty and order, an ardent sympathy for the ideal,' was visible through its negation.[5] Grigor'ev left no doubt that this elusive ideal was to be found in nationality, the exposition of which constituted the positive task of *Iakor'*: 'We know one thing only: that we have a positive haven (*pristan'*), – nationality, with its historically typical features – a profound faith in its power – and an anchorage in the continuous bond of its traditions. We put down our anchor in this haven.'[6]

The positive side could not, Grigor'ev argued, be as clearly defined as the negative: 'It would be unjust to demand from us greater definition than from the other "native soil" tendencies which are related to us. As with all of them, our positive task is more a feeling than a definite, theoretical idea – the difference is that we had, and have, a unique claim – that is, the greatest freedom and spontaneity of feeling in comparison with them.'[7] Grigor'ev declared the solidarity of his journal with *Den'* and with *Vremia* but wished *Iakor'* to be less exclusive than the former and bolder and more definite than the latter. *Iakor'* sought neither to reconcile East and West, nor to reverse the reforms made by Peter. Great as was his respect for Slavophilism, Grigor'ev continued to differ with it on several points. First, he conceived of nationality as an organic phenomenon in which elements from before and after Peter were combined. Second, he saw the 'people' not as just the 'old nobility' (*boiarstvo*) and the 'steppe peasants,' but as all the strata of Russian society as a whole. As he had as a 'young editor,' he believed that the merchant class best embodied this integrated nationality.[8] *Iakor'* rejected the Slavophile ideal of the past and turned instead to literature and art as the source of a new ideal, even though the Slavophiles judged literature and art to be rotten and false.[9]

While sharing *Vremia's* profound faith in the people, Grigor'ev felt that the tendency of Dostoevsky's journal was inadequate in a number of respects. He believed that the reconciliation of the principles of the westernized élite in Russia with the principles of the common people was primarily a national endeavour without universal significance. Dostoevsky, in contrast, viewed this synthesis as the universal reconciliation of the fundamental principles of East and West, and hence of the peoples of East and West. Grigor'ev felt also that *Vremia* inadequately understood the national ideal, because it had not fully accepted the importance of Orthodoxy: 'Apart from our sincere belief in the highest dogmatic essence of Orthodoxy – we believe in its enormous, historical significance ... In spite of all its numberless schisms, which indicate among other things the full vitality of its fluids, Orthodoxy is a vigorously alive phenomenon, and like everything alive is strongly united with its essence. The life of the land may have deviated from the norm on many points but, all the same, it stubbornly adhered to its spiritual independence, to its collective and national mores.'[10]

Although in his organic criticism he had done much to foster it himself, Grigor'ev had been uncomfortable with the psychological interpretation of nationality in *Vremia*. By the end of 1863, Dostoevsky, as will be seen, had also begun to conceive of Russian nationality in religious rather than psychological terms. Both men had by this time accepted the view of Orthodoxy that the Slavophile A.I. Koshelev had encapsulated in the late 1850s: 'Nationality alone does not give us universal significance ... Only faith can ... create something organic ... With Orthodoxy, our nationality has world significance. Without Orthodoxy, our nationality is empty.'[11] Grigor'ev's view that Orthodoxy was a universal principle destined to replace a moribund Catholicism may have influenced the formation of Dostoevsky's later religious outlook.

In *Iakor'*, Grigor'ev firmly adhered to his belief in localism. He published one of his own letters to Strakhov from Orenburg; in it he had defended the Siberian historian Shchapov as a phenomenon as important as Ostrovsky and pointed out that the two men had much in common.[12] An unsigned leading article, perhaps not written by Grigor'ev but, nevertheless, expressing his views, upheld the right of Ukrainian nationality to a life of its own. Grigor'ev drew no separatist conclusions from his doctrine of localism.[13] He was a cultural federalist and a political decentralist who believed in regional self-administration but not in political separation. The idea that cultural nationalism could lead to demands for political independence appears never to have occurred to him.

He expressed his spare political views in another leading article in *Iakor'*. The government, he reasoned, was about to undergo not a political but a moral change. By this, he meant that the bureaucracy and the big landowners were losing their grip on the nation's administration and that a period of free and immediate intercourse between the tsar and his people was beginning.[14] Grigor'ev was a true conservative in that he rejected any form of political restraint on the monarch. The liberal slogan 'liberty, equality and fraternity' was to him a formula for despotism.[15] He stressed the importance of giving freedom and land to the nation's 'lesser brothers'; he entered the debate about legal reform with a demand for public and legally correct court procedures; he advocated, as did the Slavophiles, freedom of expression and conscience. Like Dostoevsky, Grigor'ev expected social relations to be based on love and mutual respect; it was a moral, and not a political, revolution that he hoped for in Russia, a revolution based on Christian love and Orthodox brotherhood.[16]

Grigor'ev brought to the pages of *Iakor'* an acute sensitivity to the nature of the period through which the nation was passing. 'In it, this murky epoch which we are experiencing, everything is a struggle, a struggle of thought with fact.'[17] He returned to the central theme of the native soil movement, the separation of thought and life. Consciousness was divided; the real and the ideal lived in separate spheres, filling the age with a sense of spiritual incompleteness. Wholeness would be restored only when thought again emanated immediately from life.

Iakor' was an important phenomenon in the history of *pochvennichestvo*. It challenged the national-psychological foundation on which the doctrine of *Vremia* had been built. It also undermined the balance between the two sources of the native soil movement – romantic idealism and indigenous religious sentiment. This balance, which in *Vremia* had been weighted towards the idealist concept of an integrated, universal culture, tipped steadily after 1863 towards Orthodox messianism. The earliest manifestations of the shifting values of *pochvennichestvo* appeared in *Vremia*'s successor, *Epokha*.

During the first year and a half of *Vremia*'s publication, relations with the censorship committee were surprisingly untroubled. The conciliatory tone of Dostoevsky's journal must have compared favourably in the eyes of the censor with the acrimoniousness of *Den'* and the subtle enmity of *Sovremennik* or *Russkoe slovo*. The first discordant note was struck only in the spring of 1862 with the submission to the censor of an article entitled 'The Press Laws in France.' The Ministry of Internal Affairs felt compelled to inform the Ministry of National Enlightenment, which was in charge of the censorship, that this article contained a 'series of acute comparisons and judgments which purposed to incite the reading public against the existing censorship order.'[18] The Ministry of National Enlightenment was not to be bullied by a rival ministry, however, and the article duly appeared in print, almost certainly with cuts and emendations. A second, more serious clash with the censor soon followed. During the summer of 1862 at the height of the St Petersburg fires, the editors submitted to the censorship committee two articles that defended the students against charges of incendiarism. Both articles were suppressed on the direct order of the tsar. These incidents may have alerted the police to the possible harmfulness of the tendency of *Vremia*. Censorship surveillance was in any event being tightened over all journals in 1862, and *Vremia* found itself under closer watch.

It must nevertheless have come as a complete shock to Mikhail Dostoevsky when, in April 1863, *Vremia* was suppressed for an ostensibly loyal article entitled 'The Fatal Question' and signed 'Russkii.' The article, which was written by Strakhov, dealt with the Polish revolt, a subject about which *Vremia* had been almost completely silent previously.[19] Strakhov's purpose in the article was to uncover the reasons underlying the rebelliousness of the Poles. In his view, the Poles considered themselves to be on a level with the most civilized of European nations and so were 'roused against us ... as an educated people against a less educated, or even entirely uneducated, people.' Strakhov maintained that the Poles justifiably claimed to be Europeanized; their pride reflected the long history of their self-styled role as the civilizers of eastern Europe. Nevertheless, he regarded Polish civilization as an unhealthy phenomenon that ultimately weakened its people because it was artificial and did not harmonize with the fundamental elements of Polish national life. Russia, in contrast, appeared to be barbaric but contained the seeds of a 'great and fruitful spirit' that was free of alien elements and promised a truly independent development. 'In European civilization,' Strakhov concluded, 'in a borrowed and external civilization, we bow to the Poles; but we would like to believe that in national, fundamental, healthy civilization, we surpass them or at least can claim not to bow to them or to any other people.'[20]

Possibly anticipating a snag with the censor, the editors had submitted with the article a lengthy explanation of Russkii's intentions. The first part of the article, the explanation ran, showed how the Poles and Europeans viewed the Russians; the second part demonstrated that while Russians were a people full of the forces of civilization though as yet undeveloped, the civilization of the Poles had 'death at its very roots.'[21] The censorship committee judged the article favourably; one member went so far as to welcome it as a useful tool of propaganda against the Poles. The piece appeared in print in April and, to the astonishment of all concerned, was immediately greeted by a blast from one Peterson, who in Katkov's *Moskovskie vedomosti* accused 'Russkii' of virtual treason and maliciously demanded to know why the author had been afraid to admit to his real identity.

At this crucial juncture 'The Fatal Question' may have become a pawn in the struggle between the Ministry of Internal Affairs and the Ministry of National Enlightenment over control of the censorship committee. The former ministry insisted on an explanation from V.A. Tsee, the chairman of the committee. Tsee unwisely attempted to exonerate *Vremia.* He assured the ministry that Mr Dostoevsky's journal was scholarly, moderate in comparison to other journals, and devoted to serious and useful subjects. He apologized for the article on behalf of the censorship committee and recommended that no serious measures be taken against *Vremia* since such action could disaffect the 'best and most loyal part of our public, the opinion of which it is impossible not to value.'[22] P.A. Valuev, the minister of the interior, perhaps on the grounds that loyalty was surer for the testing, disregarded Tsee's advice and on 26 May 1863 proscribed *Vremia* for its 'harmful tendency.'[23] Valuev had already dismissed Tsee, whom he considered deficient in 'ability, intellect, frankness and honesty,' two days previously.[24] In so disposing of a journal it had considered harmful since the summer of 1862 and in firing a salvo in its campaign to wrest control of the censorship committee from the Ministry of National Enlightenment, the interior ministry had scored a double victory.

Strakhov appealed unavailingly to Katkov and to Aksakov to intercede with the ministry and to petition on behalf of *Vremia*. A.V. Nikitenko, who was a member of the St Petersburg censorship committee, felt, however, that the suppression of the journal provided the enemies of Russia with a stick with which to beat a tsar too sensitive to withstand a bit of criticism.[25] Although he personally disapproved of Strakhov's article, he worked steadily in the committee along with the poet F.I. Tiutchev, who was a close friend of Grigor'ev, to defend it. Nikitenko knew and liked Mikhail Dostoevsky and was aware that he had been financially ruined by the proscription of his journal.[26] It appeared that Katkov, too, was having second thoughts. As early as May, he had prepared an account of the affair in which he exonerated Strakhov. So anxious was he to have *Vremia* rehabilitated that he refused to publish the May number of *Russkii vestnik* until the censors had approved his explanation.[27] It finally appeared at the beginning of July.

On 15 November 1863 Mikhail wearily petitioned for permission to publish a monthly journal named *Pravda*. The authorities temporized, and Mikhail, who was on the verge of desperation, had to watch the precious period for new-year subscriptions slip by. On 11 January 1864 he submitted another impassioned plea in which he pathetically detailed his financial plight and swore his intention to serve Russia through the new journal. It would, he declared, reveal to its readers those great powers concealed in Russian life which promised a great future and which were treated so negatively by society and writers. Permission was at last granted on 27 January 1864, and *Epokha*, so renamed because someone else held the copyright on the name *Pravda*, was launched.[28] No reference was made by the authorities to the 'harmful tendency' of *Vremia*, but *Epokha* was subjected to severe restrictions. The editor was obligated to 'preserve an irreproachable tendency,' and 'appropriate supervision for the discharge of this obligation' was imposed.[29]

It was not the closeness of government supervision that most damaged

Epokha, but the long delay in getting permission to publish it in the first place. A joint issue of the new journal for January–February 1864 appeared only on 21 March, when the hope of gaining subscriptions was slight, and the periodical consistently ran a few months late. By April, *Epokha* could boast only 1,900 subscribers. By the time it ceased publication in February 1865, the number had fallen to 1,300. It is true that *Epokha* was not the only Russian journal to experience a dramatic decline in subscriptions at this time. Most of its competitors faced a similar crisis, but the late start imposed on *Epokha* by the authorities made its road doubly arduous.

The climate in which *Epokha* had to function differed remarkably from that in which *Vremia* had operated only a few months before. Disillusionment, dissension, and pessimism had replaced the optimism and camaraderie among the intelligentsia of the early days of *Vremia*. The government had taken measures to check and control the enthusiasm for change that had swept the nation almost from the moment it had initiated it. The tiny flame of constitutionalism which had burned among the Tver gentry was unceremoniously smothered, the best representatives of the radical intelligentsia had been arrested, steps had been taken to reimpose authority in the universities, and the censorship was tightened. The Polish revolt in 1863 sparked a wave of chauvinism in the public which tended more and more to associate even moderately progressive ideas with treason.

A new mood in journalism prevailed as well. Katkov's *Russkii vestnik*, which until the end of 1861 had, for all its stridency, remained a moderate voice, abandoned its more liberal tone in the face of the nihilist threat within and the Polish menace without. The conservative gentry, which had at first been stunned into silence by Emancipation, had found a voice in the journal *Vest'*, which openly campaigned for the reconsolidation of gentry privileges. The reform movement lost its momentum as the Russian public settled into the new structures and relationships created by the Emancipation reforms. Indifference and apathy replaced enthusiasm among the informed public.

The situation of the intelligentsia had also changed as a result of the Emancipation reforms. Though many limitations on their activity still remained, opportunities for a more satisfying interaction with society and the organs of administration were opening up to the *intelligenty*. The Emancipation and its accompanying reforms provided the professionalization of Russian life with considerable impetus and contributed to the breaking up of the homogeneity of the intelligentsia. With the growing

INTELLIGENTSY —→ importance of public opinion as a political force, writers and journalists, too, were finding ways to exert an influence on public policy. The painful inception of the modernization of Russian social and political life was already beginning to mitigate the alienation of the intelligentsia, themselves the creatures of modernization. All of these changes did not make the intelligentsia any less idealistic, but it did blunt the visionary edge of their idealism. As one historian has pointed out, in the post-Emancipation period an integrated 'dramatic culture' gave way to a specialized culture of 'small perspectives.'[30] None of this precluded extremism from either the right or the left. On the contrary, it probably encouraged the growth of extreme views. But such extremism now appeared remote from the more sober concerns of the new order, which encouraged a policy of 'small deeds.'

The circumstances of *Epokha* also differed markedly from those of *Vremia*. The close supervision of the censorship committee made it more difficult to present a defined and consistent tendency. Dostoevsky lamented this misfortune to his brother, Mikhail, and regarded the failure of *Epokha* to evolve a clear tendency as its greatest weakness.[31] Of greater significance for the fate of *Epokha* was the fact that Fedor was able to exert very little influence on the new journal in its early days because of his first wife's illness, which ended in her death in April 1864, and his own ill health, which confined him to Moscow. His letters to Mikhail at this time conveyed his feelings of helplessness. 'From here, it is impossible to *collaborate* in Petersburg ... Here I could only write stories, and I cannot even do that.' Mikhail was also despondent: 'Yes, brother, I very much sense the extent of the damage of your absence for the journal.'[32] These fears were not unjustified. In Fedor's absence, the influence of the other members of the editorial board was enhanced. Strakhov emerged as the most powerful voice of the journal through his monthly 'chronicle.' Dmitrii Averkiev, who had played only a minor part in *Vremia*, published frequently in *Epokha*. He was already exhibiting some of the more reactionary tendencies of his later years, and at least on one occasion Dostoevsky insisted that Averkiev's articles be signed so that they could not too readily be confused with official editorial policy.[33]

A further calamity soon descended on *Epokha*. On 10 July 1864 Mikhail Dostoevsky, the only *pochvennik* with a modicum of business acumen, died, leaving a wife and children in desperate straits. Fedor Dostoevsky faced the crisis squarely. With A.U. Poretsky as the new nominal editor, he launched a colossal effort to make a success of *Epokha*. He borrowed 10,000 rubles from his aunt, with which he expected to purchase popularity by attracting better contributors.[34] After Mikhail's death most of his brother's energies were absorbed by the financial and production side of the journal which once again deprived him of the opportunity to express himself regularly in its pages. Only on the literary side of the journal was his presence felt, with the publication of his *Notes from the Underground*.

Fate continued to toy with *Epokha*. On 25 September 1864 Grigor'ev suddenly died. His death struck at the very heart of *pochvennichestvo*. Not only had he originated it but also he had remained its principal ideologue. Without the nagging of Grigor'ev and with the reduced role of Fedor Dostoevsky, the contributors to *Epokha* began to speak more as individuals than as representatives of a tendency. Differences, which had always existed, now emerged more strongly. After the failure of *Epokha* and the dispersal of the original *pochvenniki* these differences became even more pronounced.

The basic principles of *pochvennichestvo* were not lost in *Epokha*. Dostoevsky's notebooks for the period testify that he still regarded the disease of Russia to be the separation of thought and life.

We are *pochvenniki* because in the first place we believe that nothing comes into the world abstractly (outside real, historical life) and by leaps ... Your path to the attainment of the universal human ideal seems wrong to us; for in order to *outlive* former ideas and to master and *acquire* new ideas, inclinations and aspirations, one has really to live, through real life, and not just through the mind and general thinking ... And in order to have a real form, i.e., to live truly, it is necessary to live according to the self, to the soil, the land, etc. and to experience everything in practice ... We believe that our, uniquely our, Russian ideal of the soil is incomparably higher than the European ... but that it will also restore the whole of humanity to life.[35]

Everything useful in life derived not from theory but grew out of practical experience. Progress depended as before on the development in Russia of an 'organic, independent life based on the soil' because 'everything living came into being and lived of itself.'[36]

Dostoevsky's insistence that nothing comes into the world 'by leaps' was a reaffirmation of his anti-revolutionary gradualism. The source of all beneficial change remained, for the *pochvenniki*, the autonomous workings of social life, free from all external coercion. Revolutionary change represented the principal threat to the normal and organic unfolding of Russian nationality. It was for this reason that the *pochvenniki* stoutly upheld in *Epokha* the new all-class institutions of local self-government, the *zemstva*, created in 1864. They regarded such institutions, which drew all the social estates together in a common endeavour, as the most effective organs for the dissemination of civic education in the masses and the reconciliation of class differences.[37]

The idea of Russian universality did not recede in *Epokha*. Dostoevsky reasserted his view that the future of Russia lay not with the Slavophile ideal of withdrawal and interiorization but with the broad penetration of Russian nationality into general European culture. Russia had still to shake off its 'centuries' long seclusion' and widen the 'circle of its independent activity both in economic and spiritual relations.'[38]

The idealist underpinnings of *pochvennichestvo*, which had received growing prominence in *Vremia* as Dostoevsky turned his back to the radicals, become a dominant feature of *Epokha*. Strakhov, in his old role of N. Kositsa, set the tone. 'Impoverishment of the ideal, that is the obvious disease with which our era is afflicted.'[39] He went on to repeat the arguments against materialism and utilitarianism already made in *Vremia*. The philosophy of utility was inadequate because it failed to take into account the aesthetic and ethical concerns of men. To act morally, even though such action was opposed to one's immediate interests, was a source of greater satisfaction and enjoyment for man than was an act inspired by motives of utility only. Further, luxury did not guarantee the maximum happiness for an individual. Aesthetic pleasure transcended the enjoyment derived from satisfying one's physical needs. If guided only by considerations of utility, human endeavour was too narrow and fruitless. The highest aim of life was not to be happy, but to follow one's own innate nature according to one's own ideal.[40]

Given these views it is not surprising that the polemics with *Sovremennik* and *Russkoe slovo* continued even more vigorously in *Epokha* than they had in *Vremia*. Although the quarrel turned on such fundamental questions as the relationship between thought and action, the relevance of Western experience to the future of Russia, and the very nature of that future, the actual exchange between the contending parties was trivial and even mindless. It consisted of satirical, but none-too-clever, verses, plays about martlets and other maligned creatures, and degrading personal invective. Much of the little time remaining to Dostoevsky for journalism was absorbed in a barren obsession with out-quipping his opponents. He attempted to take advantage of the disagreement between *Sovremennik* and *Russkoe slovo* over Turgenev's *Fathers and Children*. Pisarev proudly accepted the name nihilist and welcomed Bazarov, the hero of the novel, as an accurate portrayal of the 'realist.' Antonovich of *Sovremennik*, who was more sensitive and less talented than Pisarev, considered Bazarov to be a slanderous caricature of the young radicals. Dostoevsky jocularly referred to the 'schism in the nihilists' (*raskol v nigilistakh*) but to little practical effect.[41]

The views expressed in *Epokha* on questions of art, literature, and criticism were also unchanged from those of *Vremia*. Continuity was assured by the publication in *Epokha* of Grigor'ev's articles on the organic links between literature and life, his unfinished but absorbing memoirs of his childhood and youth, and, after his death, his letters of 1861 to Strakhov from Orenburg and of 1857–8 to E.S. Protopovova, the wife of the composer Aleksandr Borodin, from Italy. In *Epokha*'s manifesto for 1865, Dostoevsky again remarked on the many signs in literature of the growing independence of Russian life.

The question of art remained at the heart of *pochvennichestvo* in *Epokha*. For the *pochvenniki* the crisis of the modern world was rooted in the breakdown of aesthetic sensibility. Consciousness had become an illness that divided men from the immediate sources of the life of the spirit or from the 'living life.' Men had ceased to know 'immediate (*neposredstvennye*) sensations' and knew everything only abstractly. Only through art could the organic link between life and thought be restored. Dostoevsky wrote, 'We concern ourselves with art primarily in order to declare our respect for the organic manifestations of the life of the spirit which the *moralists* want to ignore.'[42] Aesthetic intuition, the conduit between the ideal and the real, remained in *pochvennichestvo* the substitute for the religious intuition of Slavophilism.

In spite of the many similarities between *Vremia* and *Epokha* a number of differences also soon became apparent. These differences, which for the most part represented shifts in emphasis rather than new positions, reflected the changes in Russian conditions that had occurred by the mid-1860s. In *Epokha* less stress was placed on reconciliation, though the idea was by no means abandoned. Rather, the contrast between Russia and the West was pointed up more sharply and there appeared a greater scepticism about the capacity of the educated to merge with the people. Even more striking was the almost complete cessation of hostilities with *Den'* which accompanied the decisive break with *Sovremennik* and *Russkoe slovo*. The sympathies of *Vremia* had in general lain with the 'progressive' journals in spite of the fundamental differences that separated them. Only towards the end of its short life had it begun to shift towards the nationalists. *Epokha*, on the contrary, leaned towards the nationalist journals and cut itself off from the radicals entirely.

Strakhov took the lead. He had always been critical of Dostoevsky's ambivalence towards the radicals and disapproved of his forays against *Den'*. Now, with Dostoevsky preoccupied with family and business affairs and experiencing doubts about the adequacy of some of his own convictions, Strakhov was presented with the opportunity to lead the journal in directions he considered desirable. A few years after the collapse of *Epokha*, Strakhov wrote, 'As *pochvenniki*, Apollon Grigor'ev and Dostoevsky asserted constantly that they were not Westernizers and not Slavophiles ... I decided that it was necessary to identify myself directly as a Slavophile.'[43] This assertion should not be taken too literally. Strakhov's interests reached far beyond Slavophilism, and his indifference to political and social concerns separated him from his Slavophile contemporaries. But neither was he an enduring *pochvennik* because ultimately he did not believe in the possibility of reconciliation.[44] It is true that as late as 1868, when his *The Poverty of Our Literature* was published, he still accepted Grigor'ev's interpretation of Russian intellectual development since Karamzin and went on to assert that Slavophilism, westernism, and even nihilism were necessary elements in the making of Russian culture.[45] *The Poverty of Our Literature* turned out to be the fullest expression of Strakhov's *pochvennichestvo*, but it represented as much a tribute to Grigor'ev as it did a statement of his own convictions. The foundations of the more exclusivist notion of the 'struggle with the west' which he later adopted were already evident in his contributions to *Epokha*.

Strakhov adopted as his own the idea that Western civilization was in a state of decline and decay. It was, of course, an old idea which stemmed from the early Slavophiles and especially from Shevyrev and Pogodin, but the concept had plenty of vitality left. In a somewhat different context Herzen had recently in his 'Ends and Beginnings' repeated the notion that western Europe had exhausted itself and concluded its mission, and Russia alone remained fresh and strong. Whereas Herzen was referring to the relative potential of the socialists in Russia and the West, Strakhov had in mind the respective capacity of Russians and Europeans to complete the work begun by the German idealists. With the idealists, he maintained, Germany had ended its intellectual mission. The Germans were themselves incapable of understanding their own great philosophers and had been distracted from the road to full intellectual development by the exigencies of their political life.

A like disease, Strakhov believed, had paralysed the movement of thought in the rest of western Europe. Western writers and philosophers had pressed the European idea to its limits, but it remained inadequate, as the pessimism of a Proudhon or the materialistic vacuity of a Feuerbach aptly illustrated. 'In this way, western criticism, as it seems to us, has fully revealed itself; it has reached its end, has uncovered all its mysteries, has disclosed its inner content.'[46] Russia alone, he concluded, still concealed 'its intellectual forces.' If the West had exhausted its intellectual and moral resources, there was little to be gained by parroting its senescent convulsions. Instead, Russia should shake off the influence of Europe and evolve its own intellectual and spiritual life.

Like the Slavophiles, Strakhov imagined that the enemy was within as well as on the borders of Russia. St Petersburg remained Russia's most Western corner and lived in splendid and arrogant isolation from the rest of the nation. Strakhov emphasized that the initiative in the matter of fostering the national spirit had passed from St Petersburgh to Moscow and hinted at a pending confrontation between the contrary principles of the two capitals.[47] Averkiev was even more blunt in predicting a war between 'so-called' civilization and fundamentally Russian principles, a war to be fought between St Petersburg and Moscow.[48] Such a spirit of confrontation was foreign to Grigor'ev's conception of nationality and alien to Dostoevsky's idea of reconciliation. They had envisaged the absorption of Western principles into the Russian ideal and not a head-on collision between two contradictory and irreconcilable ideals.

Strakhov attached considerable importance to the Polish rebellion in hastening the evolution of Russian national consciousness. He believed that during the bloody uprising, abstract ideas and detached feelings had given way in Russia to real ideas and feelings. Events displaced opinions, and flesh-and-blood persons superseded abstract concepts. 'A feeling for our nationality awoke and spoke within us more and more distinctly,' he wrote. 'This was a correct and inevitable reaction of the national organism.'[49] In Strakhov's view it was *Den'* that had guided Russia through the Polish crisis. Aksakov's journal was 'without a doubt the most remarkable, the most profound and important phenomenon in recent years.'[50] He began to align *pochvennichestvo* with the Slavophile camp and finally declared that 'Slavophilism has conquered.' 'It is possible,' he asserted, 'to dispute particular conclusions of the Slavophiles, but the truth of their basic viewpoint is indisputable, and it appears that the time is not far off when it will be accepted by almost everyone.'[51]

The surrender to *Den'*, which Strakhov had engineered, manifested itself in *Epokha* in a number of different directions. Aksakov's journal was suddenly championed as an authority in most matters, from railway construction, through the definition and history of nihilism, to the need for the Russification of Jews and Germans living within Russian borders.[52] The latter point was inspired by Aksakov's theory of religious assimilation. Since he believed that religion was the basis of nationality, Aksakov maintained that diverse ethnic groups could live within one nation only if they professed a common religion. It was impossible, he argued, to be a Russian citizen and yet to be a Jew, Moslem, Catholic or Lutheran. This rationale for Russian imperialism was directed, interestingly enough, against Katkov's *Moskovskie vedomosti*, in which the case had been made that a Russian Lutheran or Russian Catholic could very well be a loyal citizen.[53] Strakhov joined Aksakov in condemning any such notion. He felt that foreigners should Russify because in their Russification he saw the 'guarantee of a more proper spiritual life ... and their own well-being.'[54] Neither Aksakov nor Strakhov was recommending forced Russification. Each hoped to use persuasion in order to strengthen Russian national or religious consciousness among the non-Orthodox peoples of the empire. Strakhov went so far as to contend that non-Russians were in no danger of cultural suppression because 'there is no people in the world so tolerant toward strangers as the Russian people.'[55]

Strakhov edged away from *pochvennichestvo* and nearer to Slavophilism in another crucial respect as well. In his opinion, only the *narod* had retained its instinctive nationality since the reforms of Peter. In separating themselves from the soil, the educated had sacrificed their national instincts.[56] This concession struck at the very nub of the native soil movement. Grigor'ev and Dostoevsky had staunchly maintained that since no group could lose its nationality, fundamentally Russian instincts remained to the educated. The veneer of Europeanism among the educated had for many years concealed their innate nationality from them, but without being conscious of it they had remained Russians in spite of their efforts to Europeanize.

Strakhov's retreat from *pochvennichestvo* and his homage to Aksakov were motivated less by a complete conversion to Slavophilism than by the desire to create in Russian journalism a broad nationalistic and idealistic front. His primary concern was the ethical consequences of the growth of materialism in European philosophy. As a Hegelian, Strakhov believed that the western European phase of philosophical development had passed and that the initiative in advancing the cause of the Spirit belonged now to Russia. His journalistic activity was inspired by the wish to force Russians to accept their great responsibility to civilization. Moreover, Strakhov's nationalism remained outgoing and not inward-looking as was that of the Slavophiles. In August 1864 he wrote that the Russian cause was the cause of civilization and humanity because Russian religion, history, and social structure were necessary elements in the history of mankind. His Hegelianism had taught him, however, that historical change was the product of the clash of ideas and not their simple reconciliation.

Strakhov's evolution as a conservative nationalist continued after the collapse of *Epokha* in 1865. *Zaria*, which Strakhov edited from January 1869 to the spring of 1871, was the last Russian journal to carry the marks of *pochvennichestvo*. It was financed by V.V. Kashpirev who, according to Strakhov, was a child of *Vremia* and *Epokha*. Kashpirev wanted to establish a Slavophile journal that was, nevertheless, independent of early Slavophilism. Many former contributors to *Vremia* and *Epokha* reassembled in the office of the new journal. Dostoevsky, who was abroad for reasons of financial prudence, made little impact on *Zaria* although he corresponded regularly with Strakhov about it and even contributed his story 'The Eternal Husband.' In spite of the high quality of some of its contributions, *Zaria* was not a success, largely because of the weighty solemnity that Strakhov imposed on it. It was a serious journal with very little frivolity to enliven its pages.[57]

The links of *Zaria* with the two earlier journals of *pochvennichestvo* were tenuous. Strakhov loyally popularized Grigor'ev's organic criticism in his own critical articles. The same anti-nihilism and idealism that had characterized *Epokha* were also a feature of the new journal. But the basic idea of *pochvennichestvo*, reconciliation, was conspicuously absent. This was due in large measure to the ideological domination of *Zaria* by N. Ia. Danilevsky, whose *Russia and Europe*, which first was serialized in *Zaria*, fully embodied the tendency of the journal: 'Our journal considers itself to be organically linked to the opinions and to the spirit of this article, in which, although it was begun, planned and even half written before the idea of a new journal arose, [our] journal, nevertheless, found a firm basis for its position in literature, recognized it as the best, unexpectedly broad and full expression of our tendency and deliberately adhered to its essential views.'[58]

Danilevsky's *Russia and Europe* rested on a theory of cultural-historical types that involved the adaptation of biological methods of classification to history. Danilevsky argued that there had been ten types in history. Each type existed autonomously in accordance with its own internal laws. 'The principles of the civilization of one cultural-historical type,' he insisted, 'cannot be transmitted to another type. Every type works [its civilization] out for itself.'[59] Danilevsky's theory was designed to refute the idea of universal human civilization in general, and of the westernizer ideal of Europe as the universal and final centre of civilization in particular. Although he denied that culture could be transmitted from one type to the next, Danilevsky did allow for a common bin into which every civilization poured the best fruits of its labours and upon which other types could draw.[60]

Strakhov identified the motivating idea of *Zaria* as the Slavophile idea, which he distinguished from historical Slavophilism. The essence of this idea, he believed, was the search for internal freedom and spiritual independence. It was his purpose to broaden the Slavophile movement into a general protest against European authority. Slavophilism, he held, should not be a narrow school or dogmatic faith but a broad protest against Europeanization.[61] He excluded on the authority of Danilesky, the possibility of a universal synthesis of all previous ideas on Russian soil and sternly upbraided Katkov's *Moskovskie vedomosti* for attempting to 'unite what could not be united,' Europeanism with a strong feeling for Russian national interests, faith in the principles of Europe with faith in Russia.[62] Strakhov's *pochvennichestvo*, therefore, ended in a narrow nationalism and he spent his remaining years ardently propagating the 'struggle with the West.'

Dostoevsky was meanwhile experiencing an evolution of his own. Although his presence was not strongly felt in the positive program of *Epokha*, his notebooks suggest that his views were undergoing a fundamental revision at this time. In his original formulation of *pochvennichestvo* in 1861 Dostoevsky had interpreted the role of Russia primarily in psychological terms. Russians were destined to reconcile and synthesize the conflicting ideals of the gentry and the people, and hence of Russia and the West, through the agency of education. By 1864, pressured by Grigor'ev and probably under the influence of the early Slavophiles, whose works he read in the summer of 1863, he began to revise his view of the meaning of Russia's mission. Like the Slavophiles, Dostoevsky came to identify the culture of a country with its religion. The European principle, he argued, was defined by Catholicism, which was characterized by egoism. All of the manifestations of western European social life, including socialism, were the products of Catholicism. The Russian principle was defined by Orthodoxy which was characterized by love and embodied in Russian fraternity.[63] It was this religious view, which had been with him in a confused form since his return from exile, that emerged at last to dominate his outlook from 1864.

For Dostoevsky, socialism represented the most extreme development of individualism and embodied the greatest social atomization. Only in true Christianity were freedom and unity reconciled because only through Christianity could the individual understand that the greatest act of freedom was to sacrifice the ego to the all:

After the appearance of Christ *as the ideal of man in the flesh*, it became as clear as day that the highest, final development of the personality must reach the point at which ... man discovers, knows and believes with all the strength of his nature that the supreme use that man can make of his personality, of the fullness of the development of his *ego*, is to eliminate this *ego*, to surrender it wholeheartedly and selflessly. And this is the greatest happiness. In this way, the law of the ego joins with the law of humanism, and in their mingling, both the *ego* and the *all* ... mutually annihilate one another, and at the same time, each one also attains separately the pinnacle of its individual development.

Here is Christ's paradise. The whole history of mankind ... is only the development of, struggle for, aspiration toward and attainment of this goal.

But if this is the final goal of mankind, then it follows that man on attaining it completes his earthly existence. So man on earth is being, only developing being, consequently, not finished, but transitional.[64]

This entry in Dostoevsky's notebook for 1864 marked his conversion to the Christian conception of history and historical development which characterized his mature works.

The original subtleties of the gradual cultural synthesis present in Dostoevsky's thinking on his return from exile gave way in 1864 to a sweeping theodicy. In the new scheme, a society developed from a primary, patriarchal order, through civilization, which represented a retreat from the spontaneity and unity of patriarchal society into egoism and atomism, to Christianity, which saw a return to spontaneity and wholeness as an act of freedom.[65] Dostoevsky believed that Russian Orthodoxy was the key to the final act of man's earthly evolution and that the Russian people were the bearers of true Christianity. Consequently, his faith in the universality of the Russians was reinforced. He wrote that the *pochvenniki* did not seek to narrow the horizons of nationality or limit the scope of the people. They did not do so because they were Christians and the 'first tenet of Christianity is the community of the law for all, the community of the ideal, all are brothers.'[66]

Under the influence of his grand new theological design, Dostoevsky redefined the tendencies in Russia as three only: westernizer, Slavophile, and realist. *Pochvennichestvo* apparently had, at least for the time being, been subsumed in Slavophilism. But like Strakhov, Dostoevsky wanted to define Slavophilism more broadly: 'The Slavophiles do not believe in any of the European institutions, not in one of the conclusions of Europe – for Russia. They reject constitutional, social and federalist mechanistic doctrines. They believe in Russian principles and are convinced that they take the place of both constitutions and socialism of themselves, carrying within them the embryo of Russia's own truth and, of course, having the right to live and to develop independently, just as the West lived and developed independently.'[67] Dostoevsky rejoiced that the 'Westernizer idols have been smashed' but worried that Russian society lacked a conservative moral attraction that it could 'love, respect and idolize.' Katkov, he concluded, could not provide such an attraction. 'Aksakov remains.'[68] Dostoevsky became increasingly aware of his affinity for Slavophilism. In 1866, he wrote to Katkov that he 'was, and apparently will always remain, by conviction a real Slavophile, except for some tiny disagreements.'[69]

Epokha collapsed financially early in 1865, and Dostoevsky began his strange odyssey of gambling and destitution in the spas and capitals of the West. One of the principal themes of his novels in this period was the consequences for the individual of separation from the native soil. Some of his characters were driven to commit unspeakable crimes, others to suicide. All of his heroes suffered spiritual death. Some, like Raskolnikov in *Crime and Punishment,* were resurrected through suffering and renewed contact with the soil; others, like Stavrogin in *The Devils,* perished spiritually and physically. Nihilistic youth was pictured by Dostoevsky as irredeemably degenerate. In these novels, the soil was plainly identified with Orthodox Christianity, the principle of Russia, which stood in stark contrast to the atheism of the West and of the Western principle in Russia. The contrast between Russia and the West predominated in these novels over the theme of universal reconciliation.

But Dostoevsky's *pochvennichestvo* was far from dead, and his 'tiny disagreements' with the Slavophiles were to set him apart from them for the rest of his life. On his return to Russia in the summer of 1871 after four years in western Europe, Dostoevsky was reunited with many of his former friends. In the intervening years a number of these friends had become associated with the more reactionary circles of Russian society. In January 1873 Dostoevsky took up the editorship of *Grazhdanin,* a journal published by Prince Vladimir Meshchersky, a stupid and vulgar retrograde with pretensions to ideological leadership. Although Dostoevsky worked energetically at his new job and created a new literary form with his 'Diary of a Writer,' which first appeared in *Grazhdanin,* he became increasingly uncomfortable in the company of the contributors to the journal. In March 1874, he finally resigned on the grounds of ill health.

While editing *Grazhdanin,* he had also been working on a new novel which he offered to Katkov for publication in *Russkii vestnik.* Katkov, who had just signed a contract to publish Tolstoy's *Anna Karenina,* was unable to accommodate him. Dostoevsky was, therefore, pleased to be approached by Nekrasov, his old friend of the 1840s and enemy of the 1860s, who was by now the editor of *Otechestvennye zapiski,* the leading radical journal of the 1870s. In spite of some anxiety that his old rivals would try to compromise his most fundamental convictions, he agreed to submit his *A Raw Youth* to Nekrasov's journal. As Konstantin Mochulsky has said, 'It is impossible to explain this rapprochement with Nekrasov's group simply as opportunism: a reversal took place in Dostoevsky's ideas; after his collaboration with Meshchersky, he realized that his path was not with the reactionaries.'[70] Dostoevsky's decision to collaborate with a populist journal was in fact not a reversal at all but merely a renewed emphasis on earlier themes. The rapprochement was made possible because the hard-nosed materialism and westernism of nihilism, which had so alienated Dostoevsky in the 1860s, had given way to the humanism and quasi-religious faith in the people of populism in the 1870s. These changes within the radical camp restored Dostoevsky's belief in the possibility of reconciliation.

It is clear from the notebooks for *A Raw Youth* that Dostoevsky wanted to explore in his novel the relationship between the predatory (*khishchnyi*) and the humble (*smirnyi*) types that Grigor'ev had first discovered in Russian literature.[71] The main character, Versilov, a member of the gentry and an educated man, is a disillusioned idealist of the 1840s. He is torn between a profound need to believe in the native soil and his fatal attraction for the ideas of the West. Versilov is the literary heir of those characters Grigor'ev had in the 1850s identified as predatory types. Sofia Andreevna, Versilov's peasant mistress, and Makar Dolgoruky, her legal husband and Versilov's former serf, now a pilgrim who wanders throughout Russia collecting alms for the construction of a church, embody two aspects of the humble type. Sofia Andreevna, who is characterized by her 'humility, submissiveness, self abasement and at the same time firmness, strength, real strength,'[72] stands for the soil itself, the Russian land. Her husband, Makar, is the embodiment not of the official church but of the real Orthodox religiosity of the people. The fates of these three are inextricably interwoven. Drawn by his passion for a certain

Princess Akmakhova, Versilov rejects Sofia Andreevna and Makar Ivanovich and is driven finally to the brink of murder and suicide. Only his mystical love of life saves him from the same fate as Stavrogin. Versilov does not perish but is resurrected and reunited with Sofia Andreevna. His betrayal of the land had marked him too deeply to permit his complete reconciliation with it. Yet it is precisely in this reconciliation, as Versilov is aware, that the future of Russia is contained. He declares to his son, the 'raw youth': 'The people's truth will unite with ours, and we will go forward together. The time is coming.'[73]

Juxtaposed to the story of Versilov is that of the raw youth Arkady, the illegitimate son of Versilov and Sofia Andreevna. He arrives in St Petersburg from Moscow, where he has been educated, to join his 'haphazard family.' His single motivating idea is to become a Rothschild. His ideal is, however, undermined by other ideals that he meets in the capital: by socialism and by his father's own high ideal. Arkady survives these conflicts to emerge with a fresh faith in the possibility of a new life. 'My old life,' he concludes at the end of the novel, 'has altogether gone, and a new one has scarcely begun.'[74] Dostoevsky's own conviction that the young people of Russia would emerge from their experiences prepared for the new life was reflected in the raw youth's transformation. The optimistic outcome of A Raw Youth was quite different from the one of general destruction and despair with which Dostoevsky had concluded The Devils a few years before.

The promise of a higher nationality in Russia – based on a synthesis of the universal culture of the educated and the principle of the native soil – which was held out to Russians in A Raw Youth would have pleased Grigor'ev. Dostoevsky, as earlier, went on to apply his belief in the universality of the Russian people to the reconciliation of East and West. In the notebooks for the novel, Dostoevsky makes Versilov say to Makar Ivanovich, 'Europe will give us science, and we will give Christ to them; in this is Russia's whole purpose.'[75] Versilov believes in an aristocracy of merit. 'The best men of Russia,' he declares, 'ought to unite.'[76] He expected that the gentry, which was best suited by education to act as the guardian of the highest ideals, could constitute the bulk of this aristocracy of merit. But the gentry had not only national but also universal significance because 'Peter the Great made us citizens of Europe, and we bear the universal amalgam of ideas.'[77] The Russian idea was the universal reconciliation of ideas, and the 'Russian cultural type is the universal human type' and the 'bearer of the world ideal.'[78]

It is evident from Diary of a Writer, which Dostoevsky began to publish in

1876, that Versilov was speaking for Dostoevsky. Many of Dostoevsky's old ideas from *Vremia* and *Epokha* were recycled in *Diary* but in a new, religious guise. In the 1870s Dostoevsky had lost none of his faith in the powers of Russian literature to lead Russians to the great truth contained in the common people. He still believed that the return to the soil by the educated had been foreshadowed in the works of the great Russian writers. The educated had learned that they had to 'bow before the people and await everything from them – both thought and form.' However, the people had to 'accept from us those many things which we brought with us.'[79] The educated neither could nor should seek to annihilate themselves before the people. Dostoevsky believed that it was better that the two halves should go their separate ways than that the educated sacrifice the wonders they had learned in the West. Among these wonders were science and all the other fruits of world civilization. Most precious, however, was the idea of the 'brotherly love of all peoples' which was the product of 150 years of Russian contact with the West. Through the reforms of Peter the Great Russians 'came to understand our universal mission, our individuality and our role among mankind.' Only Russia was truly universal because only Russians had acquired a faculty for 'revealing and discovering in every European civilization, or more correctly – in each of the individuals of Europe, the truth which they possess.'[80] Dostoevsky renewed his attack on the 'cosmopolitans' for dismissing Russian nationality. They were incapable of understanding that only it was truly universal. 'Consequently, if the national, Russian idea is, in the last analysis, no more than universal, all-human unity, then surely our entire interest consists in all of us, having left off our disputes, becoming Russian and national as quickly as possible.'[81]

A new element had entered Dostoevsky's political thinking since the days of *Vremia*. The Slavophile doctrine had come to mean for him a union of the Slavs, with Russia at their head, a union that would utter the new word of brotherly, universal reconciliation. Dostoevsky's later pan-Slavism was uncharacteristic of earlier *pochvennichestvo*. The 'young editors' had concentrated specifically on Russian nationality. While interested in the fate of other Slavs, Grigor'ev had never believed that their future rested on union with Russia. *Vremia* and *Epokha* had not specifically opposed pan-Slavism but had shown surprisingly little interest in the rest of the Slav world. Even after his conversion to pan-Slavism Dostoevsky was reluctant to raise the rest of the Slavs to equality with the Russians. His reluctance was fatal to the spirit of *pochvennichestvo* which had always valued the greatest possible cultural diversity and local autonomy. And in the event these values, which had been threatened as early as 1863 by the Polish rebellion, were too weakly entrenched in his mind to resist the growing attractions of Russian imperialist expansion.

Pochvennichestvo began as a theory of literature, and it was fitting that its last words should have been pronounced at a literary tribute to Russia's greatest poet. The honour paid to Pushkin in June 1880 by the Society of the Lovers of Russian Literature at the unveiling in Moscow of a monument to the great poet was as much a triumph for Apollon Grigor'ev, who, after Belinsky, had done more to foster the Pushkin cult than anyone else in Russia, as it was for Pushkin himself. It was a remarkable oversight that not one of the speakers, who owed so many of their ideas to Grigor'ev, paid posthumous homage to their former friend and mentor. Dostoevsky's celebrated speech was, with minor changes of emphasis, little more than a reiteration of thoughts Grigor'ev had expressed, no less well, in the late 1850s and early 1860s. Ivan Aksakov, who in 1865 could find nationality only in Boltin, Fonvizin, Griboedov, and Gogol' and one or two other writers since Gogol', announced during the Pushkin ceremonies in 1880 that Pushkin was the 'first true, great poet in Russia, and the first truly Russian poet and for this reason was national in the highest sense of this word.'[82] Grigor'ev, who had devoted half his life to this very proposition, would have been delighted by the unexpected conversion of the leader of Slavophilism.

Dostoevsky opened his famous speech with the contention that in Aleko, the hero of the poem 'The Gypsies,' Pushkin had created the prototype of the character who, detached from the people, wandered unhappily in search of universal ideals. Onegin, he continued, was a further development of the same type.[83] Here was, of course, the predatory type that Grigor'ev had discovered in Pushkin and elsewhere in Russian literature in the 1850s. Tatiana, Dostoevsky argued, was the first genuine and beautiful characterization of the Russian woman, the incarnation of Russian beauty. She was a type drawn from the Russian soil, from life itself. Dostoevsky went on to single out Lisa from Turgenev's *A Nest of Gentlefolk* as a creation worthy of Tatiana, the original. Grigor'ev had expressed exactly the same opinion about Tatiana in 1859 and had also linked Lisa with Tatiana, although he felt the former was not fully comparable to the latter.[84]

Greatest of Pushkin's virtues, according to Dostoevsky, was his ability to reincarnate (*perevoploshchat'sia*) an alien nationality in himself.[85] Pushkin was the first to grasp that the true strength of the Russian national spirit was its aspiration towards 'universality and all-embracing humanitarianism.' Peter's reforms prepared Russians for their universality; Pushkin made them conscious of it.

In his 'Explanatory Word Concerning the Address on Pushkin' published in *Diary of a Writer* in August 1880, Dostoevsky compounded the interest on his debt to Grigor'ev by explaining that the type of Aleko and Onegin created by Pushkin had given birth to a host of similar characters, including Lermontov's Pechorin, Gogol's Chichikov, and Turgenev's Rudin and Lavretsky.[86] This article provided Dostoevsky with one of his last opportunities to declare his indebtedness to Grigor'ev. A few months later, in January 1881, he died, depriving *pochvennichestvo* of its last articulate and committed voice.

Although many of its ideas lived on in the thought of its former adherents, *pochvennichestvo* lost its coherence as a movement with the folding of *Epokha* in 1865. The disintegration began with Grigor'ev's death late in 1864. As the founder of the movement, he had also served as the guardian of its purity. After his death, the differences among the main contributors to *Vremia* and *Epokha* began to emerge unchecked.

The second thoughts of the *pochvenniki* also reflected important changes in Russian social life. The Emancipation reforms had moved Russia further along the path of westernization than most conservative nationalists would willingly admit. In 1861 the ideals of the *pochvenniki* still appeared to be within the bounds of reality and could be associated with changes actually taking place. But the new forms and attitudes created by the reforms ultimately pointed not towards a conservative organic utopia, but towards a modern contractual and pluralistic society. The tension between Russia and the West was resolving itself in favour of the west. The *pochvenniki*, therefore, retreated from determinism into voluntarism and abandoned their optimism that the desired future would simply evolve out of the present. Dostoevsky's implacable hostility towards nihilism and Strakhov's 'struggle with the West' underscored the emphasis the *pochvenniki* now placed on will as the driving force of history. The growing forces of Russian imperialism, too, took their toll as national exclusiveness and pan-Slavism gradually displaced Grigor'ev's original conception of the fullness of the universe.

In spite of its demise as a movement not all of *pochvennichestvo* was lost. One Russian conservative *intelligent* who for a short time fell under the influence of the *pochvenniki* was K.N. Leont'ev. Leont'ev was charmed by Grigor'ev whom he described as a 'Slavophile of a special sort; he was so to speak, an expansive and immoral Slavophile.'[87] Leont'ev admired Grigor'ev for seeking out poetry in Russian life itself and not in the ideal. His ideal was the 'rich, expansive and passionate life of Russia' extended to its 'most extreme limits.'[88] Leont'ev also found Grigor'ev to be a better and more Russian critic than Belinsky.

It is not surprising that Leont'ev, an aesthete, should have discovered a kindred spirit in Grigor'ev, who viewed the universe entirely through art. But Leont'ev's admiration for Grigor'ev extended also to his philosophy of nationality and aligned him for a time with the legacy of *Vremia*. In November and December 1870, a two-part article signed N. Konstantinov and entitled 'Literacy and Nationality' appeared in *Zaria*. N. Konstantinov was, of course, Leont'ev. In the article, Leont'ev extolled *pochvennichestvo* as a more comprehensive and realistic continuation of Slavophilism. The positive tendency of *Vremia*, which, he argued, had arisen as a reaction to the radical ideology of *Sovremennik*, was wider than in the rival organs of Slavophilism. Every step that educated society had taken since 1856 along the path of Europeanism brought it closer to the consciousness of its own profound Russian nationality. The Europeanized section of the population, Leont'ev continued, had mastered the higher (philosophy) and the lower (temporal-practical) fruits of universal consciousness. The common people had preserved that which was uniquely Russian. The fruits of civilization, garnered by the educated, when filtered through the national and local forms of Russian life and preserved by the people, would attain a 'level of novelty and orginality which would completely renew an undoubtedly ageing world.'[89]

Leont'ev's was a classic statement of *pochvennichestvo*. He insisted that each people should develop its own nationality to its fullest extent because in doing so it best served the growth of universal civilization. He implied that the educated members of society constituted an integral part of Russian nationality but, nevertheless, urged that the common people be allowed to determine their own educational needs. Like the *pochvenniki*, he maintained that the key to the attainment of *natsional'nost'* (he used the word) in Russia was literacy.[90] Leont'ev concluded with one of the central ideas of *pochvennichestvo*, reconciliation: 'And, indeed, in the harmonious combination of our general European, conscious principles with our elemental principles of the common people lies the salvation of our national independence. In absorbing European [culture], it is necessary to use all our powers in order to remake it in our own image as the bee remakes the pollen of flowers into a wax which does not exist outside of its body.'[91]

Leont'ev's *pochvennichestvo* proved to be only a transitory phase in his intellectual development. Soon he began to fear that the Europeanism he had applauded in his articles of 1870 threatened the colourful diversity of the Slav nations which he cherished. He turned instead to an extreme and pessimistic philosophy of cultural exclusiveness. By excluding Western influences from Russia, he hoped to delay the inevitable moment of cultural homogenization which he saw as the consequence of progress and modern nationalism. He buttressed his reactionary views about progress with a conception of Orthodoxy that was rooted in feelings of dread and awe.

Leont'ev was the last to embrace the principal tenets of *pochvennichestvo* more or less whole, however briefly in his intellectual development. But the legacy of the *pochvenniki* lived on among the nationalist intelligentsia. Grigor'ev's organic criticism, which had become the hallmark of the literary outlook of all the *pochvenniki*, was admired by, among others, Aleksandr Blok. Of Grigor'ev he wrote: 'But did those of loftier repute than he, Dostoevsky and Tolstoy, possess such authority? No they did not. Grigor'ev ranks with them. He was the only bridge which stretches across to us from Griboedov and Pushkin: rickety, suspended across the awful abyss of intelligentsia stagnation, but the only bridge.'[92] Latterly, in his Nobel Prize lecture, Aleksandr Solzhenitsyn spoke in the language of organic criticism and reassigned to literature the position and mission earlier accorded it by Grigor'ev and Dostoevsky.[93]

The *pochvenniki* contributed more than a theory of literature to Russia's intellectual heritage. They confirmed and transmitted to later conservative nationalists the romantic tendency to view national diversity as the natural cultural condition of man. In the 1880s, for example, the philosopher V.S. Solov'ev turned Grigor'ev's notion of the fullness of the universe against the exponents of Russian imperialism. It was a use of which Grigor'ev would have approved. 'Nationality,' Solov'ev wrote, 'is a positive force, and every people has the right to an independent (from other peoples) existence and to the free development of their national peculiarities. Nationality is the most important element of natural-human life, and the development of national self-consciousness is a great step forward in the history of mankind.'[94] Other Russian nationalists among the intelligentsia also stressed the relativism of historical development and the separate paths of cultural nations.

A further significant and lasting contribution made by the *pochvenniki* to Russian thought was the systematic critique to which they subjected Russian radicalism. The critique turned on the theoretical and unhistorical nature of radical thought, and especially its cosmopolitanism and reliance on Western models; the materialist and determinist tendencies of the radicals; their instrumentalism with regard to the *narod* and popular education; and their revolutionism. In 1904 N.M. Sokolov in his *Ideals and Ideas of the Russian Intelligentsia* underscored the foreignness of Russian radicalism when he complained, in the spirit of *pochvennichestvo*, that the radical intelligentsia believed that there was 'no truth higher than the truth that only the Europeans know.'[95] And the lonely eccentric N.F. Feodorov was not alone among the nationalists when, in the idealist vein of the *pochvenniki*, he asked an eager young radical who was longing to sacrifice his own comfort in order to further the material level of the people, 'But what if material well-being is no more important to those for whom you are troubling yourself than it is for you? To what end is all your bother!'[96]

Perhaps the single most important restatement of the major themes of *pochvennichestvo* came in the *Vekhi* collection of 1909. The *Vekhi* contributors, who were steeped in the same idealism as the *pochvenniki*, reiterated the critique of the radical intelligentsia. They particularly insisted, as had their predecessors, on the dangers of abstraction as the foundation of social thought and action and of the weakness of revolution as a panacea. Like the *pochvenniki*, Struve and the other contributors pointed to the proclivity of the radicals to treat the *narod* only as a tool for fomenting social upheaval and stressed the need for the moral education of the masses as the prerequisite to the growth of national self-consciousness and political responsibility.[97] In *August 1914* Solzhenitsyn turned to similar themes in his search for the roots of the Russian Revolution and the Soviet system.[98]

Few conservative nationalists in Russia after the *pochvenniki* any longer accepted the backward-looking orientation of Slavophile nationalism. Orest Miller was, perhaps, overly optimistic when he declared as early as 1864 that no one in Russia doubted the necessity and utility of Peter's reforms,[99] but most conservative nationalists had by that time turned their thoughts to Russia's future. *Pochvennichestvo* played a decisive role in the transformation.

At the core of the theory of nationality of the *pochvenniki*, it will be recalled, was the concept of the reconciliation of the achievements of civilization with the national principle, through the agency, at least initially, of a group of 'best men.' After the *pochvenniki* the idea of reconciliation enjoyed a long history. Not only did it reappear in Ivan Aksakov's theory of *obshchestvo*, which he defined as 'educated people regardless of their social status,'[100] but it also became a commonplace in nationalist thought for the rest of the century and beyond. And the idea of reconciliation did not stand still. It was originally propagated by Grigor'ev as a process internal to Russia, the reconciliation of the Western principles contained in Russia's educated classes with the national principle that was possessed by all Russians but preserved in purer form among the masses. In his middle and later years, however, as is well known, Dostoevsky came to believe in a universal mission for Russia. Through Orthodox Christianity, he believed, all the conflicts of civilization would be reconciled. Hence in Dostoevsky reconciliation came to mean the reconciliation of East and West in universal Christian harmony. Solov'ev took the same idea in a different direction. Through its humility and demonstrated powers of self-renunciation, Russia would initiate the reconciliation of the churches under papal auspices.[101]

An unlikely place to find the notion of reconciliation was in the work of Danilevsky. His theory of exclusive cultural-historical types seemed to preclude all significant borrowings of one type from another. But the idea of reconciliation was too deeply entrenched in nationalist thought for Danilevsky to resist. 'Where,' he asked, 'are we to seek the reconciliation between Russian national feeling and the demands acknowledged by reason for human prosperity and progress?'[102] And he went on to argue that although the idea of pan-human unity was nonsense, the Slav type was nevertheless unique in that it was capable of absorbing and reconciling all the positive achievements of other cultural-historical types. In the twentieth century reconciliation lived on in Berdiaev's religious philosophy and in Eurasianism and has recently reappeared in Solzhenitsyn's *August 1914*.[103]

Influences are difficult to trace. To demonstrate that Grigor'ev influenced Dostoevsky whose ideas left their mark on Solov'ev whom the *Vekhi* contributors admired and who, it transpires, were important in Solzhenitsyn's intellectual evolution is possible and even interesting but not in the end very illuminating. It is more important for the historian of ideas to discover the conditions under which a body of ideas can arise and persist over decades or longer. In Russia, where disjunction characterizes so much of life, where the fashionable and dominant ideologies have rested on materialism and class struggle, where the cultural, economic, and social differences between Russia and the West are perennially of paramount concern to Russian intellectuals, and where the creative intelligentsia is condemned to a life of alienation from the régime and mass public opinion, hopes for social and cultural harmony founded on theories of the reconciliation of the contending forces will remain a vital feature of the nation's ideological repertoire. The *pochvenniki* stood near the beginning of an intellectual tradition the force of which is far from spent.

10

Conclusion

The origins of *pochvennichestvo* reached back well into the early years of Russian romanticism when writers and critics began to search for the marks of originality in Russian art and literature. It was here that the links of the native soil movement with aesthetic theory were forged and that its central metaphor, Russia and the West, was first formulated. *Pochvennichestvo* was not an isolated phenomenon. It was profoundly influenced by western European conservative organic philosophies and was part of a general European response to the new challenges to tradition posed by materialism and positivism. The *pochvenniki* owed most to Belinsky, of their many Russian predecessors. Grigor'ev laid no claim to originality and always stressed his debt to the great critic. In his organic criticism he perpetuated and elaborated one current of Belinsky's thought and furnished Dostoevsky with a framework into which to fit the vague thoughts about Russian nationality that he had formed during his term of exile.

Dostoevsky's debt to Grigor'ev was large and largely unacknowledged. His journalistic activity from 1860 to 1865 and later in his career, especially his views about nationality and its relationship to literature and criticism, was rooted in Grigor'ev's organic criticism. But Dostoevsky was both broader and shallower in his formulations. His notion, which he held until his death, that Russia was destined to reconcile the thought of East and West turned out to be a jingoistic parody of Grigor'ev's original, more modest conception that in the new Russian nationality the ancient tradition of Russian fraternity would be reconciled with the new, Western elements of Russian life, which had entered the country from the time of Peter the Great, and so overcome the nation's divisions. The triumphant culmination of Dostoevsky's nationalistic literary criticism, the Pushkin speech, was little more than an oversimplified and heated summary of Grigor'ev's major critical articles of the late 1850s.

In the periodization of Dostoevsky's creative evolution the significance of the years 1860 to 1864 has been too often underestimated. Although the novelist's conversion, or reversion, to a Christian perspective took place during his exile, he did not return to St Petersburg late in 1859 with the religious-nationalist views of his later years already in place. The intervening years constituted a middle period in his evolution, when under the influence of Grigor'ev's organic criticism and goaded by the clash with the nihilists, he moved from a still largely unexamined humanitarianism to a profoundly Christian humanism, complicated by his nationalistic hopes for the Russian people.

In keeping with its eclectic nature, *pochvennichestvo* was as intimately linked to early Slavophilism as it was to Belinsky's criticism; but it also differed significantly from the thought of Kireevsky or Khomiakov. The *pochvenniki*, who like other conservative *intelligenty* were separated from the land and were urban in their preoccupations and outlook, turned their backs on the aristocratic patriarchalism of the Slavophiles. They widened the definition of Russian nationality to embrace not just the peasantry but the entire spectrum of society. The almost democratic pathos of *pochvennichestvo* derived from the very inclusiveness of its conception of the 'people.' The *pochvenniki* transformed the idea of Russian nationality from a static entity that had to be retrieved by a quasi-religious act of contrition, as the Slavophiles understood it, into a dynamic and evolutionary principle of organic change. Whereas the early Slavophiles located the ideal in the past, the *pochvenniki* pinned their hopes on the future. In their view, the Russian ideal was naturally being realized in the gradual creation of a self-conscious *natsional'nost'* or *obshchestvo*. On this point at least the later Slavophile Ivan Aksakov, and Leont'ev in his early career, followed the *pochvenniki*. Moreover, the emphasis on the need for ethical and spiritual education as the prerequisite of the self-conscious nation, united in its pursuit of a moral ideal, has become the hallmark of Russian conservatives from Struve to Solzhenitsyn.

The young editors and the *pochvenniki* reflect many of the characteristics of intelligentsia conservatism in nineteenth-century Russia. Intelligentsia conservatism was less a reaction to intelligentsia radicalism than it was its paired opposite. Both arose more or less simultaneously as two related responses from within a single group, the socially unattached intelligentsia, to the same social, cultural, and personal experiences and needs. The socially unattached intelligentsia, which was largely the product of the intensification of urban culture in the closing years of the reign of Nicholas I, addressed itself to the tensions in Russian thought and life that were generated by the slow process of modernization. These tensions were encapsulated in the metaphor Russia and the West. The outlook of both radicals and conservatives among the *intelligenty* was shaped not only by their common intellectual roots in romanticism and utopian socialism, but also by their vehement rejection of the individualistic values and mechanical social arrangements that they believed characterized life in the bourgeois West. Both sides, consequently, ended by advocating remarkably similar collectivist or communalist social objectives.

The *Weltanschauung* of the socially unattached intelligentsia was formed by its experience and not as the product of its class of origin. Seeking to overcome their own feelings of displacement and disorientation in a society that had little room for them and a state that oppressed them, members of the socially unattached intelligentsia usually pursued one of two possible routes. The radicals, for the most part, advocated peasant revolution in order to emancipate the primitive forms of Russian peasant communalism from state and gentry domination and the bonds of a traditionalist peasant mentality and translate them into the advanced socialism of the Western theorists. The conservatives, in contrast, attempted to reconcile class divisions through the agency of a higher, self-conscious form of Russian nationality in which the cultural and technological achievements of the West, contained in the educated classes, were infused with the communalism and Christian fraternity preserved in the peasant class. The routes chosen by the *intelligenty* reflected personal preference and life experiences and cannot with any certainty be related to social origins.

The conservative intelligentsia in Russia borrowed extensively from the European conservative tradition, especially from German romanticism and idealism, and its story constitutes a distinctive chapter in the history of European conservatism. It viewed history as an organic process of the growing consciousness of innate ideals that were contained and, in time, were consciously expressed in the lives of nations. Its members were antirationalists who sought to reintegrate reason with intuition and faith and to ground thought in the experience of concrete reality. They persistently warned the Russian intelligentsia against the dangers of excessive abstractionism.

In keeping with their organic view of history, the intelligentsia conservatives were gradualists, who deplored revolutionary change or reforms inspired by foreign or abstract models. They looked instead to the particularist tradition of Russia. There they found the principles of autocracy and communalism which, they believed, secured Russians from the corrupting influence of politics and the social atomization and impersonal legalism of the liberal, contractual state and assured them a communal life inspired by Christian fraternity.

In spite of the stress that most Russian conservatives placed on historical experience as the only reliable guide to action, the conservative conception of Russian nationality rested far less on an objective reading of European and Russian history than it did on a theory of spiritual types. These types, which were contained in the metaphor Russia and the West, were rooted both in Russia's religious experience and in the literary formulations of the Russian romantics. They had early become entrenched in Slavophilism. The *pochvenniki*, who professed to have discovered in literature the ideal essence of living types, tended to reinforce the basically non-historical character of conservative thinking about Russian nationality and to encourage an even greater reliance on a typology. The whole idea of spiritual types almost inevitably fostered thoughts of national exclusiveness and fuelled not only nationalism but also the politically more explosive pan-Slavism as well. In his last years, Dostoevsky carried the idea of national types to militancy. And it was not by chance that Danilevsky's theory of cultural-historical types should first have seen the light of day in Strakhov's *Zaria*, a journal professing to perpetuate in some measure the spirit of *Vremia* and *Epokha* but which had already abandoned much of that spirit for a more nationalistic and exclusive approach to Russia and the West.

By perpetuating the myth of the apolitical nature of Russians, the conservative members of the intelligentsia formed an unwitting alliance with the radicals. The defence of the autocratic principle gave ideological sustenance to the autocracy at a time when its traditional bases of legitimacy were steadily being eroded by the forces of social and economic change. Although the conservative intelligentsia, particularly the *pochvenniki*, emphasized individual moral responsibility as the basis of social life, the sharp distinction they drew between the internal life of the land and the external life of the state, their critique of liberal constitutionalism, and their indifference to legal order contributed significantly to retarding the growth of a strong liberal consciousness among the Russian public. Linked as they were by a complex of internal psychological and intellectual affinities and predilections, the conservative and radical intelligentsia inadvertently conspired to polarize Russian political and social thought at the extremes and to prejudice a moderate outcome to the political strivings of their century.

Notes

INTRODUCTION

1 The Slavophiles have as a matter of course received the greatest attention, but a few studies of other conservative individuals are available. A comprehensive list appears in the bibliography. Two useful works, which attempt to draw together elements of the conservative tradition are E.C. Thaden, *Conservative Nationalism in Nineteenth-Century Russia* (Seattle 1964), and Andrzej Walicki, *The Slavophile Controversy: History of a Conservative Utopia in Nineteenth-Century Russian Thought* (Oxford 1975).

2 Two works of Soviet scholarship have been particularly important for the present study: B.F. Egorov, 'Apollon Grigor'ev – kritik,' *Uchenye zapiski Tartuskogo gos. universiteta*, xcviii (1960), 194–246 and B.G. Bazanov et al, *Neizdannyi Dostoevskii, Literaturnoe nasledstvo*, lxxxiii (Moscow 1971).

3 Richard Pipes has provided the most satisfactory working definition of Russian conservatism. Conservatism in Russia, he writes, is the 'ideology which advocates for Russia an authoritarian government subject to restraints neither by formal law nor by an elected legislature but only of such limitations as it sees fit to impose on itself'; R. Pipes, 'Russian Conservatism, in the Second Half of the Nineteenth Century,' *Slavic Review*, xxx no. 1 (March 1971), 121.

4 For a penetrating analysis of this aspect of the mentality of the Russian peasantry, see Daniel Field, *Rebels in the Name of the Tsar* (Boston 1976).

5 The great diversity of use of the term *intelligentsia* has prompted a few historians to abandon it altogether. See, for example, Daniel Brower, 'The Problem of the Russian Intelligentsia,' *Slavic Review*, xxvi no. 4 (December 1967), 638–47. Most historians prefer, however, to go on using the word

because the advantages of abandoning it and finding substitutes are often more apparent than real. In the case of the individuals discussed in this book, it is difficult to find an adequate substitute for 'intelligentsia conservatives.' The varieties of conservatism in nineteenth-century Russia were too great for 'conservative' to stand alone, but the addition of 'educated,' 'intellectual,' or 'philosophical' to 'conservative' is very far from satisfactory. None of these adjectives is as precise in meaning as intelligentsia and none conveys the oppositional character of the attitude of these particular conservatives towards the existing order as well as does intelligentsia. Most of the men discussed in this book were 'publicists' but by no means all conservative publicists of their day shared either the social characteristics or the specific views of the 'young editors' or the *pochvenniki*. Nor were all 'conservative nationalists' opposed to the existing régime. It may, indeed, be argued that only the phrase 'intelligentsia conservatism' adequately describes both the social characteristics and the peculiar ideological amalgam of loyalty to tradition and opposition to the established order of the 'native soil' movement.

6 For an intelligent and balanced discussion of relations between the state and society in the first half of the nineteenth century, see N.V. Riasanovsky, *A Parting of Ways. Government and the Educated Public in Russia, 1801–1855* (Oxford 1976).

7 Cited in ibid, 249–50

8 The literature concerning the Russian intelligentsia is extensive. Particularly helpful works include Marc Raeff, *Origins of the Russian Intelligentsia. The Eighteenth-Century Nobility* (New York 1966); Richard Pipes ed, *The Russian Intelligentsia* (New York 1961); Allan Pollard, 'The Russian Intelligentsia,' *California Slavic Studies*, III (Berkeley 1964), 8–19; Vladimir Nahirny, 'The Russian Intelligentsia: From Men of Ideas to Men of Convictions,' *Comparative Studies in Society and History*, IV (1962), 403–35; and Michael Confino, 'On Intellectuals and Intellectual Traditions in the Eighteenth- and Nineteenth-Century Russia,' *Daedalus* (Spring 1972), 117–49.

9 John Weiss, *Conservatism in Europe, 1770–1945. Traditionalism, Reaction and Counter-Revolution* (London 1977), 60

10 These behavioural patterns of the Russian intelligentsia conform to the model suggested by Karl Mannheim in his discussion of what he calls the 'socially unattached intelligentsia.' See Karl Mannheim, *Ideology and Utopia: An Introduction to the Sociology of Knowledge* (New York 1936), 155–61.

11 In his study of the Russian nihilists, Brower points out the dangers of linking ideology to social origins; Daniel R. Brower, *Training the Nihilists. Education and Radicalism in Tsarist Russia* (Ithaca and London 1975), 117–18.

CHAPTER ONE: CONSERVATISM AND THE SEARCH
FOR NATIONAL ORIGINALITY

1 The following brief account of the European conservative tradition rests
  on the work of a number of scholars. I have relied extensively on Klaus
  Epstein, *The Genesis of German Conservatism* (Princeton 1966); Russell Kirk,
  The Conservative Mind. From Burke to Santayana (Chicago 1953); Noel O'Sullivan, *Conservatism* (London 1976); and John Weiss, *Conservatism in Europe,
  1700–1945. Traditionalism, Reaction and Counter-Revolution* (London 1977).
2 O'Sullivan, *Conservatism*, 10–11
3 Ibid, 11
4 Edmund Burke, *Reflections on the Revolution in France* (Indianapolis and
  New York 1955), 70
5 Ibid, 99
6 Joseph de Maistre, *On God and Society. Essay on the Generative Principle of
  Political Constitutions and Other Human Institutions*, Elisha Greifer ed and
  trans (Chicago 1967), 84
7 Weiss, *Conservatism*, 18
8 O'Sullivan, *Conservatism*, 12
9 Weiss, *Conservatism*, 42
10 S.T. Coleridge, *The Friend* (London 1850), 268
11 Weiss, *Conservatism*, 53
12 The best introduction to the political thought of the German romantics is
  Reinhold Aris, *History of Political Thought in Germany from 1789–1815*
  (London 1936).
13 F.K. von Savigny, 'On the Vocation of Our Age for Legislation and Juris-
  prudence' in H.S. Reiss ed, *The Political Thought of the German Romantics
  1793–1815* (Oxford 1955), 204
14 For a discussion of this aspect of Herder's thought, see Isaiah Berlin, *Vico
  and Herder: Two Studies in the History of Ideas* (London 1976), 153ff.
15 Shcherbatov's *O povrezhdenii nravov v Rossii* was written in 1786–9 but
  published for the first time, by Herzen, only in 1858.
16 For population figures see William L. Blackwell, *The Beginnings of Russian
  Industrialization, 1800–1860* (Princeton 1968), 96–7, 427.
17 Ibid, 435
18 On this point see Jacob W. Kipp and W. Bruce Lincoln, 'Autocracy and
  Reform: Bureaucratic Absolutism and Political Modernization in Nineteenth
  Century Russia,' *Russian History*, VI pt 1 (1979) 1–21.
19 Hans Rogger has traced this development in his *National Consciousness in
  Eighteenth-Century Russia* (Cambridge, Mass, 1960).

20 N.M. Karamzin, 'Love of Country and National Pride,' in Marc Raeff ed, *Russian Intellectual History: An Anthology* (New York 1966), 110 (Karamzin's emphasis)

21 Russian romantic and idealist thought in the first half of the nineteenth century is discussed in a number of sources. Most useful are D.I. Chizhevskii, *Gegel' v Rossii* (Paris 1939); Alexandre Koyré, *Études sur l'histoire de la pensée philosophique en Russie* (Paris 1950) and *La Philosophie et le problème national en Russie au début du XIXe siècle* (Paris 1929); and I.I. Zamotin, *Romantizm dvadtsatykh godov XIX stoletiia v russkoi literature,* I (Warsaw 1903) and *Romanticheskii idealizm v russkom obshchestve i literature 20–30x godov XIX stoletiia* (St Petersburg 1907).

22 P.K. Christoff, *The Third Heart: Some Intellectual Currents and Cross-Currents in Russia, 1800–1830* (The Hague 1970), 36

23 P. Ia. Chaadaev, 'Apologia of a Madman' in Raymond T. McNally ed, *The Major Works of Peter Chaadaev* (Notre Dame and London 1969), 213–14

24 V.F. Odoevskii, *Russian Nights* (New York 1965), 251–3

25 A.S. Pushkin, 'On Nationality in Literature' in Carl R. Proffer ed, *The Critical Prose of Alexander Pushkin* (Bloomington and London 1969), 41

CHAPTER TWO: THE YOUNG EDITORS OF MOSKVITIANIN

1 The careers of Pogodin and Shevyrev have been examined in Nicholas V. Riasanovsky, *Nicholas I and Official Nationality in Russia, 1825–1855* (Berkeley 1959).

2 For relations between the young editors and the Countess Rostopchina, see N.V. Berg, 'Salon E. Rostopchinoi' in N.L. Brodskii ed, *Literaturnye salony i kruzhki: Pervaia polovina XIX veka* (Moscow 1930), 414–18.

3 The origins of the young editors' circle are discussed in N. Barsukov, *Zhizn' i trudy M.P. Pogodina,* XI (St Petersburg 1897) 64–72. See also S. Vengerov, 'Molodaia redaktsiia *Moskvitianina,*' *Vestnik Evropy,* I no. 2 (1886), 581–612.

4 A.A. Grigor'ev was the son of a bureaucrat who had attained hereditary nobility on the Table of Ranks, E.N. Edel'son was the son of a gymnasium teacher in Riazan', A.N. Ostrovsky was from a priestly family which had later entered the bureaucracy, A.F. Pisemsky came from the impoverished gentry, Ia. P. Polonsky was the son of a bureaucrat, and L.A. Mei was the son of a disabled army officer of German origin.

5 See, for example, Vengerov, 'Molodaia,' 590–5 and F. Nelidov, 'A.N. Ostrovskii v kruzhke molodogo *Moskvitianina,*' *Russkaia mysl'* III (St Petersburg 1901), 17–19.

6 Baruskov, *Pogodina*, XI, 90

7 A.G. Dementev, *Ocherki po istorii russkoi zhurnalistiki, 1840–1850 gg.* (Moscow-Leningrad 1951), 235

8 Pogodin outlined his ideas about Russian history and nationality in *Moskvitianin* in 1845. The article is reproduced in part in Barsukov, *Pogodine*, VIII (1894), 53–7.

9 A contemporary later noted that the young editors lived in an orgy of song; S.V. Maksimov, 'A.N. Ostrovskii po moim vospominaniiam,' *Dramaticheskie sochineniia A.N. Ostrovskogo*, XI (St Petersburg n.d.), 12–16.

10 A.A. Grigor'ev, *Materialy dlia biografii A. Grigor'eva*, Vl. Kniazhnin ed (Petrograd 1917), 184–5. *Neposredstvennost'* may be translated also as 'spontaneity.'

11 The influence of Herder on Grigor'ev and the native soil movement will be discussed in greater detail in chapter 3.

12 A.N. O[strovskii], '"Oshibka", povest' G–zhi Tur,' *Moskvitianin* (April 1850), 88–9. Evgeniia Tur was the pseudonym of Elizaveta Vasil'evna Salias-de-Turnemir (1815–1892), a minor novelist.

13 Apollon Grigor'ev, 'Russkaia literatura v 1851 godu,' *Sochineniia I. Kritika*, V.S. Krupitsch ed (Villanova 1970), 27

14 Ibid, 29

15 V.V. Zenkovsky refers to the young editors' romantic proclivity for immediately felt experience as the 'cult of immediacy'; V.V. Zenkovsky, *A History of Russian Philosophy*, I (London 1953), 402.

16 E.N. Edel'son, 'Zhurnalistika,' *Moskvitianin* (November 1854), 81–2. A month earlier Edel'son had deplored critics who greeted any work of art, no matter how devoid of talent, as a 'welcome phenomenon' so long as it was useful; Edel'son, 'Zhurnalistika,' *Moskvitianin* (October 1854), 188. Grigor'ev's views on art were outlined in his 'Russkaia literatura v 1851 godu.'

17 A.A. Grigor'ev, 'Kritika i bibliografiia,' *Moskvitianin* (May 1851), 169

18 A.A. Grigor'ev, *Sochineniia Apollona Grigor'eva*, I, N. Strakhov ed (St Petersburg 1876), 120

19 E.N. Edel'son, 'Kritika,' *Moskvitianin* (March 1854), 2

20 See, for example, N.L. Rubinshtein, 'Apollon Grigor'ev,' *Literatura i marksizm*, II (Moscow 1929), 104–6; and U.A. Gural'nik, '*Sovremennik* v bor'be s zhurnalami Dostoevskogo,' *Izvestiia Akademii Nauk SSSR. Otdelenie literatury i iazyka*, IX no. 4 (Moscow 1950), 268.

21 E.N. Edel'son, 'Zhurnalistika,' *Moskvitianin* (July 1854), 84

22 Alfred J. Rieber, 'The Moscow Entrepreneurial Group: The Emergence of a New Form in Autocratic Politics, I,' *Jahrbücher für Geschichte Osteuropas*, XXV no. 1 (1977), 13

23 A. Walicki views the Slavophiles as the defenders of the pre-capitalist social structure as a whole and not simply of their own gentry class: 'Slavophilism was the ideology of the hereditary Russian nobility who were reluctant to stand up on their own behalf as a privileged group defending its own selfish interests and therefore attempted to sublimate and universalize traditional values and to create an ideological platform that would unite all classes and social strata representing "ancient Russia"'; Andrzej Walicki, *The Slavophile Controversy* (Oxford 1975), 177–8. The traditional values which they sought to universalize remained, however, the patriarchal values of rural Russia.

24 Barsukov, *Pogodina*, XIV (1900), 200

CHAPTER THREE: GRIGOR'EV AND ORGANIC CRITICISM

1 Recent Soviet works include A. Grigor'ev, *Izbrannye proizvedeniia*, D.O. Kostelianets ed (Leningrad 1959); A. Grigor'ev, *Literaturnaia kritika*, B.F. Egorov ed (Moscow 1967), hereafter *Literaturnaia kritika*; B. Ia. Bukhshtab, '"Gimny" Apollona Grigor'eva,' *Bibliograficheskie razyskaniia po russkoi literature XIX veka* (Moscow, 1966), 27–49; and I.Z. Serman, 'Dostoevskii i Ap. Grigor'ev,' *Dostoevskii i ego vremia* (Leningrad 1971), 130–42. In the West, a selection of Grigor'ev's critical works has appeared in Apollon Grigor'ev, *Sochineniia I. Kritika*, V.S. Krupitsch ed (Villanova 1970); one of his critical essays has been translated into English in Paul Debreczeny and Jesse Zeldin eds, *Literature and National Identity. Nineteenth-Century Russian Critical Essays* (Lincoln 1970).

2 The main exception is E.C. Thaden, who included a useful chapter on Grigor'ev in his *Conservative Nationalism in Nineteenth-Century Russia* (Seattle 1964).

3 The best short biographical essay available in English is Krupitsch's introduction to his edition of Grigor'ev's selected essays cited above. Grigor'ev's own autobiography is available in English: see Apollon Grigoryev, *My Literary and Moral Wanderings*, Ralph Matlaw trans (New York 1962).

4 Grigor'ev reminisced about his childhood years in his 'Moi literaturnye i nravstvennye skital'chestva. Avtobiografiia.' *Sobranie sochinenii*, I–XIV, V. Savodnik ed (Moscow 1915–16), 7ff.

5 A.A. Fet, the poet, lived as a boarder in the Grigor'ev home from 1839. He later provided invaluable information about Grigor'ev's childhood and painted an intimate portrait of life in the family during Grigor'ev's university years; A.A. Fet, 'Rannie gody moei zhizni' in A.A. Grigor'ev, *Vospominaniia*, R.V. Ivanov-Razumnik ed (Moscow-Leningrad 1930), 387–413.

6 For details about Grigor'ev's circle, see ibid, 400–3 and Ia. P. Polonskii, 'Moi studencheskie vospominaniia,' *Niva* (December 1898), 642–87.

7 Grigor'ev to M.P. Pogodin, Vl. Kniazhnin ed., *Materialy dlia biografii A. Grigor'eva* (Petrograd 1917), 101, hereafter *Materialy*.

8 Fet made it clear that by 'dogmatic structure' Grigor'ev meant the humiliating restrictions placed on him by his mother; 'Rannie gody moei zhizni,' 394–7.

9 The play is reproduced in A.A. Grigor'ev *Izbrannye proizvedeniia*, Kostelianets ed, 183–268.

10 V.G. Belinskii, *Izbrannye filosofskie sochineniia*, II (Moscow 1948), 313

11 Apollon Grigor'ev, 'Gogol' i ego "perepiska s druz'iami",' *Sochineniia I. Kritika*, Krupitsch ed, 1–22

12 For Grigor'ev's efforts to revive *Moskvitianin*, see I.S. Zil'bershtein, 'Apollon Grigor'ev i popytka vozrodit' *Moskvitianin* (nakanune sotrudnichestva v zhurnale *Vremia*),' *Literaturnoe nasledstvo*, LXXXVI (Moscow 1973), 567–80.

13 Grigor'ev to A.I. Koshelev, *Materialy*, 150–2

14 Grigor'ev to A.N. Maikov, ibid, 175

15 Grigor'ev to M.P. Pogodin, ibid, 227

16 Nicholas Berdyaev, *Leontiev* (Orono, Me, 1968), 151

17 On Grigor'ev and Bergson, see L. Grossman, 'Apollon Grigor'ev. Osnovatel' novoi kritiki,' *Russkaia mysl'* (November 1914), 2–10.

18 A.A. Grigor'ev, 'I.S. Turgenev i ego deiatel'nost',' *Literaturnaia kritika*, 355. For a discussion of Grigor'ev's relationship to Belinsky, see Victor Terras, *Belinskij and Russian Literary Criticism: The Heritage of Organic Aesthetics* (Madison 1974), 34–5 and 214–15.

19 A.N. Maikov to A.I. Maikova, *Literaturnoe nasledstvo*, LXXXVI, 398

20 Belinskii, *Izbrannye*, I, 72 (Belinsky's emphasis)

21 Ibid, I, 145–6 (Belinsky's emphasis)

22 Ibid, II, 443

23 Ibid, II, 278

24 Belinsky discusses the relationship of the author to his environment and the theory of types in ibid, II, 432–46.

25 Grigor'ev, 'I.S. Turgenev,' 324

26 A.A. Grigor'ev, 'Posle "Grozy" Ostrovskogo,' *Sochineniia*, I, N.N. Strakhov ed (St Petersburg 1876), 458

27 A.A. Grigor'ev, 'O pravde i iskrennosti v iskusstve,' ibid, 141–2

28 A.A. Grigor'ev, 'Vzgliad na russkuiu literaturu so smerti Pushkina,' *Literaturnaia kritika*, 187

29 Grigor'ev, 'O pravde,' 142

30 A.A. Grigor'ev, 'Kriticheskii vzgliad na osnovy, znachenii i priemy sovremennoi kritiki iskusstva,' *Literaturnaia kritika*, 125

31 Grigor'ev, 'Posle "Grozy",' 451

32 Heinrich Stammler, 'Dostoevsky's Aesthetics and Schelling's Philosophy of Art,' *Comparative Literature*, VII (Fall 1955), 317

33 Grigor'ev, 'I.S. Turgenev,' 324

34 Ibid

35 Grigor'ev, 'Vzgliad na russkuiu literaturu,' 166–7

36 Grigor'ev, 'Kriticheskii vzgliad,' 127

37 Ibid, 129

38 For an excellent discussion of nineteenth-century European idealism, on which my own summary relies, see Maurice Mandelbaum, *History, Man and Reason. A Study of Nineteenth Century Thought* (Baltimore 1971), chapter 1.

39 Belinskii, *Izbrannye*, 1, 65 and 74

40 Ibid, 1, 495

41 G.W.F. Hegel, *The Philosophy of History* (New York 1956), 78

42 F.W.J. von Schelling, *Of Human Freedom*, James Gutmann trans (Chicago 1936), 62

43 Ibid, 95

44 Ibid, 108

45 Grigor'ev, 'Kriticheskii vzgliad,' 134

46 For a discussion of Setschkareff's findings, see Lauren Leighton, *Russian Romanticism: Two Essays* (The Hague 1975), especially 44 and 104.

47 For the following interpretation of Herder's thought, I have relied extensively on the work of F.M. Barnard. See his introductory essay in *J.G. Herder on Social and Political Culture* (Cambridge 1969), 3–60.

48 J.G. Herder, 'Journal of My Voyage in the Year 1769,' Barnard ed *J.G. Herder*, 66

49 Grigor'ev discussed 'historical feeling' in his 'Kriticheskii vzgliad,' 146–50. Khomiakov, too, had identified two stages in the development of rationalism: 1) Enlightenment, and 2) Hegel.

50 J.G. Herder, 'Yet Another Philosophy of History,' Barnard ed, *J.G. Herder*, 214

51 Odin iz mnogikh nenuzhnykh liudei [Grigor'ev], 'O postepennom no bystrom i povsemestnom rasprostranenii nevezhestva i bezgramotnosti v russkoi slovesnosti,' *Vremia* (March 1861), sect IV, 40–1

52 Herder, 'Yet Another,' 204

53 Grigor'ev, 'Kriticheskii vzgliad,' 134

54 Ibid

55 Herder, 'Yet Another,' 194

56 Grigor'ev, 'Kriticheskii vzgliad,' 134
57 For a more detailed discussion of Herder's understanding of the *Volk*, see Barnard's introduction in *J.G. Herder*, especially 31–2.
58 I.V. Kireevskii, *Polnoe sobranie sochinenii*, II (Moscow 1911, reprint 1970), 149
59 Grigor'ev, 'O komediiakh Ostrovskogo i ikh znachenie v literature i na stsene,' *Sochineniia Apollona Grigor'eva*, I, Strakhov ed, 119; or 'Posle "Grozy",' 477–8
60 Belinskii, *Izbrannye*, I, 343
61 Barnard, *J.G. Herder*, 50
62 Grigor'ev, 'Vzgliad na russkuiu literaturu,' 167 (emphasis added)
63 Herder, 'Yet Another,' 215
64 Grigor'ev, 'Kriticheskii vzgliad,' 134. Robert Williams regarded the emphasis placed on the soul (as opposed to the Hegelian spirit) as the distinguishing characteristic of the native soil movement; R.C. Williams, 'The Russian Soul: A Study in European Thought and Non-European Nationalism,' *Journal of the History of Ideas*, XXXI no. 4 (1970), 573–88.
65 A.A. Grigor'ev, 'Vzgliad na istoriiu Rossii. Sochineniia S. Solov'eva,' *Russkoe slovo* (January 1859), 39–44
66 Grigor'ev to M.P. Pogodin, *Materialy*, 246
67 Grigor'ev to A.N. Maikov, ibid, 217
68 Grigor'ev outlined his views on the predatory and humble types in Russian literature in Grigor'ev, 'Vzgliad na russkuiu literaturu,' 175–85.
69 Grigor'ev, 'I.S. Turgenev i ego deiatel'nost,' 297. In this passage, Grigor'ev completely identifies art and reality.
70 Ibid, 316
71 [Anon] A.A. Grigor'ev, 'Nasha pristan', '*Iakor*', no. 3 (1863), 41

CHAPTER FOUR: INTELLIGENTSIA CONSERVATISM
IN THE EMANCIPATION PERIOD

1 V.S. Nechaeva, *Zhurnal M.M. i F.M. Dostoevskikh 'Vremia', 1861–1863* (Moscow 1972), 5
2 Cited in I.I. Zamotin, *Sorokovye i shestidesiatye gody* (Moscow-Petrograd 1915), 227
3 N.N. Strakhov, 'Vospominaniia o Fedore Mikhailoviche Dostoevskom,' *Biografiia, pis'ma i zametki iz zapisnoi knizhki F.M. Dostoevskogo*, O. Miller and N. Strakhov eds (St Petersburg 1883), 198–9 and 232
4 See N. Barsukov, *Zhizn' i trudy M.P. Pogodina*, XVI (St Petersburg 1902), 307–38 for the program of *Parus* and extracts from the most important articles that appeared in the only two issues that were published.

5 F.M. Dostoevskii, *Pis'ma*, I A.S. Dolinin ed (Moscow-Leningrad 1928–59), 150

6 Leonid Grossman, *Dostoevskii* (Moscow 1965), 174

7 Dmitrii Chizhevskii, 'Dostoevskii – psikholog,' *O Dostoevskom – Sbornik statei*, II, A.L. Bem ed (Prague 1933), 71

8 V.G. Belinskii, *Izbrannye filosofskie sochineniia*, I (Moscow 1948), 341–2

9 Dostoevskii, *Pis'ma*, I, 165

10 Ibid, 183

11 Ibid, 167

12 Ibid, 597

13 A.N. Plescheev to F.M. Dostoevsky, April 1859, in *F.M. Dostoevskii. Materialy i issledovaniia*, A.S. Dolinin ed (Leningrad 1935), 444

14 Dostoevskii, *Pis'ma*, II, 587

15 A.S. Dolinin, 'Zhurnaly Dostoevskogo i tsenzura,' in A.S. Dolinin ed, *F.M. Dostoevskii. Stat'i i materialy*, II (Leningrad 1924), 562.

16 Dostoevskii, *Pis'ma*, II, 593

17 For the story of *Russkoe slovo*, see L.E. Varustin, *Zhurnal 'Russkoe slovo'* (Leningrad 1966), especially 7–30. Also see G.R. Prokhurov, 'G.E. Blagosvetlov, Ia. P. Polonskii, G.A. Kushelev-Bezborodko, Pis'ma i dokumenty,' *Zven'ia*, no. 1, Vl. Bonch-Bruevich et al eds, 298–303. For Pisemsky's abortive efforts to take over the *Biblioteka dlia chteniia*, see A.F. Pisemskii to A.N. Ostrovskii in M.D. Prygunov ed, *Neizdannye pis'ma iz arkhiva A.N. Ostrovskogo* (Moscow-Leningrad 1932), 370–1.

18 Strakhov, 'Vospominaniia o Dostoevskom,' 172–5

19 D.I. Kalinovskii, 'Vstupitel'noe slovo,' *Svetoch*, I (January 1860), vii

20 Ibid, x. Cf 'Ob"iavlenie,' *Svetoch*, VIII (August 1860), v–vii.

21 Kalinovskii, 'Vstupitel'noe slovo,' v

22 A.P. Miliukov, 'Zakliuchitel'noe slovo *Russkoi Besede*,' *Svetoch*, II (February 1860), 27

23 'Ot redaktsii,' *Svetoch*, VIII (August 1861), back cover

24 'Russkaia khronika,' *Svetoch*, IV (April 1861), 19

25 Miliukov, 'Zakliuchitel'noe slovo *Russkoi Besede*,' 18–21

26 'Kriticheskoe obozrenie,' *Svetoch*, x (October 1861), 13

27 M.M. Dostoevskii, '*Groza* A.N. Ostrovskogo,' *Svetoch*, II (March 1860), 7–8. For a Soviet view of this article and of *Svetoch*, see G.M. Fridlender, 'U istokov "pochvennichestva". (F.M. Dostoevskii i zhurnal *Svetoch*),' *Izvestiia akademii nauk SSSR. Otdelenie literatury i iazyka*, xxx (September–October 1971), sect v 400–10.

28 Dostoevskii, *Pis'ma*, III, 294

29 Strakhov, 'Vospominaniia o Dostoevskom,' 170 and 177. Nikolai Nikolae-

vich Strakhov (1828–1896), the son of a priest, was born in Belgorod near Kharkov. He received his early education in a seminary. In 1844, he came to St Petersburg and registered at first in the juridical faculty as an auditor. In 1845, he transferred to the mathematical faculty. Owing to a family quarrel, he lost his stipend after a little more than a year and was forced once again to transfer, this time to the Chief Pedagogical Institute. This move obligated him to ten years' teaching service after graduation. After completing his studies, he was posted to Odessa but within a year was assigned to a gymnasium in St Petersburg. Here he remained for nine years. Along with his teaching, he pursued graduate work in biology, and in 1857 he received a master's degree. Apart from his interest in the natural sciences, he had acquired a wide knowledge of philosophy and European literature. His publishing career began in 1857 and occupied him fully until his death. For a detailed study of Strakhov's life and work, see Linda Gerstein, *Nikolai Strakhov. Philosopher, Man of Letters, Social Critic* (Cambridge, Mass, 1971).

30 N.N. Strakhov, 'Vospominaniia ob A.A. Grigor'eve,' *Epokha* (September 1864), 3

31 See I.S. Zil'bershtein, 'Apollon Grigor'ev i popytka vozrodit' *"Moskvitianin"* (nakanune sotrudnichestva v zhurnale *"Vremia"*),' *Literaturnoe nasledstvo*, LXXXVI (Moscow 1973), 575–6

32 Strakhov, 'Vospominaniia o Dostoevskom,' 202

33 Fridlender, 'U istokov "pochvennichestva"' 404. Besides members of the *Svetoch* group, other contributors included Ia. P. Polonsky, A.F. Pisemsky, the economist I. Shill, F. Berg, K. Babikov, M. Semevsky, V. Fuks, and P. Bibikov.

34 Strakhov, 'Vospominaniia o Dostoevskom,' 205

35 Gerstein, *Nikolai Strakhov*, 53. Also see Nechaeva, *Zhurnal 'Vremia'*, 17.

36 Strakhov, 'Vospominaniia o Grigor'eve,' 7. Strakhov pointed out also that the editors of *Vremia* printed Grigor'ev's articles as if they were editorials; ibid, 29.

37 A.A. Grigor'ev, 'Zhurnal'nyi mir i ego iavleniia, I,' *Iakor'*, no. 6 (1863), 102

CHAPTER FIVE: NATIVE SOIL

1 In *Fathers and Children*, I.S. Turgenev epitomized the realist in the character of Bazarov. Less well known are some of his attempts to portrary the urge to return to Russia. In the following passage from *Rudin*, Turgenev wrote: 'Rudin's misfortune consists in the fact that he does not know Russia, and that is truly a great misfortune. Russia can get along without any one of us, but none of us can get along without her. Woe to him who thinks he can,

woe twice over to him who actually does get along without her. Cosmopolitanism is nonsense; the cosmopolitan is a cipher, and worse than a cipher; outside nationality there is neither art, nor truth, nor life. Without a distinct physiognomy, there is no such thing even as an ideal face; only a vulgar face is possible without a distinct physiognomy'; I.S. Turgenev, *Sochineniia*, IV (Moscow 1860), 115–16.

2 From the manifesto of *Vremia* for 1860 in F.M. Dostoevskii, *Biografiia, pis'ma i zametki iz zapisnoi knizhki F.M. Dostoevskogo*, O. Miller and N. Strakhov eds (St Petersburg 1883), 177

3 F.M. Dostoevskii, 'Riad statei o russkoi literature. Poslednie literaturnye iavleniia. Gazeta *Den*',' *Vremia* (November 1861), sect II 71

4 N.K. [N.N. Strakhov], 'Literaturnye zakonodateli,' *Vremia* (November 1861), sect II 117

5 See, for example, A.S. Khomiakov, 'O vozmozhnosti russkoi khudozhestvennoi shkoly,' *Polnoe sobranie sochinenii*, I (Moscow 1861), 80.

6 Anon [F.M. Dostoevskii], 'N.A. Dobroliubov,' *Vremia* (March 1862), sect II 46

7 N.K., 'Literaturnye zakonodateli,' 118

8 Anon [F.M. Dostoevskii], 'N.A. Dobroliubov,' 45

9 A.A. Grigor'ev, 'Belinskii i otritsatel'nyi vzgliad v literature,' *Vremia* (April 1861), sect II 203

10 Anon [Dostoevskii], 'N.A. Dobroliubov,' 45 (Dostoevsky's emphasis)

11 F.M. Dostoevskii, 'Neizdannyi Dostoevskii,' *Literaturnoe nasledstvo*, LXXXIII (Moscow 1971) 186 (Dostoevsky's emphasis)

12 Robert C. Williams, 'The Russian Soul: A Study in European Thought and Non-European Nationalism,' *Journal of the History of Ideas*, XXXI, no. 4 (1970) 584

13 N. Kositsa [N.N. Strakhov], 'Primer apatii,' *Vremia* (January–February 1862), sect II 65

14 F.M. Dostoevskii, 'Riad statei o russkoi literature. Vvedenie,' *Vremia* (January 1861), sect II 11

15 N.K., 'Nechto o polemike,' *Vremia* (August 1861), sect II 147–8

16 Dostoevskii, 'Neizdannyi Dostoevskii,' 172 (Dostoevsky's emphasis)

17 Dostoevskii, 'Riad statei ... Vvedenie,' 11; and from the 'manifesto' for 1860 in Dostoevskii, *Biografiia, pis'ma*, 178

18 F.M. Dostoevsky, *Winter Notes on Summer Impressions* (Toronto 1955), 89. It is interesting that Grigor'ev had used the analogy of the anthill to describe the social vision of Western socialists as early as December 1857 in a letter to Edel'son; A.A. Grigor'ev, *Materialy dlia biografii A. Grigor'eva*, Vl. Kniazhnin ed (Petrograd 1917), 196.

19 A.S. Dolinin, among others, has drawn attention to certain similarities

between *Winter Notes on Summer Impressions* and Herzen's *Letters from Italy and France*. That Dostoevsky visited Herzen in London in 1862 has lent further credence to the view that Herzen influenced *Winter Notes*. See A.S. Dolinin, 'Dostoevskii i Gertsen,' in A.S. Dolinin ed *F.M. Dostoevskii. Stat'i i materialy*, I (Petersburg 1922), 308. There are undeniable parallels between the two works, but the ideas shared by the two writers, such as the decline of the West and its inability to escape from its dilemma through its own resources, were common currency at the time. E.H. Carr suggests that coincidence played a greater role than did imitation in the similarities; E.H. Carr, *Dostoevsky 1821–1881* (London 1962), 75. Herzen also at this time shared with Dostoevsky the notion that Russians were capable of the reconciliation of classes and the creation of social harmony. But this, too, was a view common to many of the 'unattached' intelligentsia of the day and not an exclusive characteristic of the conservatives.

20 Dostoevskii, 'Riad statei ... Vvedenie,' 15
21 For the Slavophile view of Russia and the West, see I.V. Kireevskii, 'O kharaktere prosveshcheniia Evropy i o ego otnoshenii k prosveshchenii Rossii,' *Polnoe sobranie sochinenii*, I (Moscow 1911, reprint 1970), 182–98; and A.S. Khomiakov, 'Po povodu stat'i I.V. Kireevskogo,' *Polnoe sobranie sochinenii*, I (Moscow 1861), 210–11.
22 K.S. Aksakov, 'O vnutrennem sostoianii Rossii,' in *Rannie slavianofily: A.S. Khomiakov, I.V. Kireevskii, K.S. i I.S. Aksakovy*, N.L. Brodskii ed (Moscow 1910), 91
23 A.S. Khomiakov, 'Zamechaniia na stat'iu g. Solov'eva: Shletser i anti-istoricheskoe napravlenie,' *Polnoe sobranie sochinenii*, I, 603. The entire passage is stressed in the original.
24 A.S. Khomiakov, 'Mneniia inostrantsev o Rossii,' ibid, 16. Cf A.I. Koshelev, *Zapiski, 1812–1883* (Berlin 1884), 77.
25 A.S. Komiakov, 'To the Serbians. A Message from Moscow,' in P.K. Christoff, *An Introduction to Nineteenth Century Slavophilism. A.S. Khomiakov* (The Hague 1961), 256
26 From the 'manifesto' of *Vremia* for 1860 in Dostoevskii, *Biografiia, pis'ma*, 179–80
27 A.A. Grigor'ev, 'Lermontov i ego napravlenie, II' *Vremia* (November 1862), sect II 55; and Dostoevskii, 'Riad statei o russkoi literature. Vvedenie,' *Vremia* (January 1861), sect III 18
28 Anon [F.M. Dostoevskii], 'Dva lageria teoretikov,' *Vremia* (January–February 1862), sect II 154
29 From the 'manifesto' of *Vremia* for 1860 in Dostoevskii, *Biografiia, pis'ma*, 179

30 F.M. Dostoevskii, 'Riad statei o russkoi literature. Knizhnost' i gramotnost', I,' *Vremia* (July 1861), sect II 50

31 V.G. Belinskii, 'Deianiia Petra Velikogo,' *Izbrannye filosofskie sochineniia*, I (Moscow 1948), 343–4

32 Nicholas Berdiaev, *Dostoevsky* (Princeton 1969), 167

33 Dostoevskii, 'Riad statei o russkoi literature. Knizhnost' i gramotnost',' 45 (Dostoevsky's emphasis)

34 The triadic structure that was characteristic of German idealism is apparent in this construction. It should be noted, however, that what appear to be the thesis and antithesis are not antithetical at all but are complementary, and the synthesis is not the product of a struggle between thesis and antithesis but their harmonious mingling.

35 Strakhov was to endorse Grigor'ev's analysis fully in 1868 in his *Bednost' nashei literatury. Kriticheskii i istoricheskii ocherk* (St Petersburg 1868), 33–4.

36 A.A. Grigor'ev, 'Narodnost' i literatura,' *Vremia* (February 1861), sect III 92

37 Ibid, 98–9

38 Ibid, 100–2

39 Ibid, 104–10

40 A.A. Grigor'ev, 'Zapadnichestvo v russkoi literature,' *Vremia* (March 1861), sect III 6–8

41 Ibid, 9

42 Anon [Dostoevskii], 'Dva lageria teoretikov,' 144

43 Grigor'ev, 'Zapadnichestvo v russkoi literature,' 22

44 Ibid, 33

45 F.M. Dostoevskii, 'Riad statei o russkoi literature. Poslednie literaturnye iav-leniia. Gazeta *Den'* ,' *Vremia* (November 1861), sect II 72. Dostoevsky's comments in this passage were aimed specifically at the early Slavophiles rather than at Ivan Aksakov. Cf A.A. Grigor'ev, 'Graf Tolstoi i ego sochi-neniia, I,' *Vremia* (January–February 1862), sect II 10.

46 Anon [Dostoevskii], 'Dva lageria teoretikov,' 144

47 Ibid, 151

48 A.A. Grigor'ev, 'Stikhotvoreniia N. Nekrasova,' *Vremia* (July 1862), sect II 25

49 Anon [Dostoevskii], 'Dva lageria teoretikov,' 150

50 Ibid, 151. See also Anon, 'Opisanie nekotorykh sochinenii napisannykh russkimi raskol'nikami v pol'zu raskola,' *Vremia* (October 1861), sect II 79–100.

51 Grigor'ev, 'Stikhotvoreniia N. Nekrasova,' 26 (Grigor'ev's emphasis). Cf Anon [Dostoevskii], 'Dva lageria teoretikov,' 151–2. Ivan Kireevsky, too,

noted the impossibility of turning back as early as 1838. He remarked that it would be just as difficult to escape the century of European influence as it would be to shake off the thousand-year tradition that had preceded it; Kireevskii, 'V otvete A.S. Khomiakovu,' *Polnoe sobranie sochinenii*, I, 110.

52 Dostoevskii, 'Riad statei o russkoi literature. Gazeta *Den*',' 68
53 Anon [A.A. Grigor'ev], 'Vzgliad na knigi i zhurnal'nye stat'i,' *Vremia* (April 1861), sect II 175
54 Grigor'ev, 'Belinskii i otritsatel'nyi vzgliad v literature,' 186–7 and 214–15. Also see his 'Narodnost' i literatura,' 84–5.
55 Dostoevskii, 'Riad statei o russkoi literature. Gazeta *Den*',' 67
56 Ibid, 68
57 Ibid, 69. Cf Grigor'ev, 'Graf Tolstoi i ego sochineniia, I,' 10.
58 Khomiakov, 'O vozmozhnosti russkoi khudozhestvennoi shkoly,' *Polnoe sobranie sochinenii*, I, 97–8. On the voluntarism of the Slavophiles, see B.E. Nol'de, *Iurii Samarin i ego vremia* (Paris 1926), 31.
59 From the 'manifesto' of *Vremia* for 1862 in Dostoevskii, *Biografiia, pis'ma*, 32 (my emphasis)
60 From the 'manifesto' of *Vremia* for 1860 in Dostoevskii, *Biografiia, pis'ma*, 181
61 Dostoevskii, 'Riad statei o russkoi literature. Vvedenie,' 10. The difference between Slavophilism and *pochvennichestvo* on this point was a matter of emphasis. The *pochvenniki* saw a positive value in the ideals of the West because they vastly expanded the potential of Russian nationality. The Slavophiles, in contrast, believed that Russia already possessed the best that had been formulated in the West. Frank Fadner has written that, in the eyes of the Slavophiles, 'The Russian people would accomplish [the realization of Western ideals] through the development of its own natural and native talents; the highest manifestations of the European spirit and the deepest beliefs of the Russian people were *essentially the same*. Thus the early Slavophiles looked inward'; Frank Fadner, *Seventy Years of Pan-Slavism in Russia. Karamzin to Danilevskii, 1800–1870* (Georgetown 1963), 183–4. The early Slavophiles remained ambivalent on the relationship of European to Russian ideas, however. Khomiakov wrote, 'We also renounced ourselves and humiliated ourselves more, a hundred times more than Germany. I hope, I am certain that when we return home (and we shall return home – and soon), we shall bring with ourselves a clear understanding of the entire world, such as the Germans did not even dream of'; cited in N.V. Riasanovsky, *A Parting of Ways. Government and the Educated Public in Russia, 1801–1855* (Oxford 1976), 190. Such views anticipated *pochvennichestvo* and encouraged Grigor'ev in his belief that his views were a natural continuation of the best of Slavophilism.

62 Dostoevskii, 'Riad statei o russkoi literature. Knizhnost' i gramotnost',' 51–2
63 From the 'manifesto' of *Vremia* for 1860 in Dostoevskii, *Biografiia, pis'ma,* 180–1
64 Cited in ibid, 210

CHAPTER SIX: NATIVE SOIL AND SOCIAL AND POLITICAL CULTURE

1 P.V. Bykov, *Siluety dalekogo proshlogo* (Moscow-Leningrad 1930), 51
2 F.M. Dostoevskii, 'Neizdannyi Dostoevskii,' *Literaturnoe nasledstvo,* LXXXIII (Moscow 1971), 176
3 Ibid
4 From the 'manifesto' of *Vremia* for 1862 in F.M. Dostoevskii, *Biografiia, pis'ma i zametki iz zapisnoi knizhki F.M. Dostoevskogo,* O. Miller and N. Strakhov eds (St Petersburg 1883), 32–3
5 On Dostoevsky and the fires, see N.G. Rozenblium, 'Peterburgskie pozhary 1862 g. i Dostoevskii,' *Literaturnoe nasledstvo,* LXXXVI (Moscow 1973), 16–43.
6 F.M. Dostoevskii, *Pis'ma,* I (Moscow-Leningrad 1928), 312–13
7 M. Lemke, *Epokha tsenzurnykh reform 1859–1864 gg.* (St Petersburg 1904), 192. For Aksakov's figures, see I.S. Aksakov, *I.S. Aksakov v ego pis'makh,* IV pt 2 (St Petersburg 1896), 86.
8 Anon, '19 fevralia 1861 goda,' *Vremia* (March 1861), sect I 584
9 F.M. Dostoevskii, 'Riad statei o russkoi literature. Knizhnost' i gramotnost', I,' *Vremia* (July 1861), sect II 38. In the first number of *Den'*, Ivan Aksakov also welcomed Emancipation as beginning a movement forward of Russian life corresponding to the movement of thought (Slavophile) in the preceding fifty years; I.S. Aksakov, 'Moskva, 14 oktiabria,' *Den'* (15 October 1861), 1.
10 From the 'manifesto' of *Vremia* for 1861 in Dostoevskii, *Biografiia, pis'ma,* 177
11 F.M. Dostoevskii, 'Riad statei o russkoi literature. Vvedenie,' *Vremia* (January 1861), 11
12 Ibid, 19
13 Ibid, 11
14 Ibid, 12. Cf Anon [Dostoevskii], 'Dva lageria teoretikov,' *Vremia* (January–February, 1862), sect II 158–9
15 From the 'manifesto' for 1861 in Dostoevskii, *Biografiia, pis'ma,* 180
16 Dostoevskii, 'Riad statei o russkoi literature. Vvedenie,' 28
17 Anon., 'Nashi domashnie dela,' *Vremia* (October 1862), sect II 63
18 A.A. Grigor'ev to A.N. Maikov, January 1858, in A.A. Grigor'ev, *Materialy dlia biografii A. Grigor'eva,* Vl. Kniazhnin ed (Petrograd 1917), 215

19 Grigor'ev to N.N. Strakhov, ibid, 283
20 Dostoevskii, 'Neizdannyi Dostoevskii,' 186
21 Anon, 'Nashi domashnie dela,' *Vremia* (October 1861), sect III 171
22 Anon [Dostoevskii], 'Dva lageria teoretikov,' 157. In his notebooks Dostoevsky observed that the radicals were arguing about whether science (*nauka*) was universal or national. He went on, 'That's nonsense; science is everywhere and always in the highest degree national– one could say, science is in the highest degree nationality (*natsional'nost'*)'; Dostoevskii, 'Neizdannyi Dostoevskii,' 176.
23 From the 'manifesto' for 1863 in Dostoevskii, *Biografiia, pis'ma*, 30. The *pochvenniki* used civilization in at least two senses. In the first sense, they meant simply those philosophical, artistic, scientific, and technological achievements of mankind that had accumulated over centuries. In the second sense, they meant the aggregate of those fundamental, national ideals that various nations had so far contributed to the universal idea of man.
24 Dostoevskii, 'Riad statei o russkoi literature. Knizhnost' i gramotnost', II,' *Vremia* (August 1861), sect II 91–130. By May 1864 the Slavophile journal *Den'* had taken up the argument that education must accord with the national spirit and not be presented to the people in patronizing, scientifically prescribed doses; N. K–v, 'Kak uchit' prostoi narod?,' *Den'* (20 May 1864), 10–14.
25 Anon, 'Sobranie literaturnykh statei N.I. Pirogova,' *Vremia* (April 1862), sect II 6–7
26 Anon [N.N. Strakhov], 'Iasnaia-Poliana,' *Vremia* (March 1862), sect II 65–8
27 F.M. Dostoevskii, 'Vopros ob universitetakh,' *Vremia* (November 1861), sect II 96
28 For an account of the Sunday schools, see Ia. V. Abramov, *Nashi voskresnye shkoly* (St Petersburg 1900).
29 Anon [A.U. Poretskii?], 'Vnutrennie novosti,' *Vremia* (January 1861), sect IV 15–16
30 Dostoevskii, 'Riad statei o russkoi literature. Knizhnost' i gramotnost', II,' 91–130
31 Grigor'ev to N.N. Strakhov, *Materialy dlia biografii*, 275
32 Grigor'ev to Strakhov, ibid, 283
33 Still the best available study of Slavophile political thought is N. Ustrialov, 'Politicheskaia doktrina slavianofil'stva. Ideia samoderzhaviia v slavianofil'- skoi postanovke,' *Vysshaia shkola v Kharbine. Izvestiia iuridicheskogo fakul'teta* (Harbin 1925), 47–74.
34 Anon, 'Nashi domashnie dela,' *Vremia* (August 1861), sect IV 42–3; and Anon, 'Smes',' *Vremia* (April 1862), sect III 53

35 A. Poretskii, 'Preobrazovanie gorodskogo obshchestvennogo upravleniia,' *Vremia* (January 1863), sect II 28
36 Anon, 'Nashi domashnie dela,' *Vremia* (February 1863), sect II 121
37 A.P. Shchapov, 'Zemstvo i raskol,' *Vremia* (October–November 1862), sect II 319–50, 251–97. For a discussion of Shchapov and the 'federal school' of Russian history, see Dmitri von Mohrenschildt, 'Shchapov: Exponent of Regionalism and the Federal School in Russian History,' *Russian Review*, XXXVII no. 4 (October 1978), 387–404.
38 See, for example, Anon, 'Opisanie nekotorykh sochinenii napisannykh russkimi raskol'nikami v pol'zu raskola,' *Vremia* (October 1861), sect II 79–100; and M.R.D. Ch., 'Bibliografiia,' *Vremia* (December 1862), sect II 78–102.
39 A.A. Grigor'ev, 'Severno-russkaia narodopravstva vo vremeni udel'-novechenogo uklada,' *Vremia* (January 1863), sect II 101
40 N.N. Strakhov, 'Vospominaniia o Fedore Mikhailoviche Dostoevskom,' *Biografiia, pis'ma*, 229 (Strakhov's emphasis)
41 From the 'manifesto' of *Vremia* for 1863 in *Biografiia*, 33
42 Dostoevskii, 'Neizdannyi Dostoevskii,' 158
43 K.D. Kavelin to A.I. Herzen, *Pis'ma K.D. Kavelina i I.S. Turgeneva k A.I. Gertsenu*, M. Dragomanov ed (Geneva 1892), 59
44 Anon [F.M. Dostoevskii], 'Dvorianstvo i zemstvo,' *Vremia* (March 1862), sect II 19
45 Anon [Dostoevskii], 'Dva lageria teoretikov,' 160; and Anon, 'Deviatnadtsatyi numer *Dnia*,' *Vremia* (January– February 1862), sect II 74–5
46 I. Voskoboinikov, 'Zametka po krest'ianskomu voprosu,' *Vremia* (July 1861), sect III 1–11
47 Anon [Dostoevskii], 'Dvorianstvo i zemstvo,' 24
48 Ibid, 10–11
49 Ibid, 11
50 Anon [Dostoevskii], 'Dva lageria teoretikov,' 160. Cf I.S. Aksakov, 'Moskva, 9 dekabria,' *Den'* (9 December 1861), 2
51 Dostoevskii, from the 'manifesto' for 1863; *Biografiia*, 30–1
52 Anon [Dostoevskii], 'Dvorianstvo i zemstvo,' 27 (my emphasis)
53 F.M. Dostoevskii, *Sobranie sochinenii*, VIII, L.P. Grossman, A.S. Dolinin, et al. eds (Moscow 1958), 241–2
54 Anon [Dostoevskii], 'Dvorianstvo i zemstvo,' 26
55 Letopisets [N.N. Strakhov], 'Zametka letopistsa,' *Epokha* (August 1864), 21
56 P.B. Struve, 'Romantika protiv kazenshchiny,' *Na raznye temy – Sbornik statei* (St Petersburg 1902), 205
57 Anon, [Dostoevskii], 'Dvorianstvo i zemstvo,' 25–6
58 Anon, 'Nashi domashnie dela,' *Vremia* (August 1861), sect II 31–57

59 See, for example, P. Bibikov, 'Po povodu odnoi sovremennoi povesti,' *Vremia* (January–February 1862), sect II 31–57.

60 Dostoevsky himself connected Proudhon's view with his own idea of spontaneity in his notebook; Dostoevskii, 'Neizdannyi Dostoevskii,' 186.

61 P.-J. Proudhon, *La Guerre et la paix*, II (Brussels 1861), 205–14

62 Ibid, 436

63 Anon [A.E. Razin?], 'Politicheskoe obozrenie,' *Vremia* (October 1861), sect III 33–66

64 Ibid, 41

65 Anon, 'Nashi domashnie dela,' *Vremia* (October 1862), sect II 40–1

66 Anon, 'Nashi domashnie dela,' *Vremia* (February 1863), sect II 95

67 Anon, 'Politicheskaia ekonomiia nastoiashchogo i budushchego,' *Vremia* (March 1861), sect II 74–92

68 Anon, 'Nashi domashnie dela,' *Vremia* (October 1862), sect II 42

69 Anon, 'Nashi domashnie dela,' *Vremia* (November 1862), sect II 117

70 I. Shill, 'K voprosu o postroike zheleznoi doroge na iuge Rossii,' *Vremia* (November 1862), sect. II 1–31. It is interesting that Shill, professor-financier, was brought into *Vremia* on the insistence of Grigor'ev who is all too frequently thought of as an advocate of backwardness.

71 Anon, 'O formakh promyshlennosti voobshche i o znachenii domashnego proizvodstva v zapadnoi Evrope i v Rossii,' *Vremia* (September 1861), sect II 55–62

CHAPTER SEVEN: NATIVE SOIL AND LITERATURE

1 For a discussion of the influence of Schelling on Dostoevsky, see Heinrich Stammler, 'Dostoevsky's Aesthetics and Schelling's Philosophy of Art,' *Comparative Literature*, VII (Fall 1955), 313–23. In his detailed study of Dostoevsky's aesthetic views, Robert Jackson deals with the relationship between the ideas of Grigor'ev and those of Dostoevsky in little more than a footnote; R.L. Jackson, *Dostoevsky's Quest for Form* (New Haven 1966), 196 and 253.

2 Anon [F.M. Dostoevskii], '*Svistok* i *Russkii vestnik*,' *Vremia* (March 1861), sect IV 81–2. Later in the same year, Dostoevsky wrote, 'Science is an awesome force which was born with man and will remain with him as long as man dwells on earth'; Anon [F.M. Dotoevskii], 'Razskazy N.V. Uspenskogo,' *Vremia* (December 1861), sect II 179.

3 F.M. Dostoevskii, 'Riad statei o russkoi literature. g. – bov i vopros ob iskusstve,' *Vremia* (February 1861), 202

4 A.A. Grigor'ev, 'Stikhotvoreniia N. Nekrasova,' *Vremia* (July 1862), sect II 23

5 Anon, 'Beztsvetnye iavleniia,' *Vremia* (July 1861), sect II 82

6 Anon [Dostoevskii], '*Svistok* i *Russkii vestnik*,' 75

7 A.A. Grigor'ev, 'Paradoksy organicheskoi kritiki I. Organicheskii vzgliad i ego osnovnoi printsip,' *Epokha* (May 1864), 265–6 (Grigor'ev's emphasis)

8 A.S. Khomiakov, 'O vozmozhnosti russkoi khudozhestvennoi shkoly,' *Polnoe sobranie sochinenii*, I (Moscow 1861), 75

9 Ibid, 76

10 I.S. Kireevskii, 'Obozrenie sovremennogo sostoianiia literatury,' *Polnoe sobranie sochinenii* I (Moscow 1911, reprint 1970), 149

11 N.S.K., 'Otstupniki I,' *Den'* (20 October 1862), 16–17

12 I.S. Aksakov, 'Moskva, 16 ianvaria,' *Den'* (16 January 1865), 50

13 A.A. Grigor'ev, 'Russkii teatr I,' *Epokha* (January–February 1864), 423

14 Dostoevskii, 'Riad statei o russkoi literature. g. – bov i vopros ob iskusstve,' 200

15 Anon [A.A. Grigor'ev], 'Neskol'ko slov o Ristori,' *Vremia* (February 1861), sect II 156

16 Anon [F.M. Dostoevskii], 'Vystavka v akademii khudozhestv za 1860–61 gg.,' *Vremia* (October 1861), sect II 150

17 Anon [Dostoevskii], 'Razskazy N.V. Uspenskogo,' 177

18 Grigor'ev, 'Stikhotvoreniia N. Nekrasova,' 19

19 Dostoevskii, 'Riad statei o russkoi literature. g. – bov i vopros ob iskusstve,' 169–73

20 Ibid, 173–4

21 Ibid, 204

22 Ibid, 177

23 Ibid, 193 (Dostoevsky's emphasis)

24 Ibid, 203–4 (Dostoevsky's emphasis)

25 Ibid, 193

26 Anon [N.N. Strakhov], 'Nigilizm v iskusstve,' *Vremia* (August 1862), sect II 57

27 A.A. Grigor'ev, 'Lermontov i ego napravelenie II,' *Vremia* (November 1862), sect II 54

28 Dostoevskii, 'Riad statei o russkoi literature. g. – bov i vopros ob iskusstve,' 195 (Dostoevsky's emphasis)

29 Anon [Dostoevskii], 'Razskazy N.V. Uspenskogo,' 178

30 A.A. Grigor'ev, 'Severno-russkaia narodopravstva vo vremeni udel'novechenogo uklada,' *Vremia* (January 1863), sect II 93

31 See I.I. Lapshin, *Estetika Dostoevskogo* (Berlin 1923), 19.

32 Anon [Dostoevskii], 'Razskazy N.V. Uspenskogo,' 178

33 Cited in Lapshin, *Estetika Dostoevskogo*, 19

34 A.A. Grigor'ev, 'Narodnost' i literatura,' *Vremia* (February 1861), sect III 103
35 A.A. Grigor'ev, 'Zapadnichestvo v russkoi literature,' *Vremia* (March 1861), sect III 1–2
36 A.A. Grigor'ev, 'Nashi literaturnye napravleniia s 1848 goda,' *Vremia* (February 1863), sect II 5
37 F.M. Dostoevskii, 'Riad statei o russkoi literature. Vvedenie,' *Vremia* (January 1861, sect III 33–4
38 Ibid, 34
39 These judgments are contained in Grigor'ev's 'Nashi literaturnye napravleniia s 1848 goda,' 1–38 *passim.*
40 N.A. Dobroliubov, *Izbrannoe* (Moscow 1970), 43–179 and 226–302
41 Grigor'ev, 'Russkii teatr I,' 427
42 F.M. Dostoevskii, 'Neizdannyi Dostoevskii,' *Literaturnoe nasledstvo*, LXXXIII (Moscow 1971), 136
43 Anon [Dostoevskii], '*Svistok i Russkii vestnik*,' 76
44 Anon [A.A. Grigor'ev], 'Iavleniia sovremennoi literatury, propushchennye nashei kritikoi,' *Vremia* (March 1861), sect II 67
45 Anon [A.A. Grigor'ev], 'Iavleniia sovremennoi literatury. g. – zha Kokhanovskaia i eia povesti,' *Vremia* (September 1861), sect II 29

CHAPTER EIGHT: NATIVE SOIL AND ITS RIVALS

1 N.N. Strakhov, 'Vospominaniia o Fedore Mikhailoviche Dostoevskom,' *Biografiia, pis'ma i zametki iz zapisnoi knizhki F.M. Dostoveskogo*, O. Miller and N. Strakhov eds (St Petersburg 1883), 235
2 The apparent change in *Vremia* in its attitudes towards *Sovremennik* has prompted a great deal of speculation among Soviet and Western historians. A.S. Dolinin noted a movement from liberal to conservative in the journal and argued that the change reflected Dostoevsky's personal evolution. He held Strakhov responsible for cajoling Dostoevsky away from his earlier democratic convictions; A.S. Dolinin, 'F.M. Dostoevskii i N.N. Strakhov,' in *Shestidesiatye gody*, N.K. Piksanov and O.V. Tsekhnovitser eds (Moscow 1940), 238–54. G.O. Berliner in his N.G. *Chernyshevskii i ego literaturnye vragi* (Moscow 1930) had previously arrived at a similar conclusion. S.S. Borshchevsky, in his *Shchedrin i Dostoevskii* (Moscow 1956), pp. 62–3, argued, in contrast, that Dostoevsky was a sly reactionary who in the early days of *Vremia* concealed his true views for tactical reasons but underwent no significant political evolution. Another Soviet writer rejected Borshchevsky's opinion that Dostoevsky presented one view in his journal and another in his notebooks. Instead, he argued, Dostoevsky's views simply were not yet

settled in 1861 and he was at war with himself; M. Gus, *Idei i obrazy F.M. Dostoevskogo* (Moscow 1962), 169–70.

Linda Gerstein, in a recent biography of Strakhov, offered a fresh approach. *Vremia* was never clearly in the radical camp, in her view, and Dostoevsky underwent no evolution from liberal to conservative. In her opinion, *pochvennichestvo* was a doctrine of philosophical and aesthetic idealism without any significant political content. The change in Dostoevsky had nothing to do with politics but reflected simply the gradual deeping of his idealism. Ambiguities arose, however, because it took some time for the apolitical nature of *pochvennichestvo* to become apparent. She thinks it was Strakhov's debate with *Sovremennik*, which culminated in May 1862, that gave *pochvennichestvo* its final definition. Dostoevsky's idealism, she concluded,was ultimately irrelevant to *pochvennichestvo*. See Linda Gerstein, *Nikolai Strakhov. Philosopher, Man of Letters, Social Critic* (Cambridge, Mass, 1971), 48–54. This interpretation rests on accepting Strakhov's perception of *pochvennichestvo* as the only correct one. Strakhov did not, however, specifically identify himself as a *pochvennik*. He interpreted *pochvennichestvo* very narrowly, preferring to concentrate on the philosophical task of creating a broad nationalistic and idealistic front to counter the forces of westernism and materialism and remained aloof from *pochvennichestvo* in its wider ramifications.

3 F.M. Dostoevskii, 'Neizdannyi Dostoevskii,' *Literaturnoe nasledstvo*, LXXXIII (Moscow 1971), 156

4 A.A. Grigor'ev, *Materialy dlia biografii A. Grigor'eva*, Vl. Kniazhnin ed (Petrograd 1917), 285. The fact that Grigor'ev's contributions to *Vremia* continued while he was in Orenburg suggests that he had a more pressing reason for leaving St Petersburg. He was, as usual, in desperate financial straits and went to Orenburg to take advantage of a government plan that doubled the salary of those prepared to teach in isolated districts for a period of three years. Grigor'ev was constitutionally unprepared to do so and typically compounded his monetary woes by remaining only a few months. The result was that he had to repay his advance salary. See P. Iudin, 'K biografii A.A. Grigor'eva,' *Istoricheskii vestnik* (December 1894), 779–86.

5 Anon [N.G. Chernyshevskii], '"Vremia", zhurnal politicheskii i literaturnyi,' *Sovremennik* (January 1861), 90

6 I.A. Piotrovsky, 'K voprosu o sblizhenii s narodom,' *Sovremennik* (August 1861), 240

7 M. Antonovich, 'O pochve (ne v agronomicheskom smysle, a v dukhe "Vremeni",' *Sovremennik* (December 1861), 172

8 Ibid, 174

9 Ibid, 175–6

10 Ibid, 183
11 Ibid, 184
12 Dostoevskii, 'Neizdannyi Dostoevskii,' 180
13 Antonovich, 'O pochve,' 185
14 Petr Struve, 'The Intelligentsia and Revolution,' *Vekhi*, in *Canadian Slavic Studies*, IV no. 2 (Summer 1970), 194–5
15 Dostoevskii, 'Neizdannyi Dostoevskii,' 180
16 For a detailed discussion of the Pirogov affair, see G.O. Berliner, 'Literaturnye protivniki N.A. Dobroliubova,' *Literaturnoe nasledstvo*, XXV–XXVI (Moscow 1936), 32–69.
17 Anon, 'Sobranie literaturnykh statei N.I. Pirogova,' *Vremia* (April 1862), sect II 1–20
18 Dostoevskii, 'Neizdannyi Dostoevskii,' 142
19 Ibid, 144
20 Ibid, 150
21 Anon, 'Nashi domashnie dela,' *Vremia* (May 1862), sect IV 40–1
22 A.A. Grigor'ev, 'Graf Tolstoi i ego sochineniia I,' *Vremia* (January–February 1862), sect II 22
23 F.M. Dostoevskii, 'Ob"iavlenie,' *Vremia* (September 1861), 5
24 Odin iz mnogikh nenuzhnykh liudei [Grigor'ev], 'O postepennom no bystrom i povsemestnom rasprostranenii nevezhestva i bezgramotnosti v russkoi slovesnosti,' *Vremia* (March 1861), sect IV 40–1
25 N.N. Strakhov, 'Durnye priznaki,' *Vremia* (November 1862), sect II 163
26 Ibid, 172
27 N. Kositsa [Strakhov], 'Primer apatii,' *Vremia* (January–February 1862), sect II 71
28 Anon [Dostoevskii], 'N.A. Dobroliubov,' *Vremia* (March 1862), sect II 48–50. Dostoevsky's antipathy towards the seminarists, to whom he was inclined to ascribe most of Russia's ills, is well known. The article on Dobroliubov raised a storm. It was published after the critic's death and was construed by the radicals as an unwarranted attack on the memory of a defenceless man.
29 N.K. [Strakhov], 'Nechto o polemike,' *Vremia* (August 1861), sect II 147
30 Anon, 'Vnutrennee obozrenie,' *Sovremennik* (January–February 1863), 255
31 Anon, [N.N. Strakhov], 'Ottsy i deti I. Turgeneva,' *Vremia* (April 1862), sect II 67–84
32 Dostoevskii, *Biografiia, pis'ma*, 31
33 F.M. Dostoevskii, *Zimnie zametki o letnykh vpechatleniiakh, Sochineniia*, V (Leningrad 1973), 79
34 Cited in Martin Katz, *M.N. Katkov* (The Hague 1966), 69

35 Ibid, 44–61, for Katkov's debate with Chicherin and Kavelin
36 Ibid, 85–103
37 Anon [F.M. Dostoevskii], 'Svistok i Russkii vestnik,' Vremia (March–April 1861), sect IV 71–84
38 F.M. Dostoevskii, 'Otvet Russkomu vestniku,' Vremia (May–June 1861), sect V 18
39 Ibid, 22
40 Ibid, 23–8
41 Ibid, 28
42 Katz, M.N. Katkov, 76
43 Anon [F.M. Dostoevskii], 'Shchekotlivyi vopros,' Vremia (October 1862), sect II 141–63
44 Anon, 'Nashi domashnie dela,' Vremia (December 1862), sect II 55–6
45 Ibid, 62
46 Dostoevskii, 'Neizdannyi Dostoevskii,' 186
47 Ibid
48 N.N. Strakhov, 'Tiazheloe vremia,' Vremia (October 1862), sect II 203
49 Dostoevskii, Biografiia, pis'ma, 335
50 F.M. Dostoevskii, 'Riad statei o russkoi literature. Poslednie literaturnye iavleniia. Gazeta Den',' Vremia (November 1861), sect II 65
51 Anon [F.M. Dostoevskii], 'Dva lageria teoretikov,' Vremia (January–February 1862), sect II 147
52 N.N. Strakhov, 'Vospominaniia ob A.A. Grigor'eve,' Epokha (September 1864), 43–4
53 A.A. Grigor'ev, 'Belinskii i otrisatel'nyi vzgliad v literature,' Vremia (April 1861), sect II 209
54 Aksakov's letter and Strakhov's reply may be found in Strakhov, 'Vospominaniia o F.M. Dostoevskom,' 257–8.
55 I.S. Aksakov, 'Moskva, 4 noiabria,' Den' (4 November, 1861), 1
56 S. Lukashevich, Ivan Aksakov 1823–1886 (Cambridge, Mass, 1965), 64–5
57 Aksakov was at this time, however, revising his views substantially in the direction of pochvennichestvo. See below 149–51.
58 I.S. Aksakov, 'Moskva, 1 avgusta,' Den' (1 August 1864), 1–3
59 Strakhov, 'Vospominaniia o F.M. Dostoevskom,' 258
60 Anon, 'Opisanie nekotorykh sochinenii napisannykh russkimi raskol'nikami v pol'zu raskola,' Vremia (October 1861), sect II 92
61 I.S. Aksakov, 'Moskva, 19 oktiabria,' Den' (19 October 1863), 3
62 I.S. Aksakov, 'Moskva, 16 fevralia,' Den' (16 February 1862), 1–2
63 Anon, 'Deviatnadtsatyi numer' Dnia,' Vremia (January–February 1862), sect II 164–8

64 Anon, 'Nashi domashnie dela,' *Vremia* (October 1862), sect II 50
65 Robert E. MacMaster, *Danilevsky: A Russian Totalitarian Philosopher* (Cambridge, Mass, 1967), 180
66 I.S. Aksakov, 'Moskva, 10 marta,' *Den'* (10 March 1862), 1 (Aksakov's emphasis)
67 I.S. Aksakov, 'Moskva, 24 marta,' *Den'* (24 March 1862), 2–3
68 Aksakov, 'Moskva, 10 marta,' 1–2
69 Cited in Dostoevskii, 'Neizdannyi Dostoevskii,' 237
70 Ibid, 202

CHAPTER NINE: SECOND THOUGHTS

1 N.N. Strakhov, 'Vospominaniia ob A.A. Grigor'eve,' *Epokha* (September 1864), 40
2 Ibid, 41
3 Dm. Averkiev, 'Apollon Aleksandrovich Grigor'ev,' *Epokha* (August 1864), 16. Although Grigor'ev died on 25 September 1864, *Epokha* had fallen behind its publishing schedule and Grigor'ev's obituary appeared in the August number.
4 Anon [A.A. Grigor'ev], 'Vstupitel'noe slovo o fal'shivykh notakh v pechati i zhizni,' *Iakor'*, no. 1 (1863), 1
5 Anon [A.A. Grigor'ev], 'Na poldoroge,' *Iakor'* no. 28 (1863), 566
6 Anon [Grigor'ev], 'Vstupitel'noe slovo,' 1
7 Anon [Grigor'ev], 'Na poldoroge,' 565
8 Anon [A.A. Grigor'ev], 'Nasha pristan',' *Iakor'*, no. 3 (1863), 41
9 Anon [Grigor'ev], 'Na poldoroge,' 565
10 Anon [Grigor'ev], 'Nasha pristan',' 41
11 Cited in P. Miliukov, 'Razlozhenie slavianofil'stva,' *Voprosy filosofii*, XVIII (Moscow 1889), 293
12 A.A. Grigor'ev, 'Po povodu malo zamechaemogo sovremennoiu kritikoiu iavleniia,' *Iakor'*, no. 2 (1863), 21–2
13 Anon [A.A. Grigor'ev], 'Vopros o natsional'nostiakh,' *Iakor'*, no. 5 (1863), 81
14 Anon [A.A. Grigor'ev], 'Veter peremenilsia,' *Iakor'*, no. 2 (1863), 1
15 Anon [Grigor'ev], 'Na poldoroge,' 565
16 Anon [Grigor'ev], 'Veter peremenilsia,' 1
17 A.A. Grigor'ev, 'Zhurnal'nyi mir i ego iavleniia, III,' *Iakor'*, no. 12 (1865), 226
18 V.E. Rudakov, 'Poslednie dni tsensury v ministerstve narodnogo prosveshcheniia,' *Istoricheskii vestnik* (September 1911), 971

19 The only previous article was Rusin [a Ruthenian], 'Zametka po odnu gazetnuiu stat'iu,' *Vremia* (September 1862), sect II 42–56

20 Russkii [N.N. Strakhov], 'Rokovoi vopros,' *Vremia* (April 1863), sect II 153–61

21 Cited in Rudakov, 'Poslednie', 985

22 Ibid, 985–6

23 A.S. Dolinin, 'Zhurnaly Dostoevskogo i tsensura,' *F.M. Dostoevskii. Stat'i i materialy*, I (Petersburg 1922), 566

24 P.A. Valuev, *Dnevnik, Vol. I. 1861–1864 gg.* (Moscow 1961), 266. Rudakov claimed that Tsee was not fired but resigned in order to protect his subordinates; Rudakov, 'Poslednie,' 986.

25 A.V. Nikitenko, *Dnevnik*, II (Moscow 1955), 336

26 Ibid, 440

27 N.N. Strakhov, 'Vospominaniia o Fedore Mikhailoviche Dostoevskom,' *Biografiia, pis'ma i zametki iz zapisnoi knizhki F.M. Dostoevskogo*, O. Miller and N. Strakhov eds (St Petersburg 1883), 255

28 Dolinin, 'Zhurnaly,' 570. In 1916 A.S. Volzhskii speculated that on his return from exile Dostoevsky was passing through a crisis in which he was struggling to come to grips with the new people of his time or epoch. He cited the names Dostoevsky chose for his journals, *Vremia* and *Epokha*, as evidence; A.S. Volzhskii, 'Na puti krestnom,' *Khristianskaia mysl'* (December 1916), 27. *Vremia* was, in fact, named by Mikhail Dostoevsky without prior consultation with his brother, and Fedor's first choice of name for *Vremia*'s successor was *Pravda*

29 L. Grossman, *Zhizn' i trudy F.M. Dostoevskogo* (Moscow-Leningrad 1935), 130

30 Robert E. MacMaster, 'In the Russian Manner: Thought as Incipient Action,' *Russian Thought and Politics. Harvard Slavic Studies IV* (Cambridge, Mass, 1957), 297

31 F.M. to M.M. Dostoevskii (26 March 1864), F.M. Dostoevskii, *Pis'ma*, I, A.S. Dolinin ed (Moscow-Leningrad 1928), 352

32 F.M. to M.M. Dostoevskii (9 February 1864), ibid, 347–8; M.M. to F.M. Dostoevskii (23 March 1864), A.S. Dolinin, *F.M. Dostoevskii. Materialy i issledovaniia* (Leningrad 1935), 550

33 F.M. to M.M. Dostoevskii (2 April 1864), Dostoevskii, *Pis'ma*, I, 354

34 F.M. Dostoevskii to A.E. Wrangel (31 March 1865), ibid, 400

35 F.M. Dostoevskii, 'Neizdannyi Dostoevskii,' *Literaturnoe nasledstvo*, LXXXIII (Moscow 1971), 256 (Dostoevsky's emphasis)

36 F.M. Dostoevskii, 'Ob"iavlenie,' *Epokha* (September 1864), iii

37 Anon, 'Nashi domashnie dela,' *Epokha* (June 1864), 282–4

38 Dostoevskii, 'Ob"iavlenie,' ii
39 N. Kositsa [N.N. Strakhov], 'Pis'mo v redaktsiiu *Epokhi*,' *Epokha* (January–February 1864), 578
40 Ibid, 583–6
41 F.M. Dostoevskii, 'Gospodin Shchedrin ili raskol' v nigilistakh,' *Epokha* (May 1864), 274–94
42 Dostoevskii, 'Neizdannyi Dostoevskii,' 250 (Dostoevsky's emphasis)
43 Cited in *Shestidesiatie gody*, N. Piksanov and O. Tsekhnovitser eds (Moscow 1940), 256
44 For Strakhov and his relationship to Slavophilism see Linda Gerstein, *Nikolai Strakhov. Philosopher, Man of Letters, Social Critic* (Cambridge, Mass, 1971), 102–3. For his relationship to *pochvennichestvo* see V.V. Zenkovskii, *Russkie mysliteli i Evropa* (Paris 1955), 175.
45 N.N. Strakhov, *Bednost' nashei literatury. Kriticheskii i istoricheskii ocherk* (St Petersburg 1868), 39–54
46 N.N. Strakhov, 'Opyty izucheniia Feierbakha,' *Epokha* (June 1864), 153
47 Kositsa, 'Pis'mo v redaktsiiu *Epokhi*,' 578
48 Dm. Averkiev, 'Po povodu samopriznanii Peterburzhtsev,' *Epokha* (December 1864), 14
49 Letopisets [Strakhov], 'Zametki letopistsa,' *Epokha* (June 1864), 237
50 Ibid, 240
51 Letopisets [Strakhov], 'Zametka letopistsa,' *Epokha* (December 1864), 25
52 See respectively Anon, 'Nashi domashnie dela,' *Epokha* (December 1864), 1–25; Letopisets [Strakhov], 'Zametka letopistsa,' *Epokha* (December 1864), 21–2
53 I.S. Aksakov, 'Moskva, 28 noiabria,' *Den'* (28 November 1864), 2–3
54 Letopisets [Strakhov], 'Zametki letopistsa,' (December 1864), 21–2
55 Ibid, 22
56 Ibid
57 V.G. Avseenko, 'Kruzhok,' *Istoricheskii vestnik* (May 1909), 442–3
58 Anon [N.N. Strakhov], 'Kriticheskie zametki,' *Zaria* (December 1869), 152. This article was a statement of editorial policy and reflected Strakhov's own views.
59 N. Ia. Danilevskii, *Rossiia i Evropa*, 5th edition (St Petersburg 1895), 95
60 Ibid, 104. Strakhov hailed *Russia and Europe* as a new theory of universal history. From Danilevsky's work he concluded that Russia must purge itself of foreign accretions. Russia had no universal task to perform because Danilevsky had shown that there was no universal task to have; N.N. Strakhov, 'Bibliografiia,' *Zaria* (March 1871), 10–12.
61 N.N. Strakhov, 'Vzgliad na nyneshnuiu literaturu,' *Zaria* (January 1871), 2

62 Ibid, 11
63 Dostoevskii, 'Neizdannyi Dostoevskii,' 244. Dostoevsky himself cites Khomiakov in connection with this idea.
64 Ibid, 173 (Dostoevsky's emphasis)
65 Ibid, 248–50
66 Ibid, 256
67 Ibid, 234
68 Ibid, 251
69 Dostoevskii, *Pis'ma*, IV, 280
70 Konstantin Mochulsky, *Dostoevsky. His Life and Work* (Princeton 1971), 482
71 F.M. Dostoevskii, 'F.M. Dostoevskii v rabote nad romanom *Podrostok*. Tvorcheskie rukopisi,' *Literaturnoe nasledstvo*, LXXVII (Moscow 1965), 62
72 F.M. Dostoevskii, *Sobranie sochinenii*, VIII, L.P. Grossman, A.S. Dolinin, et al eds (Moscow 1956–8), 139
73 Dostoevskii, 'Dostoevskii v rabote,' 422
74 Dostoevskii, *Sobranie sochinenii*, VIII, 619
75 Dostoevskii, 'Dostoevskii v rabote,' 167
76 Ibid, 372
77 Ibid, 410
78 Ibid, 421
79 F.M. Dostoevskii, *Dnevnik pisatelia*, II (Paris 1951), 61
80 Ibid, 253–4
81 Ibid, III, 26–7
82 I.S. Aksakov, *Sochineniia*, VII (Moscow 1887), 833
83 Dostoevskii, *Dnevnik pisatelia*, III (Paris 1951), 510–11
84 Ibid, 515–20. Cf A.A. Grigor'ev, 'I.S. Turgenev i ego deiatel'nost',' *Literaturnaia kritika*, B.F. Egorov ed (Moscow 1967), 363–4.
85 Dostoevskii, *Dnevnik pisatelia*, III, 523–5
86 Ibid, 527
87 Cited in P. Gaidenko, 'Naperekor istoricheskomu protsessu,' *Voprosy literatury*, V (May 1974), 169
88 Ibid, 169–70
89 N. Konstantinov [N.K. Leont'ev], 'Gramotnost' i narodnost' I,' *Zaria* (November 1870), 197–8
90 N. Konstantinov [N.K. Leont'ev], 'Gramotnost' i narodnost' II,' *Zaria* (December 1870), 294
91 Ibid, 301
92 Aleksandr Blok, 'Sud'ba Apollona Grigor'eva,' *Stikhotvoreniia Apollona Grigor'eva* (Moscow 1916), xxxiii
93 See Wayne Dowler, 'Echoes of *Pochvennichestvo* in Solzhenitsyn's *August*

1914,' Slavic Review, XXXIV no. 1 (March 1975), 119–21, for a discussion of Solzhenitsyn's views about literature and their relation to organic criticism.

94 Vladimir Solov'ev, *Natsional'nyi vopros v Rossii*, II (St Petersburg 1891), 159
95 Cited in Christopher Read, *Religion, Revolution and the Russian Intelligentsia, 1900–1912* (London 1979), 100
96 Cited in George M. Young, *Nikolai F. Fedorov. An Introduction* (Belmont 1979), 24–5
97 See, for example, P.B. Struve, 'The Intelligentsia and Revolution,' *Vekhi*, in *Canadian Slavic Studies*, IV no. 2 (summer 1970), 193–5.
98 Dowler, 'Echoes,' 114–15
99 Orest Miller, *Slavianstvo i Evropa. Stat'i i rechi, 1865–1877 g.* (St. Petersburg 1877), 15
100 Cited in Stephen Lukashevich, *Ivan Aksakov 1823–1886. A Study in Russian Thought and Politics* (Cambridge, Mass, 1965), 75
101 Solov'ev, *Natsional'nyi vopros*, I (St Petersburg 1891), 32–42
102 Robert E. MacMaster, *Danilevsky: A Russian Totalitarian Philosopher* (Cambridge, Mass, 1967), 197
103 Dowler, 'Echoes,' 117

Bibliography

PRIMARY SOURCES

Journals

Den'. Moscow, 1861–5
Epokha. St Petersburg, 1864–5
Iakor'. St Petersburg, 1863–5
Moskvitianin. Moscow, 1841–56
Russkoe slovo. St Petersburg, 1859–66
Sovremennik. St Petersburg, 1846–66
Svetoch. St Petersburg, 1861–3
Vremia. St Petersburg, 1861–3
Zaria. St Petersburg, 1869–72

Collected Works

Aksakov, I.S. *Sochineniia*. 7 Vols. (Moscow 1886–7)
Aksakov, K.S. *Polnoe sobranie sochinenii*. I (Moscow 1861)
Barnard, F.M. ed. *J.G. Herder on Social and Political Culture* (Cambridge 1969)
Belinskii, V.G. *Izbrannye filosofskie sochineniia*. 2 vols. (Moscow 1948)
Brodskii, N.L. ed. *Rannie slavianofily: A.S. Khomiakov, I.V. Kireevskii, K.S. i I.S. Aksakovy* (Moscow 1910)
Debreczeny, Paul, and Jesse Zeldin eds *Literature and National Identity. Nineteenth-Century Russian Critical Essays* (Lincoln 1970)
Dobroliubov, N.A. *Izbrannoe* (Moscow 1970)
Dostoevskii, F.M. *Dnevnik pisatelia*. 3 vols. (Paris 1951)
– *Polnoe sobranie sochinenii v tridtsati tomakh*. I–XXII (Leningrad 1972–81)

- *Sobranie sochinenii.* L.P. Grossman, A.S. Dolinin, et al eds. 10 vols. (Moscow 1956–8)
Grigor'ev, A.A. *Izbrannye proizvedeniia.* D.O. Kostelianets ed (Moscow 1959)
- *Literaturnaia kritika.* B.F. Egoroved (Moscow 1967)
- *Sobranie sochineniia.* I–XIV. V. Savodnik ed (Moscow 1915–16)
- *Sochineniia Apollona Grigor'eva,* I, N. Strakhov ed (St Petersburg 1876)
- *Sochineniia I. Kritika.* V.S. Krupitsch ed (Villanova 1970)
Grigoryev, Apollon, *My Literary and Moral Wanderings.* Ralph Matlaw trans (New York 1962)
Khomiakov, A.S. *Polnoe sobranie sochinenii.* 1 (Moscow 1861)
Kireevskii, I.V. *Polnoe sobranie sochinenii.* 2 vols. (Moscow 1911, reprint 1970)
Miller, Orest. *Slavianstvo i Evropa. Stat'i i rechi, 1865–1877 g.* (St Petersburg 1877)
Solov'ev, Vladimir. *Natsional'nyi vopros v Rossii.* 1 and 11 (St Petersburg 1891)
Strakhov, N.N. *Bednost' nashei literatury. Kriticheskii i istoricheskii ocherk* (St Petersburg 1868)
- *Bor'ba s zapadom v nashei literature.* 3 vols. 3rd ed (Kiev 1897–8)
- *Iz istorii literaturnogo nigilizma (1861–1865)* (St Petersburg 1890)
- *Kriticheskie stat'i (1861–1894)* (Kiev 1902)
- *Kriticheskie stat'i ob I. Turgeneve i L. Tolstom* (St Petersburg 1885)
Turgenev, I.S. *Sochineniia.* IV (Moscow 1860)

Memoirs, letters, and notes

Aksakov, I.S. *I.S. Aksakov v ego pis'makh.* IV pt 2 (St Petersburg 1896)
Avseenko, V.G. 'Kruzhok.' *Istoricheskii vestnik* (May 1909), 438–51. A memoir of the *Zaria* group
Berg, N.V. 'Moskovskie vospominaniia Nikolaia Vasilovicha Berga.' *Russkaia starina* (October 1884), 53–71. Berg was a close observer of the young editors in the 1850s.
Berg. N.V. 'Salon E. Rostopchinoi,' in N.L. Brodskii ed *Literaturnye salony i kruzhki: Pervaia polovina XIX veka* (Moscow 1930), 414–18
Boborykin, P.D. *Vospominaniia I. Za polveka* (Moscow 1965)
Brodskii, N.L. ed. *Literaturnye salony i kruzhki. Pervaia polovina XIX veka* (Moscow 1930)
Bykov, P.V. *Siluety dalekogo proshlogo* (Moscow-Leningrad 1930). Bykov was a devoted admirer of Grigor'ev and a familiar figure around the office of *Vremia.*
Dolinin, A.S. ed. *F.M. Dostoevskii v vospominaniakh sovremennikov.* 1 (Moscow 1964)

– *F.M. Dostoevskii. Materialy i issledovaniia* (Leningrad 1935). Includes a number of letters to Dostoevsky from A.N. Pleshcheev and Mikhail Dostoevsky.
– *F.M. Dostoevskii. Stat'i i materialy.* 2 vols. (Petrograd 1922 and 1924)
Dostoevskii, F.M. *Pis'ma.* A.S. Dolinin ed. 4 vols. (Moscow– Leningrad 1928–59).
Egorov, B.F. ed. 'Apollon Grigor'ev – kritik.' *Uchenye zapiski Tartuskogo gos. universiteta.* XCVIII (1960), 194–246. Includes some of Grigor'ev's previously unpublished letters
– 'Materialy ob Ap. Grigor'eve iz arkhiva N.N. Strakhova.' *Uchenye zapiski Tartuskogo gos. universiteta.* CXXXIX (1963), 343–50
– 'Publikatsiia i soobshchenie perepiska Ap. Grigor'eva s. N.N. Strakhovym.' *Uchenye zapiski Tartuskogo gos. universiteta.* CLXVII (1965), 163–73
Fet (Shenshin), A.A. *Moi vospominaniia.* 2 vols. (Moscow 1890)
Grigor'ev, A.A. 'Neizvestnye pis'ma A. Grigor'eva.' *Voprosy literatury.* No. 7 (1965), 254–6
Grigor'ev, A.A. (son of above). 'Odinokii kritik.' *Knizhki nedeli* (August 1895), 5–23. A memoir of Grigor'ev by his son
Iudin, P. 'K biografii A.A. Grigor'eva.' *Istoricheskii vestnik* (December 1894), 779–86. Iudin knew Grigor'ev in Orenburg and sheds some light on this obscure period in Grigor'ev's life.
Ivanov-Razumnik, R.V. ed. *A.A. Grigor'ev. Vospominaniia* (Moscow–Leningrad 1930). Grigor'ev's memoirs and memoirs about him, including Fet's 'Rannie gody moei zhizni'
Kniazhnin, Vl. ed. *Materialy dlia biografii A. Grigor'eva.* (Petrograd 1917). Includes the largest compilation of Grigor'ev's letters
Kohn, Hans ed. *The Mind of Modern Russia. Historical and Political Thought of Russia's Great Age* (New York 1962)
Koshelev, A.I. *Zapiski, 1812–1883* (Berlin 1884)
Literaturnoe nasledstvo. LXXVII, LXXXIII, LXXXVI (Moscow 1965, 1971, 1973). All three volumes contain previously unpublished materials from Dostoevsky's notebooks.
Maksimov, S.V. 'A.N. Ostrovskii po moim vospominaniiam.' *Dramaticheskie sochineniia A.N. Ostrovskogo.* XI (Moscow n.d.)
Miliukov, A.P. *Literaturnye vstrechi i znakomstva* (St Petersburg 1890)
Miller, O. and N. Strakhov eds. *Biografiia, pis'ma i zametki iz zapisnoi knizhki F.M. Dostoevskogo* (St Petersburg 1883)
Nikitenko, A.V. *Dnevnik.* II (Moscow 1955)
Ostrovskii, A.N. *Neizdannye pis'ma iz arkhiva A.N. Ostrovskogo.* M.D. Prygunov ed (Moscow–Leningrad 1932)
Piksanov, N.K. ed. *Iz arkhiva Dostoevskogo* (Moscow-Petrograd 1923). Includes a variety of letters to Dostoevsky

Polonskii, Ia. P. 'Moi studencheskie vospominaniia.' *Niva* (December 1898), 642–87. Polonsky was Grigor'ev's close friend in youth and was later an associate of *Vremia*.

Prokhorov, G.R. ed. 'G.E. Blagosvetlov, Ia. P. Polonskii, G.A. Kushelev-Bezborodko. Pis'ma i dokumenty.' *Zven'ia*. No. 1 (1932), 298–305

Serova, V.S. *Vospominaniia* (St Petersburg 1914). Memoirs by the wife of the composer; Serov was among Grigor'ev's closest friends in his last years.

Strakhov, N.N. 'Novye pis'ma A.A. Grigor'eva.' *Epokha* (February 1865), 152–82

– 'Pis'ma N.N. Strakhova F.M. Dostoevskomu.' In Piksanov, N.K. and O.V. Tsekhnovitser eds. *Shestidesiatye gody* (Moscow 1940)

– 'Vospominaniia o Fedore Mikhailoviche Dostoevskom.' In Miller, O., and N. Strakhov eds. *Biografiia, pis'ma i zametki iz zapisnoi knizhki F.M. Dostoevskogo* (St Petersburg 1883)

– 'Vospominaniia ob A.A. Grigor'eve.' *Epokha* (September 1864), 1–55

– 'Zhizn' i trudy N. Ia. Danilevskogo.' In Danilevskii, N. Ia. *Rossiia i Evropa*. 5th ed (St Petersburg 1895)

Valuev, P.A. *Dnevnik. I. 1861–1864 gg.* (Moscow 1961)

Other sources cited

Burke, Edmund. *Reflections on the Revolution in France* (Indianapolis and New York 1955)

Chaadaev, P. Ia. 'Apologia of a Madman.' In McNally, Raymond T. ed. *The Major Works of Peter Chaadaev* (Notre Dame and London 1969), 199–218

Coleridge, S.T. *The Friend* (London 1850)

Danilevskii, N. Ia. *Rossiia i Evropa*. 5th ed (St Petersburg 1895)

de Maistre, Joseph. *On God and Society. Essay on the Generative Principle of Political Constitutions and Other Human Institutions.* Greifer, Elisha, ed and trans (Chicago 1967)

Dostoevsky, F.M. *Winter Notes on Summer Impressions* (Toronto-New York 1955)

Dragomanov, M. ed. *Pis'ma K. D. Kavelina i I.S. Turgeneva k A.I. Gertsenu* (Geneva 1892)

Hegel, G.W.F. *The Philosophy of History* (New York 1956)

Karamzin, N. 'Love of Country and National Pride.' In Raeff, M. ed. *Russian Intellectual History: An Anthology* (New York 1966), 107–12

Khomiakov, A.S. 'To the Serbians. A Message from Moscow.' In Christoff, P.K. *An Introduction to Nineteenth Century Slavophilism: A.S. Khomiakov* (The Hague 1961), 247–68.

Labedz, Leopold ed. *Solzhenitsyn: A Documentary Record.* 2nd ed (London 1974)

tiia Akademii nauk SSSR. Otdelenie literatury i iazyka, xxx (September–October 1971), sect v 400–10

Gaidenko, P. 'Naperekor istoricheskomu protsessu (Konstantin Leont'ev – literaturnyi kritik),' *Voprosy literatury*, v (May 1974), 159–205

Gerstein, Linda. *Nikolai Strakhov. Philosopher, Man of Letters, Social Critic* (Cambridge, Mass, 1971)

Grossman, L. 'Apollon Grigor'ev. Osnovatel' novoi kritiki,' *Russkaia mysl'* (November 1914), 1–19

– *Tri sovremennika (Dostoevskii, Tiutchev, Grigor'ev)* (Moscow 1922)

– *Zhizn' i trudy F.M. Dostoevskogo* (Moscow-Leningrad 1935)

Gural'nik, U.A. '*Sovremennik* v bor'be s zhurnalami Dostoevskogo,' *Izvestiia Akademii nauk SSSR. Otdelenie literatury i iazyka*, ix no. 4 (1950), 265–85

Gus', M. *Idei i obrazy F.M. Dostoevskogo* (Moscow 1962)

Ivanov, I.I. *Istoriia russkoi kritiki s XVIII v.* 2 vols. (St Petersburg 1898–1900)

Jackson, R.L. *Dostoevsky's Quest for Form. A Study of His Philosophy of Art* (New Haven 1966)

Jerkovich, G.C. *A. Grigor'ev as a Literary Critic*. Unpublished PHD. thesis. University of Kansas (1970)

Kantor, V. 'M.N. Katkov i krushenie estetiki liberalizma,' *Voprosy literatury*, no. 5 (1973), 174–212

Katz, Martin. *M.N. Katkov* (The Hague 1966)

Kedourie, Elie. *Nationalism* (London 1971)

Kipp, Jacob W. and W. Bruce Lincoln. 'Autocracy and Reform: Bureaucratic Absolutism and Political Modernization in Nineteenth Century Russia,' *Russian History*, vi pt 1 (1979), 1–21

Kirk, Russell. *The Conservative Mind. From Burke to Santayana* (Chicago 1953)

Kirpotin, V. Ia. *Dostoevskii i Belinskii* (Moscow 1960)

– *Dostoevskii v shestidesiatye gody* (Moscow 1966)

Kitaev, F.A. 'Slavianofily v pervye poreformennye gody,' *Voprosy istorii*, no. 6 (June 1977), 19–36

Kogan, G.F. 'Razyskaniia o Dostoevskom I. Zhurnal *Vremia* i revolutsionnoe studenchestvo 1860-kh godov,' *Literaturnoe nasledstvo*, LXXXVI (Moscow 1973), 581–93

Koyré, Alexander. *Études sur l'histoire de la pensée philosophique en Russie* (Paris 1950)

– *La Philosophie et le problème national en Russie au début du XIX siècle* (Paris 1929)

Kozmin, N. 'Iz istorii russkogo romantizma,' *Zhurnal Ministerstva Narodnogo Prosveshcheniia* (January, February, March 1903), 1–50

Lampert, E. *Sons against Fathers* (Oxford 1965)

Lapshin, I.I. *Estetika Dostoevskogo* (Berlin 1923)

Lavrin, Janko. *Russia, Slavdom and the Western World* (London 1969)

Leighton, Lauren. *Russian Romanticism: Two Essays* (The Hague 1975)

Lemke, M. *Epokha tsenzurnykh reform 1859–1864 gg.* (St Petersburg 1904)

Lincoln, W. Bruce. *Nicholas I: Emperor and Autocrat of All the Russias.* (Bloomington and London 1978)

Lord, Robert. *Dostoevsky: Essays and Perspectives* (London: 1970)

Lukashevich, S. *Ivan Aksakov 1823–1886. A Study in Russian Thought and Politics* (Cambridge, Mass, 1965)

MacMaster, Robert E. *Danilevsky: A Russian Totalitarian Philosopher* (Cambridge, Mass, 1967)

– 'In the Russian Manner: Thought as Incipient Action.' In *Russian Thought and Politics. Harvard Slavic Studies IV* (Cambridge, Mass, 1957)

Maksimovich, G.A. 'Uchenie pervykh slavianofilov,' *Kievskie universitetskie izvestiia*, no. 1 (January 1907), 1–53, no. 3 (March 1907), 54–100; no. 5 (May 1907), 101–22

Mandelbaum, Maurice. *History, Man and Reason, A Study of Nineteenth-Century Thought* (Baltimore 1971)

Mannheim, Karl. *Ideology and Utopia: An Introduction to the Sociology of Knowledge* (New York 1936)

Marchik, A.P. '"Organicheskaia kritika" Apollona Grigor'eva,' *Izvestiia Akademii Nauk SSSR. Otdelenie literatury i iazyka*, xxv (1966)

Masaryk, T.G. *The Spirit of Russia.* 3 vols. (London 1955)

Miliukov, P. 'Razlozhenie slavianofil'stva,' *Voprosy filosofii.* xviii (Moscow 1889)

Mochulsky, Konstantin. *Dostoevsky. His Life and Work* (Princeton 1971)

Mohrenschildt, Dmitri, 'Shchapov: Exponent of Regionalism and the Federal School in Russian History,' *Russian Review*, xxxvii no. 4 (October 1978), 387–404

Morozov, P. 'Iz zhizni i literatury. A.A. Grigor'ev,' *Obrazovanie* (November 1899), 40–50

Nahirny, Vladimir. 'The Russian Intelligentsia: From Men of Ideas to Men of Convictions,' *Comparative Studies in Society and History*, iv (1962), 403–35

Nechaeva, V.S. *Zhurnal M.M. i F.M. Dostoevskikh 'Epokha', 1864–1865* (Moscow 1975)

– *Zhurnal M.M. i F.M. Dostoevskikh 'Vremia', 1861–1863* (Moscow 1972)

Nelidov, F. 'A.N. Ostrovskii v kruzhke molodogo *Moskvitianina*,' *Russkaia mysl'*, iii (1901), 1–36

Nol'de, B.E. *Iurii Samarin i ego vremia* (Paris 1926)

O'Sullivan, Noel. *Conservatism* (London 1976)

Petrovich, M.B. *The Emergence of Russian Panslavism 1856–1870* (New York 1956)

Pipes, Richard. 'Russian Conservatism in the Second Half of the Nineteenth Century,' *Slavic Review*, xxx no. 1 (March 1971), 121–8

Pipes, Richard ed. *The Russian Intelligentsia*. (New York 1961)

Pollard, Allan. 'The Russian Intelligentsia,' *California Slavic Studies*, iii (Berkeley 1964), 8–19

Raeff, Marc. *The Origins of the Russian Intelligentsia. The Eighteenth-century Nobility* (New York 1966)

– 'Codification et droit en russie imperiale. Quelques remarques comparatives,' *Cahiers du monde russe et sovietique*, xx no. 1 (January–March 1979), 5–13

Read, Christopher. *Religion, Revolution and the Russian Intelligentsia, 1900–1912* (London 1979)

Riasanovsky, N.V. *Nicholas I and Official Nationality in Russia, 1825–1855* (Berkeley 1959)

– *A Parting of Ways. Government and the Educated Public in Russia, 1801–1855* (Oxford 1976)

– *Russia and the West in the Teaching of the Slavophiles* (Cambridge, Mass, 1952)

Rieber, Alfred J. 'The Moscow Entrepreneurial Group: The Emergence of a New Form in Autocratic Politics, i and ii.' *Jahrbücher für Geschichte Osteuropas*, xxv nos. 1 and 2, (1977), 1–20 and 174–99

Rogger, Hans. *National Consciousness in Eighteenth-Century Russia* (Cambridge, Mass, 1960)

– 'Reflections on Russian Conservatism: 1861–1905,' *Jahrbücher für Geschichte Osteuropas*, xiv (1966), 195–212

Rogger, Hans and Eugen Weber eds. *The European Right. An Historical Profile* (Los Angeles 1966)

Rozenblium, L.M. 'Peterburgskie pozhary 1862 g. i Dostoevskii,' *Literaturnoe nasledstvo*, lxxxvi (Moscow 1973), 16–43

– 'Tvorcheskie dnevniki Dostoevskogo,' *Literaturnoe nasledstvo*, lxxxiii (Moscow 1973), 9–92

Rubinshtein, N.L. 'Apollon Grigor'ev,' *Literatura i marksizm*, ii (1929), 95–121

Rudakov, V.E. 'Poslednie dni tsenzury v ministerstve narodnogo prosveshcheniia,' *Istoricheskii vestnik* (September 1911), 962–87

Schapiro, Leonard. 'The *Vekhi* Group and the Mystique of Revolution,' *Slavonic and East European Review*, xxxiv no. 82 (December 1955), 56–76

Serman, I.Z. 'Dostoevskii i Ap. Grigor'ev,' in Bazanov, B.G. and F.M. Fridlender eds. *Dostoevskii i ego vremia* (Leningrad 1971), 130–42

Shiliaev, E. 'Apollon Grigor'ev – kritik,' *Novyi zhurnal*, XCIII (1968), 127–42

Skabichevskii, A.M. *Istoriia noveishei russkoi literatury 1848–1892* (St Petersburg 1893)

Spiridonov, Vasilii. 'Napravlenie "Vremeni" i "Epokhi",' *Dostoevskii. Odnodnevnaia gazeta russkogo bibliograficheskogo obshchestvo* (30 October 1921), 2–9

Stammler, Heinrich. 'Dostoevsky's Aesthetics and Schelling's Philosophy of Art,' *Comparative Literature*, VII (fall 1955), 313–23

Struve, P.B. 'Romantika protiv kazenshchiny.' In *Na raznye temy – Sbornik statei* (St Petersburg 1902), 203–20

Terras, Victor. *Belinskij and Russian Literary Criticism: The Heritage of Organic Aesthetics* (Madison 1974)

Thaden, Edward C. *Conservative Nationalism in Nineteenth-Century Russia* (Seattle 1964)

Tsimbaev, N.I. *I.S. Aksakov v obshchestvennoi zhizni poreformennoi Rossii* (Moscow 1978)

Ustrialov, N. 'Politicheskaia doktrina slavianofil'stva. Ideia samoderzhaviia v slavianofil'skoi postanovke,' *Vysshaia shkola v Kharbine. Izvestiia iuridicheskogo fakul'teta* (Harbin 1925), 47–74

Varustin, L.E. *Zhurnal 'Russkoe slovo'* 'Leningrad 1966)

Vengerov, S. 'A.A. Grigor'ev.' *Entsiklopedicheskii slovar'*. IX (St Petersburg 1893), 721–3

– 'Molodaia redaktsiia *Moskvitianina*,' *Vestnik Evropy*, I no. 2 (1886), 581–612

Volzhskii, A.S. 'Na puti krestnom,' *Khristianskaia mysl'* (December 1916), 3–33

Vucinich, Alexander. *Social Thought in Tsarist Russia. The Quest for a General Science of Society* (Chicago and London 1976)

Walicki, Andrzej. *The Slavophile Controversy: History of a Conservative Utopia in Nineteenth Century Russian Thought* (Oxford 1975)

Weiss, John. *Conservatism in Europe, 1770–1945. Traditionalism, Reaction and Counter-Revolution* (London 1977)

Wellek, René. *A History of Modern Criticism, 1750–1950*. IV (New Haven 1965)

Whittaker, Cynthia H. 'The Ideology of Sergei Uvarov: An Interpretive Essay,' *Russian Review*, XXXVII no. 2 (April 1978), 158–76

Williams, Robert C. 'The Russian Soul: A Study in European Thought and Non-European Nationalism,' *Journal of the History of Ideas*, XXXI no. 4 (1970), 573–88

Woehrlin, W.F. *Chernyshevskii. The Man and the Journalist.* (Cambridge, Mass, 1971)

Yaney, George L. *The Systematization of Russian Government. Social Evolution in the Domestic Administration of Imperial Russia 1711–1905.* (Urbana 1973)

Young, George M. *Nikolai F. Fedorov. An Introduction.* Belmont 1979

Zamotin, I.I. *Romanticheskii idealizm v russkom obshchestve i literature 20–30kh godov XIX stoletiia* (St Petersburg 1907)

– *Romantizm dvadtsatykh godov XIX stoletiia v russkoi literature.* I (Warsaw 1903)

– *Sorokovye i shestidesiatye gody* (Moscow-Petrograd 1915)

Zenkovsky, V.V. *A History of Russian Philosophy.* 2 vols. (London 1953)

– *Russkie mysliteli i Evropa* (Paris 1955)

Zernov, N. *Three Russian Prophets: Khomiakov, Dostoevskii, Solov'ev* (London 1944)

Zil'bershtein, I.S. 'Apollon Grigor'ev i popytka vozrodit' *Moskvitianin* (nakan-une sotrudnichestva v zhurnale *Vremia*).' *Literaturnoe nasledstvo,* LXXXVI (Moscow 1973), 567–80

Index

Aksakov, I.S. 12, 64, 97, 119, 158, 165, 170, 174; and education 150–1; and individualism 148; and *narod* 147, 150–1; and *obshchestvo* 150–1, 178, 181; and Orthodoxy 166; and *pochvenniki* 147–9; and reconciliation 147, 151, 178; and Slavophilism 145–6, 149–50

Aksakov, K.S. 42, 145; and education 82; and literature 119; and Peter the Great 81

Alexander I 6, 22

Alexander II 62, 69, 97

alienation 8, 75–6, 144

Almazov, B.N. 28, 29

Antonovich, M.A. 140, 162–3; and *pochvennichestvo* 133–5

art 102, 128; and Belinsky 45–6; and conservatives 11, 20; and Dostoevsky 117, 120–4; and Grigor'ev 46–9, 117, 118, 120–1; and nationality 20, 45–6, 102, 116, 117–18, 119–20, 124–5; and *pochvennichestvo* 128, 140, 163; and Slavophiles 117, 119; and Strakhov 122–3; and young editors 32–4, 35

artel': and *pochvenniki* 110–11, 113–14; and *Svetoch* 70

autocracy 4, 6, 20–1, 61–2; and Chernyshevsky 63, 134; and conservatism 4, 183; and Grigor'ev 155; and Katkov 142–3; and *pochvenniki* 109–10, 115, 183; and Slavophiles 103

Averkiev, Dmitrii 160, 165

Bakunin, M.A. 11, 50

Belinsky, V.G. 9, 11, 50, 55; and art 45–6; and Dostoevsky 66; Dostoevsky on 139; and Grigor'ev 45–7, 86, 180; on Grigor'ev 42; and Leont'ev 176; and literary criticism 31, 34; and nationality 46, 56, 83; and *pochvennichestvo* 181; and Pushkin 174

Berdiaev, Nikolai: and Grigor'ev 44; and reconciliation 179; and Slavophilism 83

Bergson, Henri: and Grigor'ev 44

Bibikov, P. 112

Blok, Aleksandr: on Grigor'ev 177

bureaucracy 22, 62; Grigor'ev on 155; *pochvenniki* on 110

romanticism: and art 129; and capitalism 111; and conservatism 17–19;
and individualism 148; and intelligentsia 9, 10, 24, 26, 45, 180, 182;
and *pochvenniki* 116; and young
editors 32
Rostopchina, E.P. 28
Rousseau, J.-J. 107
Russia and the West 8, 23, 25–6;
and intelligentsia conservatives
182–3; and *pochvenniki* 76, 84, 89,
91–2, 152, 154, 163, 175, 179, 180;
and Slavophiles 80; and *Svetoch*
75; and young editors 38
Russkii vestnik 72, 96, 97, 108, 130,
132, 142–4 passim, 151, 158, 159,
171
Russkoe slovo 43, 45, 67–8, 96, 131,
140, 156, 162, 163

Saltykov-Shchedrin, M.E. 140
Samarin, Iu. 119
Savigny, F. von 19, 52
Schelling, F.W.J. von 19, 30, 45, 46,
48, 50–2, 116–17, 118, 123; Gri-
gor'ev on 52
Schiller, F. 18
Schlegel, F. 52
science 62, 70; Dostoevsky on 172–3;
Grigor'ev on 117; *pochvenniki* on
100, 111, 113, 114–15, 138, 140
Scott, Walter 85–6
Serov, A. 152–3
Shchapov, A.P. 155; and regionalism
104–5
Shcherbatov, M. 21
Shevyrev, S.P. 28, 32, 164
Slavophilism 9, 11, 12, 106, 155; and
Antonovich 132–3; and art 117,
119; and Berdiaev 83; and Dostoev-

sky 87, 88, 91; and education
81–2, 99, 150; and Grigor'ev 43,
86–7, 88, 104, 125, 127; and I.
Aksakov 64, 145–7; and law 107;
and literature 118–19, 154; and
nationality 36, 55, 56, 88, 90, 119,
151, 178; and Orthodoxy 80–1,
163; and peasantry 36, 37, 82, 149–
50; and Peter the Great 55, 81–4,
90; and *pochvenniki* 73–4, 78,
90, 92–3, 102–3, 109, 115, 181;
and politics 103; and reason 76–7;
and society 103; and Strakhov
164–5; and Struve 110; and *Svetoch* 69–70; and *zemskii sobor* 103
socialism: Dostoevsky on 135, 168–9;
Herzen on 164; *pochvenniki* on
111, 114
society 6–7, 92, 94; Dostoevsky on
95, 136, 170; and liberalism 106;
pochvenniki 103–4, 106–7, 115,
127; Slavophiles on 103
Sokolov, S.M. 178
Solov'ev, S.M. 41, 58, 104
Solov'ev, V.S. 177, 179
Solzhenitsyn, A.I. 3, 177, 178, 179,
181
Sovremennik 30, 31, 73, 96, 130–1,
132–3, 136–7, 140–1, 142, 151,
156, 162, 163
Stankevich, N. 35, 50, 76
Stellovsky, F.T. 153
Strakhov, N.N. 40, 69, 71–2, 99,
102, 131, 155, 158, 163; on art 122;
on Danilevsky 167–8; and definition of 'native soil' 78; on history
79; and I. Aksakov 163–4, 165; on
idealism 76–7, 162, 164–5; on
liberalism 105; on materialism
122, 162, 167; on nihilism 122, 132,